BITTERROOT

AMERICAN INDIAN LIVES

Series Editors

Kimberly Blaeser
University of Wisconsin, Milwaukee

Brenda J. Child
University of Minnesota

R. David Edmunds
University of Texas at Dallas

Clara Sue Kidwell
University of Oklahoma

K. Tsianina Lomawaima
University of Arizona

Bitterroot

A Salish Memoir of

Transracial Adoption

Susan Devan Harness

UNIVERSITY OF NEBRASKA PRESS | LINCOLN AND LONDON

Portions of chapter 14 originally appeared in *Mixing Cultural Identities through Transracial Adoption: Outcomes of the Indian Adoption Project (1958–1967)* (New York: Mellen, 2009). Used with permission.

"Bad Wine" is reprinted from Victor Charlo, *Put Sey (Good Enough)* (Kalispell MT: Many Voices, 2008). Used with permission.

Library of Congress Cataloging-in-Publication Data
Names: Harness, Susan Devan, author.
Title: Bitterroot: a Salish memoir of transracial adoption / Susan Devan Harness.
Other titles: Salish memoir of transracial adoption
Description: Lincoln: University of Nebraska Press,
[2018] | Series: American Indian lives
Identifiers: LCCN 2017056173
ISBN 9781496207463 (cloth: alk. paper)
ISBN 9781496210869 (epub)
ISBN 9781496210876 (mobi)
ISBN 9781496210883 (pdf)
Subjects: LCSH: Harness, Susan Devan. | Salish Indians—Biography. | Indian women—Montana—Biography. | Adopted children—West (U.S.)—Biography. | Interracial adoption—Montana. | Salish Indians—Social life and customs. | Flathead Indian Reservation (Mont.)—Biography. | Women anthropologists—West (U.S.)—Biography. | Adult children of alcoholics—West (U.S.)—Biography. | Women—Montana—Biography.
Classification: LCC E99.S2 H37 2018 | DDC 978.6004/9794350092 [B]—dc23
LC record available at https://lccn.loc.gov/2017056173

Set in Janson by Mikala R Kolander.
Designed by N. Putens.

This is a work of nonfiction. Some names and identifying details have been changed.

To Vern, Ronni Marie, and James Allen
And to all my families

CONTENTS

ILLUSTRATIONS

ACKNOWLEDGMENTS

As much as our culture would like us to believe otherwise, our social world is not dichotomous. There is no right/wrong, good/bad, even/ or, black/white, or, in my case, white/red. These concepts define the edges of a continuum filled with many ideas and perspectives far more descriptive of who we are and what we do. To accept the dichotomy means we don't have to be uncomfortable or experience the pain brought about by examination. But if we explore that space in between the defined concepts, if we rub those ideas between our fingers and bring that scent to our nose, we are changed. If we close our eyes and listen to the stories and think about the hues and textures of a lived life, we grow to know the perspectives of others, which leads us to understand and, eventually, accept ourselves.

This book is not just about me. It is also about the people whose lives intertwined with my life, thereby defining it, shaping it, and teaching me to wholly and unapologetically accept it. I have so many to thank for their additions to this work. I apologize to the number of people I am unable to detail here for their invaluable stories and their research.

First, thank you, Dr. Matthew Bokovoy, my editor at University of

Nebraska Press, for seeing this project as an important addition to the literature and conversations about and by American Indians, regarding our history and our contemporary lives. Also, thank you, Susan Silver, copyeditor extraordinaire! Your expertise polished my prose, for which I am grateful. John Calderazzo, thank you for being interested in the story from our first conversation. Your support, your instruction, and your questions made this a strong and beautiful manuscript. Swapping stories of our lives made me a better storyteller.

Kate Browne, Debby Thompson, Dan Beachy-Quick, Felicia Zamora, and Maria Haenga-Collins, your insight, careful readings, and thoughtful suggestions required me to write at a depth I'd not experienced before. It has been an amazing experience working and conversing with you, and I've learned so much. Your guidance has helped me give so much to others. Maylinn Smith, your knowledge about American Indian law and history was invaluable. And Gyda Swaney, your knowledge about life and the intensity of what it means to be us was not only much appreciated but needed. Thank you all for your support in helping me get this story told in so many different ways.

Christie Riebe, you gave me so many gifts: your perspective as an adoptive parent, your friendship, and your much-needed editing skills! Your eye for detail and your ear for a well-told, coherent story helped to make this a highly polished book. Thank you so much.

Family seems like a pretty defined word, until adoption is involved. Then it becomes more convoluted, more expansive, and, in my case, more foundational to who I am. To Mom and Vic, simply put, I wouldn't be here without you both. Vic, I miss you because I wish I'd been able to know you better; Mom, I miss you because you were the best gift I've ever received.

My family on the Flathead Indian Reservation was key in the writing of this book. Albert and Delphine Plant, your unquestioned acceptance of me turned my world around. You are kind, generous, and so very thoughtful and have helped me in any way I have asked. I treasure you.

Ronni Marie, your story was the reason I began to explore this path of our lives all those years ago. I thank you so much for sharing those pieces of you with those pieces of me. James Allen, your kindness of spirit and generosity of self are what I admire most in you. It's too bad we met at Vic's funeral, but sometimes I think that is what funerals are for—a reconnection of all those lost parts of us, as family. Vern, thank you so much for sharing your life and your lived experiences of "what it means *not* to be adopted." You gave me a much-needed perspective. I respect and admire you for so many things but most of all for just being you. I love you all so very, very much and am grateful for the time you spent with me as we shared our pain, our blessings, and hopefully a better sense of who we are in this entity called family.

To my sons, Chris and Dan, and my husband, Rick, you are the cornerstone of my being, the breath in my heart, and the wings of my spirit. Thank you for teaching me, in all those little ways life uses to educate us, of what it means to be a family. I love you all.

Prologue

Tribal Complex, Flathead Indian Reservation, Pablo, Montana, 2008.

The hallways were labyrinthine, narrow passages that twisted first one way, then another, offices shooting off in various directions. I'd gone perhaps only thirty feet and already I was lost. I caught the attention of a tall man in police blues, his black hair salted with silver.

"Do you know where I could find Vern?" I asked.

He looked me up and down, expressionless. "Yeah, he's here somewhere. Who's looking for him?"

"His sister, Vicki Charmain," I replied, giving him my birth name—a key to the secret society.

He disappeared behind yet another turn of the hall, and within moments Vern materialized from that same space, as if by magic, a genie from the lamp. "Hey, I heard you were looking for me." He smiled beneath his mustache. We didn't hug; it seemed too intimate for a person I'd seen only three other times in my life, times of uncertainty and stress, times when it would be relatively easy for him to forget that I'd ever existed. I'd been removed from my reservation family at the age of eighteen months and adopted by a white couple when I was two. He wasn't born until I was ten and living a very different life with a very different family.

As we stood in the hall and talked the mundane, safe talk of people who are essentially strangers, I studied him, looking for the familiar. Although he was not much taller than my five-foot-six stature, his frame was large and intimidating. His skin was lighter than mine, something that confused me; I figured since we shared the same mother, we'd also share the same color of skin. Both of us had black hair, except mine was streaked with swaths of white, while only silver glistened on his temples. The rest of his hair was cut close to his scalp and stood at attention. I listened to his voice, the way he spoke. I watched his gestures and saw only one other familiar characteristic: each of us had brown eyes, but his didn't blink as they studied me back.

I did much of the talking; he mainly listened. At one point he leaned back against the wall and hooked his thumbs in the pants pockets of his police blues, crossing one foot in front of the other. After a few moments of silence and that unwavering gaze, he said, "I used to dream of you."

At once I was both intrigued and confused. "How old were you," I asked, "and what did I look like?" I didn't understand how he could dream of someone he'd never met, or what role I could have possibly have played in his life.

"About eight. You looked like my sister Robin."

"What did you dream?"

He watched me for several moments before replying. "I used to dream that you would come back from wherever you were and take me away from all of this." He paused, his gaze still on me. "I used to dream that a lot."

My heart shattered, like ice on granite. It shattered for both of us, because what Vern didn't know, couldn't possibly know, was that I'd dreamed of this family as well. I dreamed that they hadn't forgotten me. I imagine he wondered about the life I might have given him, just as I wondered about the life I sought, a life where I was "real" instead of "adopted"; a life where my skin color was the same as everyone else's and I wouldn't stand out, isolated; a life where "American Indian" meant something more than "I don't know."

So, as we stood in that hallway and regarded each other, deep in our own dreams, each of us was looking to be rescued by the other.

1. Susan, age eighteen months. Adoption photo from Montana Department of Social and Rehabilitation Services. Courtesy of the author.

I

I Wasn't Born; I Was Adopted

Billings, Montana, May 1974.

Two months ago I turned fifteen.

Now my father and I sit at the dining room table, watching the mists of rain drizzle against the pane of the large picture window. Our back-yard is bordered by chain-link fencing. Pine trees stand sentry along the back edge, while rows of lilac bushes, alternating in purple and white, flank the yard's sides. Lilacs are my favorite flowers. I look forward to inhaling their pungent aroma, soft and sweet, carried on an evening's breeze. I look forward to their displays, floral cones that bend gently in their heft. But I, more often, look forward to their announcement of spring. It is quiet, this space between Dad and me, one of the few times we are able to sit in each other's company with relative ease. Dad's an alcoholic, prone to eruptions. I'm usually watchful, but today I'm relaxed. Unguarded. It just feels like a good day.

I stare outside and daydream, the dreams of a fifteen-year-old girl who misses her family. Against my wishes, a question sneaks out of my mouth and fills this tiny dining room with electricity, not the exciting kind but the scary kind. "What happened to my real parents?"

Dad's head snaps around. The pupils of his brown eyes have become tiny dark orbs, piercing me with their sharp gaze. The tendon of his jaw dances rhythmically, and within an instant I know I have asked the wrong question. My adoption and the reasons for it have always been actively avoided—until this moment, when time stops, and silence, awkward and deafening, fills the gaps. I'd asked Dad this question only once before, when I was six. Then Dad's reply was "They died in a car accident. They were both killed." It was an easy answer, straightforward to a child's ear, and the information remained unchallenged. Dad must have heard the need in my voice to know more, because his reaction became angry silence that deadened further conversation.

This time, however, the silence is gone, but the anger is audible in Dad's answer: "What do you mean, your '*real* parents'?" I wince at the harshness of his voice as he emphasizes the word *real*. "*We* are your real parents. *We* raised you; *we* clothed you; *we* fed you; *we* educated you. You have a roof over your head because of *us*. Never forget that," he says, drilling the words home, quiet and measured. "*We* are your real parents."

His answer is concrete, the line drawn: the question is closed. But I am no longer a child who is content with easy answers, and now I resent him shutting me out. I pull air deep into my lungs, where it calms my nerves and brings my pulse under control. My life with him seems to be filled with land mines. This land mine, however, is particularly charged, and I work to deaden the explosion. "It's not that you aren't my parents," I say, my voice quiet, soothing, while my pulse beats like timpani in my ears. "But I'm talking about before. What happened to them?"

The eggshells beneath my feet are sharp and painful, and I don't know how far I'll get in finding out more about me, more about my life before. Dad might answer or he might shut down, and this conversation will be as if it had never happened. That's what I dread, because if that is the case, that door will never be opened again. So I sit across from him, hands in my lap, and wait patiently as he stares out the window. My own thoughts are thrown around as if in a storm. Perhaps he's ignoring me.

Perhaps he's weighing his options. Perhaps he's forgotten the question altogether. But he casts a glance at me while he digs around in his sweater pocket for his familiar pipe and tobacco, and I take it as a positive sign. The odds are good that I'm going to get some kind of answer.

Dad has ritualized his pipe and tobacco; it is used to buy time. So I sit and watch while he packs the heavily grained cherry bowl with Sir Walter Raleigh, carefully tamping it down with his index finger until he is satisfied. Then, snapping a match beneath the dining room table, he brings the flame to the brown, wrinkled leaves and inhales deeply, so deep that his cheeks grow hollow and his face grows long, pulling until the embers burn fiery orange on their own. When he exhales, the smoke drifts in a cloud that dissipates throughout the room; the remainder curls out of his nostrils.

I used to be fascinated by the way his smoke curled, blue eddies that wound themselves around one another. I sought to produce the same effect the previous Christmas, when a friend and I sneaked out of her house and walked a half mile down the ice-laden road. We stopped near a copse of bushes, where I opened the pack of Salem menthols we'd purchased earlier at a nearby convenience store. I ran through the same ritual I'd seen my mom do and my dad do, before he switched to a pipe. Opening the wrapper, I unpeeled the small portion of the foil cover, carefully slapping the top of the pack against my palm, all performed in relative blindness; I'd never smoked before in my life. I extracted the smooth, white cylinder and placed it between my lips, where it felt foreign and plastic. Although there was no wind, I lit the match and cupped the flame, as I'd seen my parents do, and pulled in the smoke. It scalded my throat and assaulted my lungs, drowning them in a bluish haze. I coughed and tears ran, but still I tried to exhale the smoke through my nostrils, where it burned and singed my tender membranes. I tried smoking a few more times but gave up because it never got easier. Nothing was worth this much coolness.

But Dad's smoke from his pipe still captivates my attention, and I watch it swirl into itself, slow vortexes captured by invisible currents in the small dining room. After a few puffs he stares at the tabletop, his gaze unseeing, and sits quietly for many moments. When he looks up, he gives me a wry smile and shakes his head. Pensive, his voice becomes quiet, the menace gone. He sighs. "I wondered when this question was going to come up. I just didn't know what I was going to say." He pauses before he adds, "As you know, your parents died in a car accident."

My breath stops in my throat. The conversation I've most looked forward to, and dreaded, is actually happening. I work to keep my voice level, but it's difficult because adrenaline is taking over. "Where?"

"Near Missoula," he answers, returning his gaze to the window.

"How did it happen?"

"Drunk driving." He turns his head slightly and meets my eyes. "Happens all the time up there."

"Who was in the car?"

He gives me a blank look. I reframe the question: "Did I have brothers or sisters who were in the car when it happened?" What if I had siblings, but they weren't in the car? Suddenly my only-child status would change drastically! I hold my breath for his response. He pauses and looks out the window, sucking on his teeth while his brows furrow, calculating the amount of information he wants to share, the amount he wants me to know. "I don't know about brothers and sisters. I heard you had an uncle somewhere in Arizona. Phoenix, I think it was. But he was a drunk, a no-good bum. It's better you don't get a hold of him." He turns a warning gaze to me, his face set, his jaw hard. "He and his family would leech off of you for as long as you'd let them, and you have such a kind and generous heart, they'd realize they'd hit the mother lode."

Dad's description of Indians hangs in the air between us. He's not the only one who thinks this way. This perspective is held by so many people I know that it permeates my psyche: *that's how Indians are; everyone knows that.* Stories abound about people who've rented to a Native family. Within days there are thirteen relatives in the house; the place is trashed within a month. Or someone gets some money and suddenly the relatives show up, people who they've never seen before. Those stories are told by my classmates, my dad's friends, even in overheard conversations of strangers in restaurants. What is most shocking, however, is the fact that these people are so open about their bigotry; they are completely comfortable in these conversations, regardless of who might overhear them. My discomfort is palpable, but what can I do? I am isolated, an island in an angry white sea. Survival means silence; otherwise I know the anger will turn on me.

Dad stops talking, and it is my turn to stare out the window as I wonder what this uncle might look like. The yard fades away, and I see him, silhouetted against a saguaro cactus. He's a big guy, barrel-chested. He wears a black hat with a feather tucked in a beadwork band that encircles the crown. His black Western-style shirt has a pointed yoke and pearl snaps along the placket, and it is tucked into a pair of well-worn jeans, whose back pocket reveals a circular outline where his snuff can rests. I close my eyes for a moment and concentrate on his face, his round cheeks and dark skin; it is the same color as mine in the summer. But I can't see his eyes. They are hidden behind the dark-green lenses of a pair of aviator sunglasses. And just like every Indian I've ever seen in the movies, when he turns toward me he doesn't smile.

But I do. I like how this uncle looks.

I come out of my reverie and glance at Dad, who is still deep into his. "Where did you say they were buried, again?" I ask.

"Missoula," he answers.

My heart speeds up, and I lean forward. At least Missoula is in the same state. But I know if I show too much interest, too much emotion, this conversation will end. So I lean back in my chair and ask, in as much of an offhand tone as I can muster, "Where in Missoula?"

"I don't know," Dad says with a wave of his hand, irritation flooding his features, hardening his voice, turning his face to stone. I've pushed too far. So I say nothing while I sit and dig my nails into the palms of my hands, their pain invisible beneath the table. The silence stretches like taffy between us, interrupted only by the clock above Dad's head that ticks a steady cadence. Although it feels like hours, perhaps only five minutes pass before he finally sighs and shrugs. "One of the cemeteries in Missoula. I don't remember which one."

Adrenaline. It's a beginning, the first piece of the puzzle. The information he's just given to me churns, and I am now only half-aware that he's fished his Swiss Army knife from his jeans and is extracting the smallest blade. He scrapes it around the bowl of his pipe and drops the burned contents in a nearby ashtray. *A cemetery in Missoula. They would have records. There would be an obituary!*

When Dad is finished and our eyes meet, I watch his smile become tight, forced. "Enough of this macabre talk. It's in the past, and it needs to stay in the past." He stares at me for a sign of acknowledgment, and I, the people-pleaser, nod. But after that I think of little else. I suppose it could be called obsessing, wondering about these ghostly people who live at the edge of my consciousness, what they look like, their mannerisms, their way of talking, their way of being. Imagining them. I am desperate for them to take shape. How can I make that happen?

That night, in bed, I look out the window and stare through the branches of our front-yard tree, at the stars that dot a black sky, each one representing a new, unanswered question. How did the accident happen? Was anyone else in the car? Brothers or sisters? Was I in the car? If I was and they pulled me from the wreckage, did they take me to wherever they took kids to be adopted? And where was that? And if there were brothers and sisters, who survived, and where were they? Did the aunts and uncles take them? And if they had, why didn't they take me?

Adoption, by the very act itself, is defined by tragedy: death, the inability to be a parent (as in the case of my birth mother), and, in my case, the inability to be a whole and complete child. People typically don't want to discuss tragedy, including my mom. When I was younger, and couldn't get an answer from Dad, I'd ask Mom, who would deflect my questions, her discomfort at my curiosity visible as she waved her hand, dismissing the subject: "You're too young to ask questions like that," or, "You don't need to hear about the bad things that happen to people. You should hear only about happy things." These statements coded my mind to see adoption as a subject to be avoided. Wanting to please, I complied; I was silent. But as I would learn in years to come, an incestuous relationship lives between people pleasing and adoption.

My parents aren't the only ones uncomfortable with the questions. Friends, and even other adults, are uneasy when I bring up the subject. Typically, my interest, my forthrightness of discussion, is met with awkward silence or blank stares; both reactions essentially say that some events are better off unexamined. I interpret their silence as judgment: *Why isn't your family enough? Why can't you just be thankful for what you have?*

It's not that I'm not thankful; it's that I feel only half-full. The full half contains what I know: my memories, my sense of self, and how I fit in or don't fit in. The other half is divided. One portion is what people tell me: what kind of tribe I belong to or how I looked so sturdy but was so light when my mom first picked me up. The remaining portion is everything that had happened before, the things no one can tell me, because no one in my current life has any knowledge about them, whatsoever. And the older I get, the more aware of the emptiness I become.

When I go to friends' houses, I listen with rapt attention to the stories their parents tell, of when their darling little daughter took her first step at twelve months of age, falling so many times before she got to the couch, or when their son spit out the canned peas in horror at his first attempt at solid food. And they laugh, both parents and children, their eyes bright and animated. And although my smile is good-natured, it is pulled tight, so tight that my lips hurt. I hurt because I've never experienced these events, these stories, these bits and pieces of a lived memory informing me that I existed in peoples' realities before I was two years old. And then I wonder where this whole other family lives, this family who knew me before I was two, who knew things about me no one else knew.

My friends take their known pasts for granted. I, on the other hand, feel the absence of my past like a cold wind. Their life is an entire novel, whereas mine picks up on chapter 3, when the primary characters have already begun to take shape.

When I was six I had a pretend memory, a short clip of manufactured reality. In that memory both of my parents were Native. My mother's hair was long and black, and it tickled my face as she leaned over the gate of my crib and smiled. My father's hair was cropped short, his teeth white and straight against his brown skin. He didn't lean as far over.

I know exactly when and why I created this memory: to fit in with the lives of Christy and Jennifer, my two closest friends in first grade, who rode the same bus to school. We sat three to a seat, huddled together, protective of the secret space we created in our postures, and talked about how we came into the world—or, rather, how they did. I think someone asked where I was born, to which I probably replied, "I wasn't born; I was adopted." That's typically how those early conversations started. But I didn't stop there. Especially when the girls leaned forward, their eyes wide, waiting expectantly for me to continue. And the story came so easily in the spotlight I suddenly found myself in. I was a star.

"Why were you adopted?" Christy asked.

"My parents died in a car accident," I replied nonchalantly, as if I had told this story every day.

"Do you remember your parents?" That was Jennifer. She was almost breathless.

"Barely," I said, my voice low. It was almost like telling a ghost story. They leaned forward even more. "I have only one memory," I continued, but paused for effect and watched as they glanced at each other, ready for the secret. That's when I told the memory I had just constructed moments ago. I finally had a past, just not a real one. But at least I wasn't

2. Susan, first grade. Mom was angry that no one combed my hair prior to the photo being taken. Courtesy of the author.

left out. I smiled with their sharp intake of breath, throwing their hands over their mouths as if to keep in the secret. My story was exotic, and I became an instant celebrity.

Of course, the real story is that, because I was removed from my family when I was eighteen months old and adopted when I was two, I have no recollection of my parents. None. But six-year-olds can just make stuff up to fill in the blanks. Back then filling in the blanks wasn't called lying; it was called "imagination."

That same spring Dad's drinking had gone from a few times each day to nonstop, extending far into the early morning hours. This is when he felt most creative. How many mornings I would be awakened at three o'clock, when Dad, filled with a good dose or two of vodka (glasses, not shots), would rev up the saw in his workshop and cut deer antlers into little pieces of art that he called the "Laughing Man." The Laughing Man consisted of two forked antlers that mirrored each other. Vertical, with inverted curves, they formed the visage of a person, bending slightly at his torso, whose arms were raised into the air and whose legs were spread. He'd then cut a small piece of antler, shaving off the edges to form a head, which he'd attach at the upper fork. No other features or characteristics defined this being. There was a certain beauty in their simplicity.

One night I woke to the calcified odor of burned deer antler. After two hours of the noise and the smell, I stomped downstairs to the basement to angrily ask him to stop.

"Well, Suz!" Dad greeted me with a huge smile. "You're up late. What do you think?"

Dad had lined a few of the Laughing Men up on the workbench and was grinning as he looked from them to me. I was too annoyed to care what they looked like. I'd been awake for two hours, listening to the whine of his saw and smelling the stench of burned calcium.

I didn't say anything. Still grinning, he explained, "I decided they needed to be different colors, to represent the different races." And this was true—some were natural bone; others he'd painted with metallic bronze; still others were gold. There were no brown or black ones.

"Well, what do you think?" he pressed, weaving on his feet slightly.

"I think it's time you went to bed," I answered between taut lips, and went upstairs.

Dad had grown up in Cleveland, Ohio, in the Slovak section of town. His neighborhood and others in that city were highly contentious areas, whose boundaries fractured along ethnic lines. As a result, he was taught at an early age to distrust the Jews, hate the blacks (who, people whispered, were bringing down the housing prices), make fun of the Irish, and loathe the Italians. By five years of age I knew every ethnic slur and which group they belonged to. I would never use them because I knew they hurt.

"Kids used to call me Chinaman," Dad told me when I was in second grade. We were walking on a dusty road on the wildlife refuge, where silence reigned, bees buzzed, and grasshoppers leaped from Russian thistle to Russian thistle. I listened, but I was too young to see the pain on his face as he told the story. "They'd chant whenever I'd walk by, 'Chintzy, chintzy Chinaman, sitting on a fence, trying to make a dollar out of fifteen cents.'"

"Why did they call you a Chinaman?"

"Because of my eyes; they're slanted. And I was darker than most of the other kids." Those "slanted" eyes were the remnants of the Mongol blood that had filtered down through the centuries throughout eastern Europe. When I studied him, he did appear Asian. For years I used to sing that chant when I was alone, trying to capture what it felt like to be one of the boys singing it, trying to feel how my dad might have felt hearing it. Though catchy, I always had an oily, bitter taste in my mouth afterward.

At fifteen I didn't understand the role the Laughing Men played for my dad. I didn't grasp that these representations were his tools for fixing his lifelong discomfort with race and nationality. I also didn't understand that these figures laughed when he couldn't. It would be years before I was able to comprehend that those men with their arms raised to heaven were where Dad's humanity lay.

Dad puts his passion toward gardening. Although he has a myriad of plants inside the house, philodendrons and ferns, he turns his attention to the outdoors. Sometimes I'll sit on the step and watch him spade the soil, mixing in fertilizer and peat moss until the dirt is dark and fine, dusting through his fingers. Today he unpacks the flowers from their small plastic black boxes and places them carefully in the prepared beds, brilliant purple petunias, green daisies that have not yet produced flower heads, and tall pink carnations. He is so careful as he lifts each from the dark, molded squares, cradling the roots, setting them in the soil, and then packing dirt gently around their base. He loves these small gifts of nature.

One day after school I'm greeted by cement yard art: a toddler that stands in the very center of his circular garden in the front yard. As I lean on the wrought-iron fence of the front stairs landing, the concrete girl is just a few feet away. Her face, angelically innocent, tilts upward, while she points a pudgy finger toward an object off in the distance. The other hand, fisted, is curled near her jaw, and her index finger curves toward her lower lip. Her face is defined by curiosity and wide eyes.

"I don't know why the hell your father bought that ugly thing," Mom says, disgust edging her voice as she pulls weeds around the pedestal. "It should be thrown in the garbage."

The following Saturday afternoon I see Dad kneeling by the statue. The watercolors he has taken from my bedroom sit nearby, and in his hand is a cheap, fine brush. He's painted her dress red and her curly hair yellow. Blue stains her eyes, and now he's working on her lips, a gentle pink, not unlike the carnations that now lay trampled from his drunken staggers. He croons to her while he paints, and I watch with suspicion. What exactly does this thing mean to him?

He stands up to examine his handiwork, and he stabilizes himself by putting one hand on her head, carefully, gently. Then he sees me. "Oh, hey, Suz." When he turns to face her again, he wears a smile of total joy. "Isn't she the cutest damn thing? That smile? Always so happy? Always so curious?"

He pauses, his attention still captivated by the statue. "You know," he says, as if he's forgotten my presence, "I've always wanted a little blond-haired, blue-eyed girl. They're the cutest damned things, and now I have one."

Tears sting my eyes as I note his look of adoration. He's speaking about her as if this little cement girl will open that little bow-mouth of hers and tell him, in toddler language, what she is pointing at. It hurts to see that adoring gaze; it hurts to hear why I'm not good enough. Why I'll never be good enough. I finger my long black hair, pulled back into a sloppy ponytail, and stare at my brown arms, dark against Dad's white V-neck T-shirt that I'm wearing. They will only get darker as summer drags on. And I'm suddenly embarrassed that this is what I look like. No matter how hard I try I will never look like this statue; I will never see that adoring gaze focused on me. And then my throat closes, and I can't swallow, and the world blurs in front of my eyes, and I realize how much I hate him. What's worse, I realize I am beginning to hate myself.

My entire life I've been surrounded by people represented by that statue, people with blond hair, brown hair, red hair with flecks of gold, people with blue eyes, green eyes, brown eyes, but none of them have the same brown skin I do. I realize now what my brown skin represents to some in this town. It flags my difference and makes some people (far more than I feel comfortable admitting) see me as stupid or lazy. *Dangerous.* That's a word that sits on the edge of my consciousness, where its edge is as sharp as an oyster shell, cutting me if I hold it against my skin too long.

When I was little, in grade school, I just thought it was me—that I *was* lazy, *was* stupid. I didn't know why people stared at me longer than they stared at my friends, but I knew they did. My presence seemed to make people angry, their brows drawn together as they watched me and their words harsh from their mouths for the slightest infraction, like the time my Girl Scout leader screamed at me for accidently stepping into a mud puddle and dirtying my white anklets while petting the blond hair on my friend's head. If she could have hit me for being stupid, I had the feeling she would have. But these were just feelings, just the perceptions of a little girl who was unclear what signal had caused such displeasure. At the time I certainly had no idea that the signal was the color of my skin.

But now I know better. And I know there are only three other kids in my ninth-grade class of more than two hundred who resemble me. One of them is an Asian girl who, rumor has it, carries a switchblade. She is pointed out to me by my friend, a Viking princess with her nest of red hair and harsh green eyes, while she and I stand in the school yard after lunch. The Asian girl, slender and chic, leans with her back against the red brick of the school building, propped up on one leg while the sole of her booted foot rests against the wall. A black leather trench coat dusts her calves. Every lunch hour she is there, sunglasses hiding her eyes, her jaw sharp, her lips unsmiling, surrounded by thuggish boys and girls who look nothing like her. She rules this crowd: they laugh when she laughs; they don't talk to her unless she talks first. But they are always there. She's alluring and frightening at the same time, carrying so much power in that petite form. What I would give for that power, that sway to gather people around me for no other reason than to adore my presence. But I keep her at a distance. I won't be one of her lackeys.

There's also an Aleut boy who has just come to the school. One of my teachers tells me he's arrived from Alaska, but the teacher has no idea why he's here in town. He asks if I want to be introduced. I do! But the meeting is awkward because I can't stop staring, and I have no idea what to say. I just want to see someone who looks like me. But he looks more like the Asian girl, with his almond-shaped eyes, his unsmiling lips, and his harsh expression.

Then there is Greg.

Greg is Crow, a tribal membership he is proud of, stating it at each and every opportunity. He sits behind me in math class and puts a lot of confusing thoughts in my head. Although he lives in town and not on the reservation, he's a real Indian. He looks like it, he talks like it, and he acts like it, swaggering arrogance combined with a sweet tongue. Although I find him attractive, I'm also leery; he's dangerous in that "lived experience" kind of way. Definitely not the kind of kid Dad wants me hanging with.

But in this class Greg and I are comrades-in-arms; we hate this class together. Him, because he'd rather be doing just about anything else than sitting still in school; me, because I just hate math, and my teacher is creepy. My teacher has placed me in the front row, between him and Greg, which is awkward because sometimes I see the teacher's eyes grazing my chest if I'm wearing a sweater or a dress with a scoop neckline or following the line of my legs as I cross them beneath my desk. When I catch him in the act, he doesn't bother to hide the half smile that plays on his face.

Our teacher moonlights to make up for the skimpy salary he is paid. In the evenings and on weekends he works at a film-developing kiosk that's set up in the Montgomery Ward parking lot. I see him one day while Mom and I are passing by in a car, but I turn away as he glances in my direction, hoping he won't recognize me. That would be embarrassing for both of us. Greg and I find his moonlighting funny, and we ridicule him, laughing conspiratorially behind cupped hands. Although I say Greg is the first real Indian I know, maybe he's just the first one to admit he's Indian. And when I admit I'm Indian, we're suddenly a club.

Like mine, Greg's hair is coarse and straight, except that it sticks out in all directions; it is only about two inches long. His face is brown and his skin is smooth. His nose is long and straight, supporting black-rimmed glasses that were popular in military photos from the 1960s. Although he seems like my height, five and a half feet, he's much taller; the desk hides his long, slender legs. All I see are his broad shoulders that fall into a skinny torso, with long arms in constant movement, folded on the desk, folded across his chest—never are they raised to answer a question. He dresses like a cowboy, with his plaid cotton or flannel shirts and worn jeans that fit loosely over an old pair of shitkicker cowboy boots, scuffed and soft, their stitching looping over his instep. But what I look forward to each day is his ready smile and quick way of talking.

One day Greg taps me on the shoulder and whispers, "You know that Ted Nugent song? 'Cat-Scratch Fever'? That's what I got last night." When I turn to look at him, he is leaning forward and nodding his head, his smile lazy and knowing.

I'm appalled yet curious. I narrow my eyes and ask, "What do you mean?"

"You know," he answers slowly, his smile growing broader. "When a guy has sex with a girl, and she digs her fingernails into his back? I got claw marks deep on my back last night. Man, do they hurt."

"You don't," I counter.

"I do." His black eyes look earnestly into mine. "You been with anybody?"

"No." The question embarrasses me, and my face grows hot. But I'm also skeptical of what he's telling me. I look at him for a long time—that smile, those eyes. He's lying. He has to be.

"You're missing out," he says with a grin as he shrugs his shoulders.

"Miss Devan, class is going on?" The math teacher's voice breaks into the conversation, and I turn around to his knowing smile. My face grows hot; I am embarrassed by so many things.

"You get per capita?" Greg asks one day when we are supposed to be working on math problems.

"Yeah."

"How much?"

I shrug. "I don't know. I get it when I turn eighteen."

Per capita are the payments the tribe pays out to each tribal member.

It's the collective monies we get from grazing rights, timber rights, water rights, that kind of thing. It is essentially the benefits received from the treaties still being honored by the government. I used to think it was free money that the government gave us, a claim openly stated by adults, kids, teachers, strangers.

"They are not just giving you money," my mom said, her voice firm and unyielding when I repeated that statement to her. "That's not free. Those are your treaty rights; a lot of Indian people have died for those rights, and don't you ever forget that!"

"What are you going to do with it?" Greg asks, referring to my payments.

"Probably pay for college."

"My sister bought a brand-new Pontiac Firebird when she turned eighteen, blew it all in one lump sum." He sticks the eraser end of his pencil in his mouth and taps it against his teeth.

"What are you going to do with it?" I ask.

"Probably the same thing. Buy a car," he says with a slow half smile.

It is a middle-of-the-summer Sunday, and Mom and I are sitting in church. I'm only half listening to the reverend. The other half is thinking about my parents. *My real parents*, I think rebelliously. I stare out the window and watch the raindrops coalesce into small streams that dance down the glass, braiding their paths like the sand islands along a shallow river. I'm thinking about the cemetery where they are buried and imagining them side by side, beneath a tree, their graves marked with white gleaming headstones.

I could go there. I could take the Greyhound bus past Bozeman, past Butte, all the way to Missoula. I could watch the cottonwoods that lined the Yellowstone River slide by as I made my way back home, back to the place I was originally from. Maybe then, once I found them, they would feel real to me.

It is important that they feel real because being Indian, living in this white family in this white town, and going to school with these white kids reminds me not only how different I am but how I will never be one of them. If Greg could be proud of his Indianness, I reasoned, I could be proud of mine. But I would need to find my family to do that.

The following Saturday Dad and I are sitting on the front step. It is early in the day and the spot is cool, the cement still chilly from the previous night. The concrete toddler stands below us, her colors faded, still pointing to some distant object. In the background the sounds of National Public Radio drift through the screen door. My attention is caught by a story connected to the American Indian Movement, or AIM. The movement started in 1973, the previous year, when a lot of Native people occupied Wounded Knee, South Dakota. I don't know much about it because Dad usually turns off that kind of news when I'm around, but for some reason we continue to listen. Evidently activists involved in AIM are trying to start a chapter or something, maybe in Great Falls, Montana, and are meeting a lot of resistance from the townspeople. Probably from Montanans in general.

When the news story concludes, Dad looks at me and begins to laugh, his head shaking from side to side. I'm waiting for the joke. It arrives in staccato fashion. "What-in-the-hell-are-those-goddamn-crazy-drunken-war-whoops-up-to-now?"

I burn red. He continues to shake his head, but his laughter drifts into a confused smile, which is replaced with a snort as he looks off into the distance. "Yeah, well they're a few years too late to get in on the civil rights movement." He turns his head to look at me. "You know that's just what they're trying to do: get on the bandwagon, ride someone else's coattails. Hell, Black Power and the Black Panthers have already shook things up. There's no new news here for the Indians. As always, the Indians are late." He chuckles and adds, "But they're never on time to anything."

He pulls at the stem of his pipe, and he looks away. I look in the same direction he does, but I'm sure we're thinking about two different things. He's probably thinking about the news story. I'm thinking, *How am I going to keep from becoming a goddamn-crazy-drunken-war-whoop?*

2

Coming-of-Age without a Net

Apgar, Glacier National Park, Montana, June 1975.

Mom's silver-blue Oldsmobile Delta 88 moves slowly down the dirt road, its back bumper rocking, thrown around by the dipping mud beds and potholes. The road has yet to be graded; she has a mile to go before she gets to the highway. At her pace it will take her fifteen minutes to go that one mile. Fifteen minutes seem like forever when "good-bye" is involved.

But I'm not a kid. I'm sixteen and my anxiousness is not about celebrating my freedom but about my dread at being left behind. *Abandoned.* That thought is a wisp, a ghost. But I shove it away as I watch her car disappear into the trees. Only then do I fully appreciate that I am alone in the middle of absolute nowhere.

Welcome to the Youth Conservation Corps or, how people typically refer to it, the YCC, in Glacier National Park. The YCC is a summer program put together by the U.S. government that gives high school students a chance to learn skills, preparing them for future jobs. When Dad read the job announcement to me in January I wasn't jazzed about these skills being my future. He had always encouraged me to go to college, not be a laborer. But he felt it important that I apply and had grown increasingly frustrated with my lack of motivation to do so. Therefore, before the application's February due date, Dad filled it out himself and submitted it, and it was with a certain sense of self-righteousness that he handed me the acceptance letter two months later. So here I am, looking at the place that will be my home over the next eight weeks.

The premises consist of two constructed environments: one for the YCCers and the other for the leaders. The YCCers are housed in the center of the large open green in six military surplus tents, whose olive-green canvases are pulled tight over a wooden framework and whose floors, diagonal planks of two-by-sixes, sit several feet off the ground. The doorways face different directions, allowing for a certain amount of privacy for the occupants. Each tent contains two sets of bunk beds, guarded on each end by a dark-green footlocker. Everything we own is required to fit within that chest. As a result, the administration provided a succinct shopping list of required items: three chambray work shirts, three pairs of jeans, a pair of work boots, a pair of work gloves, clothes to relax in during the off hours, a hat, a raincoat, several pairs of wool socks, and assorted personal items, including underwear and toiletries. What-ever won't fit, the directions stated, were to go home with our parents.

The leaders and camp administrators are housed in more perma-nent structures, namely, the four dark-brown log cabins with their large wooden porches that all look inward at our cloth residences. Beyond those structures lies a forest of dark pines that, by its very nature, curbs exploration in anything but broad daylight.

I feel the tears coming on again as I, once more, am aware of my isolation.

"Hi!"

The voice takes me by surprise, and I am embarrassed by the tears that roll down my cheek, wishing I had contact lenses to blame them on as I rub them away. I look around for the disembodied voice.

"Over here."

A girl stands near the canvas tent behind me, partially hidden behind a tree. When she emerges, I am reminded of an Irish pixie, as I take in her short red hair, dark-brown eyes, and freckles that spread like the Milky Way across her pale skin. She's waving a slender hand, and her head is tilted; her mouth curves into an expression that is open, mischievous, and daring.

"It's okay," she says, walking slowly toward me, her voice bright against the overcast sky. "It's lonely at first, but that goes away quick. I'm Jackie." She smiles as she extends her hand and asks, "What tent are you in?"

My first friend. I sigh and no longer see the image of Mom's back bumper disappearing around the corner.

The camp has few rules; however, those are unquestioned. Lights out at ten, no sleepovers with people of the opposite sex, and no food of any kind allowed in the tents. The director emphasizes that this is to keep grizzly bears from busting through the canvas in the middle of the night. Therefore, all food will be consumed in the mess hall a mile away. Meal times are precisely at 0630, 1200, and 1830.

We can get to the mess hall one of two ways: catch a ride with one of the counselors five minutes before meal service or walk along the forest trail. Only once do I accept a ride and realize I don't like to be hurried. I need this time in the morning and evening to prepare myself for the day and to review the day, respectively. I look forward to the mornings the most, when moisture hangs in the air, and the acrid scent of pine wafts through my senses. I awaken a little more with each step, my head clears with each breath, and by the time I reach the mess hall I am ready for the day. After work, when I return, long-fallen needles from these same pines dampen my steps, making it easier to observe the birds and small mammals that skitter along the branches decorated with long brown beards of lichen. Grasses grow tall by the side of the trail, and in the early summer the ecru blossoms of bear grass call for my fingers' caress.

The people who join me on these walks are almost always the same. There is Judith, the twenty-two-year-old camp counselor who stands over six feet tall. She used to be embarrassed about her height and would walk stoop-shouldered wherever she went so as to not draw attention to herself. When she was eighteen she realized at six feet she was going to draw attention regardless. I listen to her soft voice tell her story as she walks with a daisy chain in her hair, lending an even more hippieish look to her cotton tunics and jeans and hiking boots. Shawn, a year younger than me, can't wait to get away from the never-ending work on his parent's wheat farm in eastern Montana. He divests me of my romantic notion of farming when he talks about his daily life: feeding the cows and chickens in the early mornings, bucking hay for winter feed, and endlessly combining in the fall when his town friends are gathering, drinking, and watching girls. Jeff came from Colorado at the beginning of summer to be a camp counselor. He's twenty-four. He told me he was shocked at how empty Montana was. "I saw maybe twenty cars between Sheridan and Billings," he said, awe tinging his soft voice.

Jeff practiced meditation, and when I showed interest he taught me how to do it. Every evening after dinner and every weekend morning after breakfast, I'd find a spot of grass on the bluffs above the Middle Fork of the Flathead River and sit. I'd close my eyes and cross my legs, touching the tips of my middle finger and thumb together while I whispered a mantra that sounded like something a meditator would say. And I would wait until the physical world melted into the background, and my thoughts became married to the sounds of the gentle currents of the river below.

There is Margaret and Ian, in their early fifties, she a nurse, he a carpenter. They tell me they'd participated in a fast a few years back, eating nothing and drinking only water. "You get weak," Ian explains. "But it's okay. It totally cleanses your system. Did you know there is ten pounds of junk that gets down into all the little crevices in your colon?"

I don't know that. And I'm not going to try it out.

Within a few weeks I no longer miss the life I lived in Billings. I don't miss my mom or her forced, awkward silliness brought on by the stress of living in a tension-filled house. I don't miss my friends or their shallow conversations of five-finger discounts or make-out sessions in the back of their family's station wagon with their older boyfriends. Nor do I miss the embarrassingly early curfews put in place by Dad, my parents' bitter arguments that stretch late into the night because of his drinking, or the sound of my dad's band saw revving up at three in the morning while he is revved up on vodka. But most of all, I don't miss being an only child. With sixteen other teens, I'm forced to compete for attention, conversation, and even food. But competition reveals pain.

"Anyone want the last potatoes?" I ask at one of our first meals. Silence. I ask twice more, looking from face to face for denial or acceptance of my offer. Still there is no answer, and now some people stare at me in confusion. By the third time a boy explodes, "If you want 'em, take 'em. Just stop asking!"

I'm embarrassed, but then how would he know how Dad has trained me? That if anything was left over I was supposed to offer it to others, and if I didn't Dad called me "selfish" and "piggy"? So I would offer. But even if I reached for it after a refusal, Dad then called me "grabby" or "greedy." No matter how many offers I gave, if I reached for the food I wanted Dad would glare at me and bark, "You've had enough."

Although I never went hungry, I was not entitled to this food without his permission. Despite his harsh words, this boy had just granted me permission to enjoy food without humiliation. I smiled before reaching for the potatoes. Welcome to coming-of-age without a net.

In 1970 I lived in the small town of Naselle, Washington, population somewhere in the low four hundreds. My sixth-grade class had about twenty students, and I was the only girl not wearing a bra, not even one of the cotton, waffle-weave training bras that slipped soft and pliable over the head without the wearer having to deal with awkward hooks. I was also the only one who didn't have a starched, white, cotton, button-down shirt that allowed people to see through opaque fabric enough to discern a bra, training or otherwise. When one acquired both, the games and mating rituals truly began, as girls paraded around in their new-found womanhood and boys snickered. I so much wanted to be a part of it.

"Mom," I said one rainy afternoon, "I need a training bra." The words came out in a rush, and although I'd practiced them for weeks, they still didn't feel comfortable, for me to say and probably for her to hear. Bras, or periods, or anything remotely associated with femaleness carried negative connotations for both of my parents. Their feelings were apparent by Mom's tensing of her body and her face and the increased shaking of her hands, and Dad's glower. All promoted feelings of discomfort that permeated the air around me, whichever parent I was with. Thank God I was never with both parents, or the air would have exploded.

A few months before my first menses, Mom didn't give me the "talk." No. Instead, she presented me with a box about two feet long, a foot wide, and eight inches deep, wrapped in plain brown paper—the kind of wrapping that covered my dad's *Playboy* magazines that sat upstairs in his bedside drawer, beneath his government-issued pistol that he kept hidden in a purple Crown Royal whiskey bag. Every so often I'd slip up there and flip through the pages, in awe and embarrassment, but mostly in awe, my heart pounding at the fear of being discovered. Of course, this took place during the sexual revolution—it wasn't unheard of for men to have this same type of magazine in their nightstand drawer. I knew because I asked my friends. Behind cupped hands we whispered about what was inside the glossy cover and giggled at the naughtiness.

"If you have any questions," Mom said, handing me the box, "let me know." Then she just walked away. Perhaps she was embarrassed, perhaps she wanted to give me privacy, but one way or the other her statement made it clear that one of us would feel discomfort if I did anything of the sort. The booklet inside explained what the box contained: "everything a young woman needs to learn about her changing body." And it did: the pads, the garter belt, and an illustrated book about the female body. That was my "talk."

Mom, however, wasn't quite as embarrassed about my request for a training bra, a point evident in her laughter. "What are you training them to do?" Mom's chortling stopped when she saw my frustration, and her amusement became a gentle smile. She sighed and looked at my chest for those first initial buds, which didn't exist. I reasoned that maybe, like fertilizer, a bra would make breasts grow. But it wasn't so much I wanted breasts; I wanted a bra, for what it represented: being grown up. I just wanted an end to the judgmental gazes that some girls threw at me out of the corners of their eyes in the lunchroom, across the classroom, or out on the playground, where we don't really play but stand around and act very suave and sophisticated.

"Okay," Mom said, realizing that what I wanted was group cohesion, and if a bra did that for me, so be it. "We'll go this weekend."

The following Saturday we drove across the five-mile bridge that spans the mouth of the Columbia River to the downtown area of Astoria, Oregon. Although Astoria was twenty miles away from where we lived, it was the only metropolis that was relatively close. That was the city we went to for my dance-recital outfits, my doctors' appointments, and my age-appropriate clothing. We parallel parked near the JC Penney store, an aging building in an aging city, and found the bra section. I scanned the shelves and almost immediately my gaze landed on the style that all the girls were wearing—the gentle waffle weave of the training bra. I took it out of the plastic bag, whose seal was already broken, and held it gently across my fingertips, where it lay, soft and pliable; a tiny, white satin bow daintily separated the two bumps where the cups would otherwise be. I stuffed the bra back into the plastic and looked around for the white, starched cotton shirts. Mom saw the direction of my gaze.

"We'll have to get a shirt another time," Mom said. Then, seeing my look of disappointment, she smiled. "Let's go to the five-and-dime and get a milkshake." I could be bought.

On the way home, as the forests and saltwater marshes slid past my window, I wondered if the other girls would notice the different "me" the following day. I didn't dare wonder about the boys. I'd been well trained that boys were not to be wondered about.

That evening after dinner I sneaked up to my room, closed the door, and tried on the bra, slipping it easily over my head. Looking at the mirror, I admitted I wasn't exactly like the girls on the Playtex commercials, but I did feel more grown-up. I acknowledged my new status as a young woman.

"Suz!" Dad called up the narrow hallway of stairs. "Someone's here and wants to see you."

A visitor! It was rare that anyone came to our house, and I'd never known anyone to just show up; it was always by invitation. Curious, I slid a red-print turtleneck sweater over my head and felt the change immediately. Now only a narrow swath of cotton came between my shirt and me instead of the long cotton undershirt. Although my clothing felt awkward, that grown-up feeling had found legs.

When I got downstairs, a man Dad worked with (I'd seen him only a few times) occupied the couch, his arm thrown across its back. My seating options were limited, nonexistent really. I could sit on one of the kitchen chairs or on Dad's lap. I was a child in a young woman's body. My mind, really, hadn't caught up to my status. Therefore, like so many times before, I sat on Dad's knee and listened to the adult conversation that passed back and forth between the two men like a ping-pong ball. And like so many times before, Dad's hand rubbed my back, absently. Until it stopped. Right at the ridge of the scooped back and then again three inches lower at the base of the strap.

I swallowed hard, my heart pounding, because when his hand stopped, his words stopped as well. A quick look revealed his anger as his black brows descended over eyes with pinprick pupils.

"What in the hell is this?"

His voice was harsh in my ear, as he reached under the back of my shirt and grabbed the fabric of the soft waffle-weave bra and pulled until the back of the bra came into view for him. I saw the look of discomfort cross the near-stranger's face as all this unfolded. I felt my own discomfort as well, as my face grew heated, reddening almost to the color of my turtleneck. Dad abruptly let go and forced me off his knee, anger shaking his voice.

"Get upstairs and get out of that right now. I don't know what the hell you're thinking, wearing that."

That night Mom and Dad argued, exchanging bitter, hard words, until I finally pulled the blanket over my head, which dampened their voices only a bit. I wore the bra the next day, but I was scared and mortified instead of proud. Growing up was something to be ashamed of, not something that happened.

What we do at the YCC is physical labor. For hours we swing Pulaskis, cutting through dense, granite-filled soil as we build new campsites; shovel rocks and spade dirt to enhance trails; or swing sledgehammers to bring down rotting foot bridges and dilapidated structures. By the end of it our backs ache and our shoulders hurt; every muscle in our bodies sends an electric shock through our system, and we wince at the touch.

"Anyone know how to give a backrub?" Joey asks one day after eight hours of building a footbridge and four more days to go. I study him—that round face; that long, slender nose; the broad shoulders that taper to a narrow waist; those almond-shaped eyes and brown skin all indicate American Indian heritage. But he doesn't say it and I don't ask. People lie sometimes when they're asked outright, especially if they can "pass" for white. What I know is that he comes from the eastern plains and wears T-shirts that hug his body, mainly because he's outgrown them. In the past few weeks his muscles have grown from the nonstop manual labor.

"I can try," I answer. With the help of a couple of guys, we set up a makeshift table outside, using one of the mattresses from a nearby tent.

I stand to one side, or the other, but the distance is uncomfortable, and I stretch in ways that twinge my joints and muscles.

"Do you mind if I sit on you?" I ask. It is a question I would never have asked a few weeks before, but by now we have worked and lived together under conditions where privacy and social mores have been tossed aside for efficiency.

"No," he mumbles into his arm. "Go ahead."

I climb on his buttocks and am immediately aware of the heat of his body as it sears the secret areas of mine, our parts separated by mere millimeters of fabric. He jumps when I pump the cool lotion onto his warm skin, and I smile at his sudden vulnerability. Then I place my palms on his shoulders and begin to knead. I manipulate the muscles' soreness and feel them give way under the pressure of my palm, while a surge of electricity shoots up my arms in an adrenaline rush unlike anything I'd experienced before. There is a hypnotic feel for both him and me as I push my thumbs along the groove of his spine and pull my fingers along his ribs, following their lines, feeling his flesh jump as I touch sensitive areas. His skin is satin beneath my hands; its heat pulses through me and drives the gentle motion of touch.

I will do this all summer. I will do this for just about every member of the camp at the end of just about every day. I know where to put the pressure and where to work out the pain. I have no idea that what I give is healing, for both them and me. I do know I need it, like a Pentecostal needs a laying on of hands. It reminds me I exist, that I am human. It also reminds me that I have control.

In the winter months of early 1972, before I turned thirteen, my father's alcoholism was nearing its zenith. Although it would get worse, this was pretty bad. Once, after a hard night of hard liquor, Dad decided it was time to "teach" me the ways in which boys would try to take advantage of me when I began dating a "few years from now."

My stomach churned with his attentions, his kissing, his nuzzling.

Within moments, tears flowing, I begged him to stop, as his hands wandered over my body, my voice high and strained from the humiliation. He did stop, although he continued petting my hair and crooning, holding me close while his body shook. "You did the right thing," he murmured, his lips close to my ear. "You know right from wrong. You did the right thing." Revulsion seethed while he held me in his arms. And I did nothing, because I'd seen his anger, experienced his anger, feared his anger.

Mom must have sensed something, because she came down the stairs. By the look in her eye, she had surmised what had happened, but she needed me to say it. "What's going on?" she asked, her voice quavering with emotion. The look she shot my father was kilned hatred. "Did he touch you?"

Mute, I shook my head vigorously.

"Did he touch you?" she asked again.

Her eyes implored that I tell the truth. *If you tell me the truth*, her eyes said, *I can do something about it. But if you don't, there's nothing I can do.* All this she said with one look. I shook my head once more, but I could not meet her gaze.

People specializing in family sexual abuse say victims will protect the abuser because of fear of reprisal. In my case, although I feared Dad's anger, I feared Mom's anger toward him more. Mom was an accomplished big-game hunter. If she learned the truth, I knew that at some point in the not-too-distant future, she would walk calmly to the portable gun case she kept in the basement and take out her shotgun, the one whose stock had been intricately hand carved by my father years ago, when he loved her. She would clean it, oil it, and put two shells in the barrel. She would then aim that gun at my father's head and pull the trigger.

Of that I had no doubt.

It is nearly the end of July in Glacier National Park, and my crew has worked all week to complete one final project before our eight weeks are finished: replace the subfloor on a historic cabin near St. Mary Lake, located on the east side of the park. Our home is a two-person tent at St. Mary campground, whose stunted aspen trees tell the story of harsh winters and endless wind. Now, however, it is warm, and winter is a long ways away.

Catherine, my tentmate, is a member of the Blackfeet tribe and an adoptee. She tells me that every weekend her adoptive family takes her to visit her "real" family. I feel a twinge of jealousy, because members of her real family are not ghosts; she knows them by name and by relationship. A few weeks ago Catherine's Indian grandmother died, and she cried, deep sobs that welled up from her chest. This told me everything I needed to know about her love for this elderly woman. And I wanted to cry with her, but the tears wouldn't come. I have no idea who my Indian grandmother is or what she's like or even if she's alive. Perhaps if I'd known these things I could have cried with her.

We've been working hard all week, so when I sleep, I sleep the way of the dead, unmoving. And I dream. I dream of someone calling my name, calling me to join him. "Come with me. Susan, come with me," he whispers, this faceless, body-less being. I walk along a corridor whose walls are silk, giving way when I push on them, following the voice that seems to be continually moving on the other side. I try to answer the voice, but my tongue is thick in my mouth, and the words won't form. Suddenly, my feet stumble over something unexpected. I hear a harsh whisper.

"What in the hell are you doing?"

I am forced back into wakefulness and realize I've stumbled over her legs. I have a sense of vertigo, and my hands and feet feel like lead. "I don't know what I'm doing," I answer. My sleep-filled brain is confused, and I am unable to fully process where I am. "I guess I'm sleepwalking."

Except that the voice continues to call for me to join him. *Him.*

"Who is it?" I ask through the fabric of the tent.

"It's me. Victor. Come with me. I need your help."

I make my way over to the tent's doorway and unzip the fabric. The high-altitude cold slaps my face, and a billion stars wink beyond his shadow.

"What time is it?" I ask, my voice a whisper.

"It's about one in the morning."

Victor's answer doesn't make sense. What does he need help with at one o'clock in the morning? I ask him the question, and he replies, "We have to get tools at the cabin. I left a bunch there this afternoon, and I have to get them before we leave tomorrow."

I pause, only momentarily. "Okay, hold on," I say and turn back into the tent.

Catherine clamps her hand on my leg. "Don't go."

"I have to," I whisper back, pulling on a cold pair of jeans and a T-shirt as well as the sweatshirt that's been worn too many days. "He's my boss."

"You don't have to go," she implores. "You're not on work hours. It's weird he's even asking you."

"I don't want to get fired," I say to her as I step through the doorway. "My dad would kill me if I get fired."

I step through the doorway, and it is immediately clear from his stumbles and the odor of liquor that seeps from every pore that Victor is drunk. My stomach churns at the smell.

"Your dad's not going to kill you," Catherine says, sticking her head out the door, giving one last appeal.

"Yeah, you don't know my dad."

No one outside my family trio knew how much my dad believed in corporal punishment. I would definitely get hit. A lot. Of that I am certain. His anger is already sparked by my dawning womanhood and its budding sexuality. He seems to sit and wait for me to screw up, to make bad decisions, which I always seem to do. And since he doesn't trust me, I've stopped trusting myself. Other people obviously know better than me, and if I just go with the flow, anger is abated. At least that's how it works in my sixteen-year-old mind.

"We gotta go get the tools," Victor says, his eyes heavy-lidded and his tongue so thick the words sloop out of his mouth in a way that makes them barely understandable. He weaves in the fertile light of the full moon.

"Why?" I still can't seem to shake the fuzziness from my sleep-drugged brain.

"Because we have to get them before we leave." His voice is edged with annoyance, and I let it roll off me because it must be me who doesn't understand. His voice indicates it is so obvious to him. Therefore, I am compliant as I follow Victor, watching him stumble toward the government truck. I am unfazed not only by his lack of coordination but by the fact that he's getting behind the wheel. His behavior is nothing new; I've witnessed it with my dad many times. "Let's go," Victor says, his words slurring as he pulls open the heavy door, losing his footing once more.

"Can you drive?" I ask.

"I'm fine. Just get in."

Victor burps and the smell of whiskey rides the steam of his breath across the cab. I look over at him and watch his deep-seated eyes fail to focus. The truck weaves beneath his unsteady hands, and the back tires fall off the asphalt. Something clunks around in the bed, and I swallow my fear, aware of the burning remnants of an ulcer that I first felt when I was ten. Victor roughly maneuvers the truck back on the road, and I lay my head back against the seat and close my eyes to all the other cues of dysfunction around me. This place where I am, physically and mentally, is out of my control, and it is familiar. So familiar that I fall asleep entirely as heat finally pours out of the vents, bringing an end to my shivering.

Glancing at my watch, I see that we arrive at the cabin at one thirty in the morning. In just a few hours we are scheduled to return to West Glacier, to our familiar camp, to my friends who weren't placed on this crew, to Victor's pregnant wife whose hip is riddled with cancer. He turns off the engine and suddenly my brain begins to wake up, processing the danger I'm in. We are in the middle of nowhere, it's pitch dark, and I haven't seen any other cars since leaving the campsite.

The screech of the truck door hinge makes me jump, evidence that my nerves are raw. Victor fishes around in the bed of the truck and finds the flashlight that has been rolling around back there, causing the clunking noise. "Well, let's get to it," he says, his slurring somewhat diminished.

Victor turns the flashlight on, and the beam weaves unsteadily in his hand, illuminating the hammers, wrenches, saws, and a myriad of other tools that lie scattered across the makeshift yard. One by one Victor and I throw these into the bed of the truck, where they slam, metal against metal. As I bend to pick up the leftovers, Victor's voice, no longer quiet and whispered, cuts through the night's eerie stillness. "There's more upstairs in the cabin." He indicates the doorway with his chin. He stumbles up the stairs of the front porch and motions me inside, without looking whether or not I'm following. Maybe he doesn't have to. Maybe he just knows.

A chill crawls up the back of my neck, and I look out at the trees, feeling that we are being watched by spirits, by animals hiding behind shrubs or crouched in the grass. I shiver then and tell myself it's only the eyes of night animals, the bats, the owls, the ones that move easily under a blanket of darkness, the ones annoyed at our presence. I turn away from the trees that guard the darkness and toward the shaking ray of light that falls on the floor of the cabin.

The beam is cast on the remnants of stairs, dismantled and not yet fully rebuilt. In their place are narrow oblong frames, on which a slab of oak will sit at some point in the future. Victor has already somehow scaled these and is standing about seven feet above me on what will be the second floor. I gingerly place a shaking foot on the two-inch width of framing and feel myself teeter. My balance has never been great, and there is no handrail to steady myself. *What if my leg slips?* I don't think long on that possibility.

Victor stumbles around in the near darkness, and suddenly I feel anger welling up in my chest, traveling at light speed through my arms and legs, my fingers, my toes. I'm angry that I've been awakened for this job, angry that I'm here with a drunk, and angry that I've let myself get into this situation. It is that anger that carries me up those stairs. It quickly turns to fear, however, when I cross the flooring and turn around, only to find Victor blocking my way to the stairs. I feel his hands on my shoulders, pushing me, forcing me backward, hoping I'll lose my footing and fall. But I stay upright. Without thinking I take a step back and watch as he stumbles forward.

"What are you doing?" I shout, fear chewing at the edges of my consciousness.

"Oh, come on. Don't play dumb," he says, his words sliding past his lips, swaggering and self-confident. He reaches his hand toward my chest, but his fingers are clumsy, and they grasp air as I take another step back. The momentum of his reach pulls him forward, and he lands on his hands and knees. Fear takes control, and I scream from the bottom of my lungs. I scream and I hear it shattering the night into a thousand aural crystals. Victor scrambles to his feet then; I'm surprised at his agility. That same agility allows him to clap his hands over my mouth. I bite into the tender flesh of his palm, and he lets go and steps back. There is anger in his eyes, and I open my mouth and scream again; this time the sound becomes even more shrill as I begin to panic. *God, let someone hear me!* I run out of breath then, and silence settles like a velvet curtain, dampening the echoes that seem to go on forever, growing weaker as they glide across the lake. They have been swallowed by the walls of the cabin, the forest, the carpet of tall grass in the meadow. All those barriers have taken huge bites, leaving only a weak strand to find its way to our camp ten miles away. No sound returns to me.

Once more Victor slaps his hand across my mouth. "Shhhh, shhhhh. Stop, stop, stop!" He pleads into my ear, misgivings saturating his words, alarm replacing the alcohol dullness in his feral black eyes. "Just stop screaming, goddamn it! I'm not trying to hurt you. Stop screaming and I'll take my hand away. I won't touch you. But you have to stop."

I stare at him, my eyes wide, as my lungs suck a weak stream of air through his fingers. I nod. He pulls away, and we measure each other up for our word. Then I wait, fear overtaking all emotion. I wait for the slap, for the physical retribution, for the pain of the payment of my transgression. But it doesn't come. We have changed positions through this dance of power, and I see the empty space behind him, where no railing stands between the first and second floor. If he moves toward me, I can push him back, where he'll drop into the nothingness seven feet below. Now I have a plan. I hold his gaze and plant my feet wide. I am grounded. I am the warrior, and I am ready.

He takes a step toward me. That's all it takes as I push, with my heart and soul, I push and watch as Victor's mouth widens into an O as my hands land on his shoulders and take his feet out from under him. His arms rotate uselessly, like windmills, to catch his balance, and his eyes, black and wild, no longer see me as he falls backward.

I watch in horror as he teeters on the edge. Then other thoughts come. *What if he breaks a leg? What if he falls so hard he hits his head and is knocked unconscious or ends up in a coma? What if he dies?* He falls backward, and I rush to the edge, feeling a confusion of emotion: he fell but not seven feet. One leg is caught in the empty frames of the future stairs.

"Help me. Help me up," he says as he lifts an arm in my direction.

But I stand and shake my head.

With a grimace he hauls himself up to a sitting position, straddling the framework. He is angry now, an anger that twists his mouth and brightens his eyes. "Jesus Christ! What in the hell did you do that for?"

I lean forward and clench my teeth, my own fear becoming as dark and dangerous as his. "Don't fucking touch me again," I say, low and measured. I feel adrenaline move like an electrical current through my arms, my legs, my jaw. I clamp my teeth shut to stop their chattering. "You touch me again, I will kill you."

No more words are exchanged as Victor hauls himself out and walks out the door, far soberer than when he walked in. We get in the truck, forgetting about the tools that still lay scattered on the second floor and litter the makeshift lawn around us, the ones we will not be bringing back to the camp. As he climbs behind the wheel, I reflect on how much we all revered this man, this Native American, who sounded so wise, so learned, at the beginning of our summer. We held on to his every word, thinking he held the key to us realizing the people we would become. Me especially. But now I'm disgusted. "Women want me," he sneers as he drives along the dark ribbon of asphalt. "I have slept with so many women; they beg me to sleep with them. You have no idea what you're missing." And it goes on, while I look out the window at the stars in the night sky, tarnished diamonds, the moon long in hiding. My shivering is back, but it's not from the cold.

As I crawl back into my sleeping bag, I know I won't tell the director or the counselors. I don't want Dad to find out. He'll wonder what I did to provoke the assault, what I said, what I wore, what vibes I gave off that would make this okay. So I will have to remain silent. In my family, sex and silence go hand in hand.

3

Coping Mechanisms

Billings, Montana, August 1976.

It's been a year since my summer in Glacier National Park, and I look back at that time with a mixture of joy, confusion, and anger. But not for long. A new chapter in my life is beginning, and I feel excited. My senior year is coming, and in my mind it will be filled with parties, sleepovers, and movies. Memories in the making. Get through this and the gate of life will be open. I will be free! I am partially there already, in the freedom department. Last month Dad, angry with the marriage, took a job in Minot, North Dakota. He'd made no invitation for us to join him. This wasn't the first time my parents had lived apart; there was the time Mom had left him, taking me with her, in Great Falls. But I think he figured the marriage would be patched up, like it was before. Therefore, he saw his leaving as a separation. Mom saw it as regaining her independence and filed for divorce. That's why we're having a garage sale.

Our garage is beneath the house, a sharp ninety-degree turn from the street. Mom never parks in the garage because her Oldsmobile Delta 88 can't make that turn. So this space has been turned into Dad's

3. Adoptive parents, Jed and Eleanor; and Susan, age three. A family photo. Photo by Jed Devan. Courtesy of the author.

woodworking shop, with shelves added for additional storage. Today, however, it's turned into a secondhand store. Mom and I have brought our dining room table, our coffee tables, and side tables down the narrow stairs from the main living floor. These will be used to show our "gently used" wares. For more counter space Mom has placed a piece of plywood over two sawhorses. These surfaces will hold, seemingly, every article we own. Mom has taken this garage sale very seriously.

"I hope no early birds show up," she says, as she carefully writes the item number and the price on tags and checks these against an inventory sheet. "I can't stand the early birds. They'll have plenty of time to buy without showing up at six in the morning." She doesn't pause in her efficiency. This afternoon her voice is unusually sharp, but I dismiss it, thinking it's just nerves. Tomorrow her space will be invaded by a hoard of strangers. Handing me a stack of price tags and a pen, she points to a box filled with my childhood: books, toys, and stuffed animals, none of which I want to sell. But what I want is immaterial. "You're too old for that junk," she says, waving away my distress. There is no arguing with her.

I fan out my set of Nancy Drew books, published in the late 1950s. Their navy cloth covers are worn and tattered along the edges, signs of the love affairs young girls have for good mysteries. I hold *The Secret of the Old Clock* to my nose and inhale the musty smell of attics, closets, and boxes garnered through my three moves and countless others by its previous owners. When I place it with the others, my heart is heavy. As if to say good-bye, I touch each gently, placing a sticker with "10 cents" written carefully across it, and turn away, a lump in my throat. Mom's voice whispers in my mind, *Imagine, crying over a book!*

These books, among others, are not just material items; they've woven themselves around my heart. As an only child, isolated in the rural landscape, they have kept me company on long, solitary days and provided a screen of distraction while my parents quarreled bitterly. I hate saying good-bye.

While I've been working on my things, Mom has hung a length of steel pipe, held in place by wires from the ceiling. It is about three feet long and acts like a clothes rod, where shirts and pants and some skirts and dresses are carefully hung on hangers. The only item I don't want to sell is the umber doeskin vest, velvety soft, constructed from the hide taken during a successful hunting season twenty-some years earlier. Mom had fashioned a beaded design, which sits gracefully above each pocket flap. It will be the first thing people will see. My fingers move gently over the glass beads, and I pull the leather close to my face, drawing in its smell. I'd worn it, just as I wore Mom's buckskin jacket (which I was able to talk her out of selling), taking pride in their representation of my American Indian heritage. Granted, it is an imagined heritage; I was not raised in an Indian family, nor was I raised in any kind of Native community. But when I slip it on, I feel more "Indian." I don't tell anyone this because it sounds ridiculous, but I see it as my heritage nonetheless.

"Why are you getting rid of this?" I ask for the third time, holding the leather gently in my palm.

"I don't wear it anymore," she answers, tying yet another tag to another piece of our past.

"But I do," I argue, unable to keep the pleading out of my voice.

"You're going to college next year; you don't need that old thing. Someone else can use it."

I sulk. Especially when I glance at the price tag: "$12."

The next morning, within ten minutes of the sale starting, the doeskin vest is purchased by a woman in her twenties, her broad smile indicating she found the deal of the century. By two in the afternoon nearly everything has been purchased. Mom is making fantastic deals in her last-minute negotiations. By three she pulls the garage door shut and goes upstairs to make a late lunch while I clean up. Bored in the silence, I turn the radio dial to a hit station and turn up the volume. Fleetwood Mac's "Don't Stop Thinking about Tomorrow" blares from the Sony speakers. I sigh as I sweep the floor. Considering this day and the ease with which my life has been carried out the door, tomorrow seems to be the only solid thing I have to think about.

The divorce is finalized three weeks after Mom filed, and Dad is astounded at how fast it was granted. "The judge didn't even ask me if I wanted it!" he says, confusion filling his voice. Montana, a no-fault state, is filled with domestic violence, drinking, and a lot of spite. The attitude is that those who want out should be allowed to do so. Quickly. So now Mom is single and filing to reclaim her maiden name; she wants nothing to do with Dad.

Tension trickles into every aspect of my life, and I no longer see my dreams of a fun senior year taking place. Mom is abrupt; Dad is absent. I turn down every invitation offered for fear friends will know how really chaotic my life is. One night in the middle of October, chaos takes a new turn, when I walk into the living room to see Mom crouched near one of the stereo speakers. "What are you trying to tell me?" she asks the speaker, then she turns her head so she can catch whatever reply might return. I have no idea what that reply might contain. All I hear is the weather report. It is calling for snow.

That night I lay in bed and wonder, how did she move from a frantic garage sale to this? I rake my memory, but nothing stands out. I can't map the change in her behavior, one gentle step leading to another. Or perhaps I don't want to map the change because it might undermine my belief that never once, in my fifteen years being raised by her, has Mom ever given me reason to doubt her actions. She's dedicated her life to me, her daughter. I was never her adopted daughter. She signed me up for all the appropriate cultural lessons: music, piano, voice, and dance—both ballet and jazz. She made sure I had access to all the activities she felt kids should be part of: Girl Scouts, 4-H, Pep Club, band, orchestra, and choir. She felt the right friends to be important, so she'd drive me sometimes fifty miles round-trip to girls' houses to encourage friendships. But more than anything, she protected me.

When I was sixteen Mom and I went to a small mall in Missoula, Montana, that contained a variety of retail shops. I wanted to go to the clothing store; Mom wanted to go next door. She'd meet me at the clothing store when she was done. Alone I moved around and between the racks, pushing clothes apart to get a better look, moving on to the next and the next and the next. I leisurely explored the bins, holding up T-shirts that I thought might be fun. But I felt the manager's eyes on me: she was predator and I was prey. I looked at her, her mouth turned down, her eyes unblinking. That changed in a moment when another woman came to the register, garment in hand. She was all smiles and bright talk. In fact, over the twenty minutes or so I was there, she seemed to have a smile for everyone except for me. Every time I looked up, she was staring at me. At some point she muttered something about dirty Indians, and I felt my face grow hot. I didn't know what to do, so I stood back, away from the clothes, near the door, and waited for Mom. When she arrived, I held a pair of jeans several sizes too large and pleaded with her just to buy them. I could alter them when we got back to Billings, I assured her. I just wanted her to help me escape the oppressive heat of hatred that filtered around me. I didn't want her to see how inferior I was. Although Mom had tried to raise me to stand up for myself, this woman behind the cash register held more power and more authority; I couldn't stand up against that. I had no self-confidence. I felt there was something wrong with me.

When I was six, Mom and I lay side by side on our stomachs looking for four-leaf clovers in the lawn. We rested on our forearms while our fingers combed through the end-of-June grass, dark green and strong against our fingers. My brown arm lay against her porcelain one, and I admired its myriad of freckles. "You have such pretty skin," I said. "I wish I had your skin."

She looked at me, her eyes wide, while she wrinkled her nose and pulled her brows playfully together. "This old, white skin? No, you don't want this skin. What I would give to have your beautiful, young brown skin."

And then she smiled. And I smiled back. But I still wanted her skin instead of my own.

By the time I was sixteen, and in that store, I was aware of what brown skin meant. I also was aware there was nothing anyone could do about it. Even me. So I gave the woman a twenty-dollar bill and, while Mom stood nearby, the manager said, just loud enough for my ears, "All you people do is come in here and steal me blind." She slammed the register closed and handed me back my change, and I felt my face burn with shame as I walked through the door. I finally got rid of those jeans before leaving for college two years later. I threw them into a trash bin, unaltered.

And Mom protected us, as a family, making sure no one was aware of how badly our family functioned, with Dad's alcoholism and abuse and her depression, which became noticeable when we lived in Naselle, Washington. At the time she'd blamed it on the rain; I now blame it on the fact that our family was volatile and fragile. She'd hidden it all so well from the public, from our friends, even from me, that I was unaware of the impact, the designs these dysfunctions etched on our lives.

So when she begins talking into the stereo speakers, there is no rational way to explain it. Therefore, it has to be something beyond my own knowing. Maybe, I think, if you flip a switch, stereo speakers can receive as well as send sounds. I have no idea; I've never thought about how electronics work. I just hope no one comes to the door when she is talking into them.

On Thanksgiving Day it is cold. The snow lies a couple of inches thick, covering the driveway, the grass, the outside stairs, while the thinning layer of clouds above indicates that the sun is going to break through at some point. Mom has been up all night talking with the person on the other end of the stereo speaker, and her eyes are wild and tired. As much as I love her, I am increasingly frustrated that she can't be quiet and just go to bed. The doorbell rings, and I glance at the clock. It's nine in the morning. We aren't expecting anyone. Mom follows me to the front door, and I pull it open. Dad stands on the concrete landing, cradling a frozen turkey in his arms. "Happy Thanksgiving," he says, his smile broad. He extends the bird toward me. A peace offering.

Mom pushes me out of the way. "You goddamned son of a bitch! Get that out of here. You're trying to kill us!" I look at her face, agitated and filled with anger. Spittle flies from her mouth as she pushes the words out. Her eyes, normally a moderate brown, now shine obsidian, glinting in the frail morning light.

Confusion replaces Dad's smile. "This is just a turkey," he explains. "I'm just bringing this for Thanksgiving. I thought you'd appreciate it."

"Susie, get in here," Mom hisses between clenched teeth. "It's a bomb. That goddamned bastard has brought a bomb into this house!" She tries pulling on the sleeve of my T-shirt, but it slips through her fingers as I step out of the house.

"Mom, it's a Thanksgiving turkey!" I bark. "That's all."

Mom looks at me as if I've just lost my mind. "That bastard has never done anything without having a plan behind it, and now he wants to blow us up." She then turns her full attention on the person she had—until recently—been married to for nearly thirty years. "I'm calling the bomb squad." And with that she closes the wooden door, clicking the lock into place.

Dad and I exchange uneasy glances. Within moments I hear sirens wail their way along Rimrock Avenue. "What the hell has gotten into her?" Dad asks. But I don't have time to answer; the police have shown up in a white van with an official emblem blazed on its side. The doors slide open, and three men get out, dressed in protective gear. They pull their plastic face guards down and warn Dad to get well away from the bird, but not to leave. They proceed then to take apart the frozen bird, the one he'd purchased at Safeway that morning after pulling into town at the end of a long night of driving. They hack, they cut, they saw at the carcass until it lay in tatters on the hood of Mom's Oldsmobile. The bomb squad seems to take it all very seriously, while I die the slow death of a seventeen-year-old girl whose mother talks into speakers and whose father is accused of burying a bomb in a frozen turkey that requires the assistance of the Billings Police Department's bomb squad. I am aware of neighbors who spy, glancing out their doors and windows, blinds and curtains falling quickly into place when I look in their direction. This is the family spectacle of the season, and it is so absurdly public. We have always been such a protectively private family.

"Ma'am, there's no bomb here," the head of the squad says, addressing the eye that peeks out of the slit of the barely opened door.

"Are you sure?"

"Yes, ma'am. We're sure. We've taken the whole thing apart, and no bomb has been found." I can't tell if he is serious, or if there is the tiniest bit of laughter being held back.

But there is no mistaking the seriousness of Mom's voice when she screams, "Then you tell that son of a bitch to get off my property!" She slams the door again and immediately turns the deadbolt.

The head of the bomb squad turns around and addresses my dad, his voice tired but measured. "Sir," he says, his eyes sympathetically averted, "you're going to have to leave the property."

"But it's my property too," Dad begins to argue, irritation tingeing the words, making them harsh and too loud in the quiet morning.

The sympathy of the officer disappears, and his voice hardens. "Sir, you need to leave the property. I have no idea what this is all about, and frankly, I don't really care. I'm sure you're a great guy, bringing a turkey to his family on Thanksgiving, but the lady wants you to leave and we need to ensure you do that."

"Come on, Dad," I state and begin to walk toward his truck. The last thing I want is a showdown with the police officer. But then I'm the peacekeeper. I've played this role for my entire life. ❧

"Susie, don't get in that truck," Mom yells from the house. I look up to see her head against the screen of a window she's just opened. "He'll kill you!"

Too many sleepless nights, too much adrenaline, and too much drama causes my temper to snap. I glare at her and yank open the door of Dad's truck and slide in. Before slamming the door shut, I yell, "He's okay. I'm okay. Go get some sleep, for Christ's sake!"

My father slides in on the driver's side, puts the truck into gear, and backs out of the driveway. We begin a slow crawl down the curved street past the empty house of my best friend, Cari. Thank God she'd moved a few months before and is not privy to what has just transpired. At the end of the street Dad pulls over and asks questions for which I have no answers. I have no explanation for her outburst; I really have no idea what's just happened. I just know there's been a break, a rupture, silently rendered, in the fabric of my reality.

"Well, maybe it's time I move back to Billings, keep an eye on things here," he says, a spoken thought, as if he's forgotten I am next to him.

"Don't move back," I tell him, quickly and without hesitation. Silence meets my statement, so we sit in the truck while the engine runs, pumping heat into the already stiflingly warm interior. "There's nothing you can do here. I can take care of it. Your moving back would just make things a whole lot worse."

Although it sounds like I'm protecting him, I'm not. I am saying I don't want him in this town. We've had a stormy and contentious relationship since I was twelve, and it hasn't gotten any better. His alcoholism has played a big role, blossoming when I was ten and hitting full bloom by the time I was thirteen. He'd quit drinking a year and a half ago, but it didn't solve the entire problem. He still had a generally angry nature, which in itself has created an irreparable schism in our relationship. To be honest, having him at a distance has given me a sense of peace, of solace, that I hadn't felt in years. I don't want that peace interrupted, especially now when I am under so much pressure trying to deal with my mom.

On the other hand, I do feel a certain amount of empathy for my dad, especially now, seeing him slumped over with his arms on the steering wheel. He seems so much older than when he'd left us a few months ago. It's clear he was blindsided not only by the divorce but also by the way his wife, now ex-wife, had met him at the front door with curses, epithets, and threats that would make any sailor proud. There is really nothing more to say.

"I guess I'll get a motel room and grab a couple hours sleep before driving back to Minot." He wipes his hand along his chin. He looks tired. Tired and beaten. When I get out of the truck, I raise a hand in farewell, but he doesn't see it. His eyes are on his dismal future. I shove my hands in my jeans pockets and begin the walk toward home, holding my elbows close to my sides as the cold seeps through my thin T-shirt.

When I get back to the house, Mom meets me at the door, and her black eyes scan the street behind me. "Where is he?" she asks warily.

"He left," I sigh. I enter the front door, tired and dazed. "Since our turkey has been disemboweled by the bomb squad, what are we doing for dinner?"

"Oh," she says airily, waving away my question with her hand. "We're having dinner. And we're having a guest." She drops her voice. "*He's bringing it.*" Anger has been abruptly replaced by a buoyant, careless attitude.

"Who is 'he'?" There's a pit in my stomach.

"Oh, you'll see soon enough," she hints, then speaks in an excited, low tone. "It's a surprise." Her eyes are still jet black, the soft brown of her irises buried beneath the madness. She's still beautiful, with her long black lashes against pale skin, and her smile at once engaging and whimsical. This look suggests a crush, the beginnings of love; I can't recall ever seeing this particular look when she was with my dad, ever. I would be happy for her except, given the state of her mind, I don't think love is a good idea. The pit in my stomach combines with heart palpitations, and her possible romance becomes a feared thing. But it's happening, regardless of what I want. I begin to set the table for a Thanksgiving Day meal that doesn't originate in our home.

At some point, when I was in grade school, Dad felt it was important that I be taught etiquette. Hence, the purchase of the book *Manners for All Occasions*, a book for older children, complete with line-drawn illustrations whose colors were limited to pastel pink and blue. I was enchanted and thumbed through it almost daily, committing its activities and behaviors to memory. I remember being quite impressed with the insistence of the author to act "just so" and telling me just how to do that. Keep in mind, this was just two years after the John F. Kennedy's assassination, and the United States wasn't yet finished with the pomp and circumstance of Jacqueline Kennedy. One chapter in particular caught my attention: formal table settings.

I was enamored by the formal setting, memorizing the placement of glasses (both water and wine), cups and saucers, silverware—including the placement of the knife after it had been used—dishes, salad plates, bread plates, bowls, and the ever important cloth napkin that cradled the forks for salad, dinner, and dessert. Our family never entertained like that; my parents were introverts and more interested in growing, hunting, and preparing food than of how to serve it. We were middle class. The book was for someone much more aristocratic than us.

Except on Thanksgiving. That was the day Mom pulled out all the stops and set a very elegant table. And because of Mom's anticipated guest, I do the same. When I am finished, I stand back and admire my work. The silverware, the Mikasa china set, and the crystal glasses all lie precisely on top of the white linen tablecloth that had been hand-embroidered in delft blue, complete with matching napkins. Standing sentry in the center of the table are a pair of colonial blue candles on their myrtle wood base. I smile. I've done it by myself, while Mom is sleeping in her bedroom, and when she wakes up I imagine her reaction of happiness, because I'll have "done her proud."

The wall clock reads three. I have no idea when he will arrive, and neither does Mom. But evidently she's not worried, and I try not to be. But when she comes out of her room an hour later, I ask with the first tinge of worry, "Are you sure he's going to bring all the food?"

It is the absence that bewilders me. The absence of aroma, the roast turkey, the dressing, the cranberry sauce, the baked rolls, and the clove-spice pumpkin pie. The absence of Dad. The absence of friends. All of it is disconcerting. But the most disturbing absence is my mom, that strong and stalwart person I knew in the springtime has been replaced with someone unrecognizable to me. Her absence has scattered my sense of self to the far corners of the world. My world.

This person who waves away my concern with her hand, an airiness to her voice, her eyes black and unreadable; I no longer know this person. "He's bringing everything," she assures me, and there is a sense of weightlessness to her soul, a faith in the universe that I no longer have.

I kneel on the couch and look out the picture window, biting my nails. Will the potatoes be already mashed with gravy on the side? Would he bring canned or fresh cranberries? What about the fruit salad that Mom always serves alongside the meal; did he know how to make it? And would he remember the pumpkin pie? And the whipped cream? I wish we had made the dinner.

Another hour goes by, and Mom is unfazed.

"Are you sure he knows he's bringing dinner?" I ask again.

"Yes," she answers easily, unperturbed by my incessant question. "I'm positive. He's taking care of it all." Again, that wave of her hand that brushes off concern, a gesture that begins to set me on edge. Usually she is the one worrying and fretting about the details, and I'm unaware of any possible glitches. We have switched roles, and I'm not prepared.

I gather up courage to ask my next question, glancing at her out of the corner of my eye, getting ready to measure her reaction. "So how do you know him?" My words come out slowly, oozing through guarded lips.

"Oh, we work together. His wife left him. Just walked out on him and his two girls." I give a silent groan. *There's going to be children too?* It's too overwhelming. And Mom's explanation makes it all sound like gossip. Except she never gossips. A knot forms in my stomach as she adds, "So I invited them." It seems straightforward enough, but the knot remains.

"What time are they supposed to be here?" Dinner was usually around three, and the clock on the wall said it was five in the afternoon.

"Oh, I don't know," she answers with a tinge of disinterest. "I haven't heard yet."

The knot tightens. "Is he going to call you to let you know?"

A smile rests on her lips, wily and teasing, as if she's got a secret. "There are other ways of communicating than through the phone," she answers with a half smile, raising her eyebrows meaningfully.

Acid coats my stomach. "What way?"

"You have to promise not to tell anyone," she whispers. Her eyes are wide, like a child's on Christmas, her lashes so long they touch her dark brows.

"Okay," I answer, doubt edging my words. "I won't."

Her voice drops conspiratorially. "He talks to me through the stereo speakers." She puts her finger to her lips and nods her head toward the speakers, mouthing the words, *Somebody's listening*. She then walks out of the room.

"But I haven't heard anybody talk to you through the speakers," I say, following her, my granite world rocking beneath my feet.

"I know," she says with a wink and a slow nod of her head. "It's because you don't know how to listen."

Mom stops for a moment and looks around, confused, as if she's suddenly disoriented. She studies the carefully set table, then her gaze wanders to the window, the door, and finally the speakers, where it rests for several moments. Then, quietly, seriously, she excuses herself. "I'm going to lie down for a while."

"But what if they come?" I know them only as a "they" because I don't know any of their names! Fingers of anxiety glide along my arms. I don't want to answer the door without her beside me. There is absolutely nothing familiar about this emotional landscape.

"It will be fine," she answers, but she sounds tired, the teasing gone. She disappears into her bedroom and shuts the door, and I sit on the couch, silence ringing in my ears. Once, twice, three times the hands of the clock rotate around its face, until it's almost eight at night. Outside it's dark, and streetlights dot the landscape. Still there is no sign of the family or of the food. Almost as if feeling my worry, Mom emerges from her bedroom and looks around and then looks at me. I watch in trepidation as her face becomes a mass of confusion, her eyebrows knitting together as if she is trying to solve the most difficult of puzzles. "He's not here yet?"

I shake my head. She glances at the speaker, the one closest to the dining room table, and cocks her head. She kneels down, placing her mouth near the woofer, and yells, "Where are you?" She pauses and sits back. Nothing. She leans forward once more, her mouth inches away from the fabric. "Aren't you coming?" Another pause. "You son of a bitch!" Now her voice is shaking with rage. "Answer me!" Mom rises and stares at me, her eyes black wells into the depth of her soul. She stares at me, expressions of hurt and anger vying with each other in a disjointed dance.

"I guess he's not coming." She tries to keep her tone light, but a tear courses unimpeded down her lined cheek, and the words are weak and far away. Suddenly, her face crumples along with her composure. "I can't believe he's not coming!" She disappears into her bedroom and slams the door. From within I hear her deep, wracking sobs, flooding through the thin veneer that covers the hollow core. I listen to them for an hour. When they stop, I open the door and see Mom curled on the bed, her ribcage rising and falling in the rhythms of sleep. I shut it once I know she's okay.

My confusion resurfaces as I disassemble the table setting, my motions robotic and repetitive. I return the good dishes to their boxes, the silverware to its flannel blanket, and the glasses to their shelves. I fold the napkins and the linen tablecloth and do anything but think about what just happened. And when the thoughts make their way in, like eels, I wonder if he even knew he was supposed to come on Thanksgiving.

4

Lost Bearings

Billings, Montana, December 1976.

Winter has begun in earnest. The three inches of snow that fell overnight now rests heavy on every surface, bending pine limbs into uncomfortable positions and resting in the crotches of the maples and the elms that surround us. It is late morning, and Mom has left the house. I heard her leave. I have no idea where she went and, frankly, I don't care. My eyes burn with the lack of sleep, and her erratic behavior has set me on edge. So I didn't watch her go. I didn't even answer her announcement of leaving.

I'm tired, and my frustration borders on anger, which is really the flip side of fear. Since Thanksgiving, the stereo speakers have still been her main access to the outside world. Last night she talked loudly into them all night long, first one, then the other. Strange ideas slid out of her mind and into the electronics, as she asked someone on the other end for directions for what she was to do next or queried the disembodied silent people about their activities, all spoken in a code I was not able to translate.

Since Thanksgiving she's become obsessed by three songs: Neil

Diamond's "I Am, I Said," Simon and Garfunkel's "I Am a Rock," and Manfred Mann's Earth Band's "Blinded by the Light." These she plays at top volume. "That's so people who are listening on the airwaves can't hear who I'm talking to or what I'm saying," she explained.

Sometimes she'll just play these songs on our turntable; other times she'll sing along in her off-key voice, while tears stream down her cheeks. Years later will I understand the meaning each song held for her. Neil Diamond made visible the invisibility she must have felt being married to my dad and his constant belittlement that cut away at both of us, like a raging creek eating away the soil that borders it. Simon and Garfunkel voiced her declaration of value and substance, reminding her of her strength that allowed her to survive. And Manfred Mann provided an interpretation of her experiences that seemed to be exploding inside her head, emotional firework displays of overwhelming proportions.

But right now I don't know these things. I know only that I own the records of Neil Diamond and Simon and Garfunkel, so she plays these constantly. I am overly familiar with the *tick-tick-tick* of the record needle as it settles into its groove. But she has to wait for Manfred Mann to play on the radio. Luckily for her, it's a hit song, so it plays several times a day. On the weekends, between the songs and her shouting and marching in time to the percussion, I am assaulted by sound twenty-four hours a day. Well, probably twenty-two: she sleeps, on and off, a couple of hours each day. I am sure this is how she sounds on the days when I'm at school; I know this is how she sounds at night. Therefore, my coping skills are wearing thin.

So when she leaves through the front door and tells me she's going for a walk, I don't really care. I just want the silence and the ability to think without interruption. I want to be able to lie on the couch with my head on my arm, my ear resting somewhere near my elbow, and listen to the blood pump rhythmically through my veins. I want to watch the snowflakes outside the window dance their way to the ground, like in Disney's *Fantasia*. I just want to sleep, which I do, falling off into a blissful silence.

Brrnnggg!!! The telephone jangles me awake. It rings three times before I am able to get off the couch and run to the kitchen, lifting the wall-mounted handset to my ear. "Hello?" My tongue is thick, and my mind is thicker as I try to wake up, to focus.

"This is Officer Kelsey with the Billings Police Department," replies an official, serious voice. "Are you Susan?"

His words zing through my sleep-addled brain, and suddenly I'm on alert. "Yes?"

"Your mom is here at Deaconess Hospital," he says without emotion. "We're at Dr. Haw's office, and we're wondering if you could come down and talk with us. When do you think you can be here?"

I glance at the clock. It is almost three. Five hours. I've been sleeping five hours! The knot in my stomach that began on Thanksgiving is now a constant, and it tightens once more. I assure him in the strongest voice I can muster that I will be there in fifteen minutes. I grab my mom's car keys from the counter and pull the coat from the closet, leaving through the same front door that Mom had closed behind her.

The car keys belong to the brand-new $7,000 peach-colored Saab Mom had purchased right before Thanksgiving. It is a beautiful car with European lines and European gadgets, like heated seats and a thick plastic ring that has to be pulled up the gearshift to allow access to reverse, the only gear in which the car can be started. This car has been a source of bitter contention, because it was purchased with the divorce settlement money. Money, Dad said, he didn't work so hard for so she could blow it in one visit to the most expensive car dealership in town. But I think that's why she did it. He said she couldn't swing it financially; she didn't really care what he thought. She was a rock, and she was an island.

I'm at the hospital within fifteen minutes and swing into a parking space, the sure-footed Saab skating easily over the snow-packed surface. This is why she'd bought it; it was trusty and great on snow. Not that she ever drove far. I scan the marquee of doctors' names and their office locations.

Dr. Haw, Psychiatrist. Third Floor.

I am embarrassed to be here. I just hope that when I ask the receptionist for directions to his office she doesn't think I require his services. I take the elevator, turn left after the metal doors open, and walk to a set of large doors, where a sign directs me to push a button. I do and am allowed into a carpeted hallway and then . . . the following several minutes are a complete blank, a movie clip washed with acid, stolen from my memory for protection.

I think I remember her being in a small, enclosed room that extended into the hallway. I think I remember seeing her face, eyes wide and wild with fear and anger, two sides of the same coin of madness, peering out through the iron bars that guarded the opening of a small window. I think her fingers were curled tightly around those iron bars that shielded her from the rest of the world. But I also think the world was shielded from her.

Then my memory returns, and I hear her angry words follow me down the hall, unmuted by the carpet. "Don't go back there, Susie! Don't you go back and talk to that son of a bitch. You run! You get out of here and run. There are a bunch of liars in here, a bunch of goddamned liars. They want to kill me, and they'll kill you too if you go back there!" Her howls increase as I continue down the hall. I don't look back. I'm scared and embarrassed and unsettled. I have no one to turn to, I realize as I walk through the conference-room door. The one person I have always been able to count on to tell me the truth or soothe the hurts or be the rock of my foundation is the one screaming incoherently now, back in that small, iron-barred room.

Dr. Haw greets me and introduces the two police officers occupying the far side of the conference table, gazing over an open manila folder filled with official documents. This will be the first of many meetings with Dr. Haw. Over the next several years Mom will refer to him as Dr. Haw-Haw-Haw and show that sly smile while she's doing it.

Dr. Haw looks intense, with his light blue, almost glacial-colored, eyes. But a small, apologetic smile that seems to say, "It's too bad we're having this conversation, but here we are," softens his angular, serious face.

My attention shifts when one of the officers clears his throat and begins to talk. "We received a call this morning around eleven." He tries to be calm, gentling his voice to put me at ease, but his efforts are wasted on me as my heart beats wildly and my throat constricts. I can feel my composure growing more fragile and brittle, threatening to shatter, and I hope he doesn't see it. He leans forward on his elbows, looks at me with his brown eyes, and continues, "Evidently the woman who called was concerned about your mom. What time did your mom leave your house?"

I pause. The pause is too elongated. "I guess about nine or so."

"When she left your house, did she say where she was going?"

I shake my head. I can't talk. Words are lodged above my heart, and I can't let them out or the torrent of emotion will follow, the ice dam will break.

"Do you know if she had a coat and shoes with her?"

I swallow and shake my head again, my blood pulsing evenly in my ears. I'm in trouble. I should have kept a closer watch on her. "Why?"

Dr. Haw and the officer exchange glances. It is Dr. Haw who replies, "Because when the officers received the call from the woman, your mom had been walking barefoot in the snow, knocking on people's doors and asking to be let in because she was cold."

I almost laugh. "That doesn't make sense."

"I know," the officer replies, a smile shadowed by pity gracing his lips. "That's why we were called. But according to the person who placed the call, she didn't feel your mom was dangerous. The woman invited her in, offered her socks, and gave her a cup of tea, which your mom took with milk and sugar," he adds, his smile now genuine. "And then she listened to your mom ramble on for about fifteen minutes before she called us." He stops then, watching me for a reaction.

My initial reaction is a silent question: *did she go to any of the neighbors we know?* But I ask, "Where did you pick her up?"

"Three blocks from where you live."

I exhale and feel sick to my stomach. Her behavior has begun to seep into the world beyond our house.

Oh, the secrets a family keeps behind closed lips, behind normal gestures and conversations. Children seem to know which secrets to hold dear to their hearts without ever having been told. They also know how to keep them away from the prying and intervening eyes of others. I was the keeper of such secrets.

I kept secrets of Dad's drinking. At his worse Dad would go through a gallon of vodka in a couple of days. He always kept a flask in his back pocket or in the side pocket of his brown jean jacket, as well as in the truck's glove box and in his desk drawer at work. One was always within easy reach. I grew adept at reading his body language, the layers of the muscles on his face, around his eyes, his mouth, watching for that muscle along his jaw to dance or seeing if his eyes shone true happiness when he smiled. All these unspoken conversations passed between him and me constantly. I was always aware of them. I don't know if he was. I was also always aware of the spoken conversations and listened carefully when he came home at night after a day at the office. I filtered every word, every cadence of his voice, to see if he would be lighthearted or heavy-handed. Would I be talking with the funny, playful Dad? Or would I be talking to the father who would bark at me at the dinner table to shut up, to quit yammering on about things no one was interested in? I had no idea if other families interacted like this. I didn't often go to people's houses, and rarely did I invite friends to ours.

I kept secrets of violence. When I was fourteen I got the flu and ran a fever of 103 degrees. Dad wanted to dump me, naked, into a bathtub filled with ice. He stumbled toward me, his arm outstretched. Mom argued that the shock might be deadly. "What the hell would you know?" he yelled and lifted the back of his palm near her face. Her eyes grew wide, and she ducked his reach and grabbed for the wall phone, dialing 911 with shaking hands. He reached around her and pulled the phone off the wall, leaving a hole that exposed the multicolored, now dead, wires.

As far as I know he never actually hit her. I think the threat of reprisal was too threatening for him. She was a good hunter, and she was not afraid of guns. It may have scared him to think of what might happen if he pressed her too far. So the wall was patched and the phone put back into place, and I got better and Dad moved out.

"We're going to keep your mom here for three days," Dr. Haw explains, as I fight my way back from the daydream. "We're going to see how she's behaving and hopefully we'll be able to get her feeling better." He pauses. "Has she been acting like this for a while?"

I shrug and nod, not wanting to be this honest; not seeing how I can't.

"A week?"

"More."

"A month?"

"At least." I stop talking because the secrets are pushing at the back of my throat, threatening to come out my eyes in the form of tears.

He lets me regain my composure by continuing his conversation. "Unfortunately, you won't be able to see her until tomorrow. We'll get her settled into a room and give her a chance to adjust. Then you can come and see her. Do you go to school?"

I nod.

"Then we'll see you tomorrow, after school."

I leave and Mom's violent cursing greets me in the same hallway, her face contorts in fear and anger at my betrayal and threatens all forms of abandonment. Only when the heavy doors shut behind me does her voice stop. Or maybe I just can't hear it anymore. Although my heart beats wildly and my stomach lurches and my knees threaten to buckle, I continue walking, out to the car that will take me back to the stiflingly silent house. Only when I get into the car and pull the door shut do the tears run, uncensored, down my face and into my lap. The loneliness is the worst.

But loneliness is a price I am more than willing to pay to keep Dad in the dark about her break with reality. I don't want to live in a house where it's just him and me. So I don't call him. I don't call him to say, "Hi"; I don't call him to ask for money; I don't call him to tell him about Mom's hospitalization. I just don't call.

It turns out that the three days Dr. Haw said he would confine Mom is actually a seventy-two-hour involuntary psychiatric hold. To put that involuntary hold into place, patients must present a grave danger to themselves or to others. Mom, walking barefoot in the snow and knocking on strangers' doors asking to be let in, met those guidelines. The hold is designed to allow doctors to diagnose and begin to treat the mental illnesses that place people into dangerous situations. I imagine those seventy-two hours provided Mom a feeling of almost overwhelming safety; she'd opted to remain on the psych ward, voluntarily, for two weeks.

The next two weeks are a blur, and she appears in my memory as a series of photographed still lifes, a slideshow of how she conducts her day when I'm around. My earliest visits find her in her hospital room, sitting on the edge of the bed. She's calmer (the meds have kicked in), but she's still saying things that don't make sense, about people watching her, people she can't trust because she doesn't know who they're reporting to. A man shuffles by outside of her door, and I am concerned for her safety.

After a few days I drop by when she's in art-therapy class, a room with a long table and a linoleum floor and several people. There is a box of cheap watercolors in front of her, and she mixes these as she has mixed hues all her life, carefully in the tin cover, swirling, dipping, swirling until she lays the brush to paper, a child's coloring book, and begins filling in the spaces between the lines. Or she's cutting snowflakes with safety scissors, the same ones used in kindergarten and first grade. She carefully snips intricate shapes and patterns, her eyes intent on her art.

Then she unfolds the paper and holds it up to me with a proud smile. As time moves on she paints the prestamped design of a leather belt.

And she does this all quietly, mechanically, as do the others in this group-therapy class. Every so often there are minor eruptions of inappropriate mutterings, shouted words, and deranged sentences strung together with no verbal punctuation whatsoever. Everyone else seems unfazed at these behaviors, even the teachers, going about their business as usual. I, however, watch with growing uneasiness as these patients wander without purpose and do the things children in elementary school do, their blank stares focusing inward as they speak and interact with whomever they think about at that moment. I remain unseen in their world. Sometimes Mom acts just like the rest of them.

How does anyone get better in this place? That is the question that keeps bobbing to the surface as I watch Mom in this world, as I give her a nod and an approving smile of the newest painting she shows me. *There is no pressure to act any differently. What if she starts acting like this all the time? What if she never comes back from the edge of this particular abyss?*

Mom's been at the psych ward for several weeks. Although she checked herself out a couple of times, those departures never lasted more than a few days. Then she'd return and check herself back in. When I ask why, she says she feels safe there.

One day when I arrive, a girl of about twelve years of age is talking to Mom, her words and body animated. With Mom's greeting, the girl turns her hyperactive attention to me, and I watch in fascination as her jade-green eyes dart back and forth, taking in every nuance of movement between Mom and me. I can tell by her speech and actions that delusions can take this young girl at a moment's notice; nothing holds her attention long. A few days later Mom relays what the girl has told her in one of her more lucid moments. Her mother, she'd explained, was a prostitute, so addicted to heroin she'd turn tricks on dirty mattresses left in the alleyways of downtown. The daughter was always within hearing distance for safety but was required to turn her back so she wouldn't see what her mom was doing. But she knew. The daughter began turning her own tricks the previous year, when she was eleven. She'd begun to take drugs soon after. That was why she was in the psych ward. One of the drugs she'd taken had given her a really bad trip. Although I listen intensely, I think, *But she's crazy! Who knows if what she's saying is really true?!*

We learn at such young ages to explain away those things we don't want to confront. I didn't want to confront the possibility that an eleven-year-old girl was prostituting herself and taking drugs to dull that pain. That was not a world I knew anything about. I didn't want to know anything about that world.

Mom is released a few days before Christmas, and I am overjoyed. I buy a tree and together we decorate it with the Mom's handblown glass bulbs, lights, and tinsel. We put out our traditional pieces of Christmas: the stockings, the candles. We drink hot chocolate, and we smile, we laugh. Just like old times. This is going to be a great Christmas, I think, a true homecoming. As I hang the tinsel on the outstretched greenery I realize it's been four months since last August's garage sale, that Mom has been "normal," that *we* have been normal. Therefore, it's been four months since I've felt grounded. So I believe that Christmas, and its roots in traditions, will make our reunion more powerful.

Except Christmas is not meant to be. The world becomes scary again, and Mom readmits herself the day before Christmas. Dr. Haw is not surprised and assures me it is the best place for her. I have no recollection of Christmas Day. Perhaps I'd sat at home or spent it with Mom at the hospital or gone to a friend's house. But that memory of what I'd done, or where I'd been, is gone, irretrievably gone. I do remember begging Dad not to come from North Dakota for Christmas, and thankfully, he agrees to stay where he is. He does not want a repeat of Thanksgiving; I'm very sure of that. And he has no idea that Mom is hospitalized.

The day after Christmas I take down all the decorations and place them carefully away in their proper boxes. I vacuum and dust the house; I wash the walls and mop the floor. I clean the bathroom, scrubbing the tub, the sink, and the toilet, polishing the chrome until it shines like a mirror. I wash the windows with water and cornmeal, letting them dry a bit until rubbing them clean with newspaper, the way mom had taught me. I do it all to take away my fear, so I don't have to think about the unknown future. I do it so something feels normal.

But I tell myself that I do it so it will be clean when she comes home. She does so in late January. She's the same, except she's "gone" a lot, difficult to reach and difficult to interact with. I continue going to school and now am thankful I don't have to leave my first-period class for the regularly scheduled hospital meetings about my mom. Kids were beginning to wonder why I had been gone so much. So I had evaded any possible questions by putting my heart and soul into orchestra and choir practice, where there's little time to talk. Now I drive to school instead of taking the bus, so my time with curious people is limited. And I'm unavailable after school. I come home, fix a snack, and do nothing. I don't even tell my best friend about the craziness. When we see each other, I act as if everything is okay, same as always. But within a couple of weeks Mom begins playing the late-night records again, turning the volume up and yelling into the speakers. And my heart is crushed. *What more can happen?*

I awaken one night with Mom violently shaking my shoulder. "Susie! Hurry! You've got to wake up!"

My whole body vibrates as I try to come out of my torpidity, forcing my eyes open to the blackest of nights and wondering how long I'd been sleeping. My clock says it's two in the morning. I went to bed at eleven.

"Come out to the living room, quickly!" Mom whispers, her words harsh and frantic in their appeal. Without question I pull on my robe and follow her along the short hall to the living room. All the lights are turned off, and the stereo is silent. Mom kneels down by the couch, getting as small as she can, and peers through our picture window. Our house sits high on the hill, near the rimrocks, and only the tallest tree tops, now bare in deep winter, block an otherwise uninterrupted view of the city.

"Do you see that?" Mom asks, pointing to the disjointed blinking red lights in the sky. "What do you think those are?" I hear the paranoia in her voice, and my stomach tightens. She looks at me, anxious and worried. Even in that darkness I see the blackness of her irises.

Here we go again.

"Well, I'll tell you what those are," she answers in my silence, her words staccato, jumping too quickly from her mouth. "Those are the Japs coming to bomb us, to get even for World War II. And you know what?"

I shake my head, dreading the explanation to come.

"Your father's fighting for those sons of bitches! He's getting ready to bomb our house."

"How do you know this," I ask, my voice hesitant, adrenaline rushing through my system, pitting my stomach even more. She points with her chin to the speakers. "They told me."

"Who? Who told you?" I try to calm my voice, but anxiety creeps into other parts of being, my psyche.

"I don't know their names; they never tell me their names." The explanation is fast, her words whiz by my ears in a flurry, so fast I can't decipher everything she says. "It's all in code. They said your father would be flying over our house, and a bomb would drop, and we needed to get out of here." She starts to move around the room, frantically looking for something, but then stops and cocks her head. Tired, sick, sleep-deprived, I have reached my limit of her nonsense.

"I'm going to bed." My words are tinged with anger, as my heart fractures yet again at her expression, which now becomes one of hurt and betrayal. But I go to bed anyway, only to be wakened again by her insistent shaking. Judging by the darkness, I have been asleep only a matter of minutes.

"Your father's dead." Mom whispers, her voice gentle. "His plane just went down. It just came on the news."

The news! Now that was real. The news wouldn't lie. "What happened?"

"It was somewhere in North Dakota. He was flying back from one of his trips to DC, and it was in a small plane. But don't cry. He's in a restful place, finally." She pauses and her voice hardens as she sees a strip of moisture trail down my cheek. "Don't you dare waste any tears on him; he certainly didn't waste any on you or me. Go back to sleep; we'll talk in the morning."

Surprisingly, I fall asleep, and in the morning she tells me to go school as usual. She'd make the necessary funeral arrangements.

In orchestra practice I tell a friend about my dad's death, but I don't cry. I can't. It's as if it is happening to someone else. He looks at me, his brows pulled together in concern. After a few moments of being unable to reply, he asks, "Why the fuck are you at school today?"

I have no idea.

Two days later when I come home from school, I am met by a note that's been left on the kitchen counter. I would never recognize the handwriting as Mom's, whose cursive has always been neat with deliberate scrolls. She'd learned penmanship in the 1930s, back when it mattered. This note is covered with scrawled words, shaky, jagged, and nearly illegible. It reads that she would be flying to Great Falls to see the Charles M. Russell Art Museum. She would be back by five.

Mom hates to fly. None of this makes sense. I check her bedroom. She hasn't packed; her suitcase is still in her closet, and all her clothes are untouched. No toiletries are missing from the bathroom. Only her purse is gone. It is three-thirty. She will be back in an hour and a half, I think. But she isn't. She isn't back at five, at six, or at seven. I call the airline at seven thirty. I introduce myself and relay my relationship to my mom and explain the situation. "Can you tell me if she got off the return flight?"

"Ma'am," the female voice drawls, "I can't give out that information."

"But she's my mom. She hasn't returned, and I need to know where she is."

"Sorry, ma'am," comes the rehearsed answer. "But I am not allowed to give out that information."

"Can you tell me if she got on the plane in Great Falls to fly to Billings?" Panic centers over my heart.

"I can neither confirm nor deny your mother's reservation on this flight." I plead for her assistance. She answers with a clipped, "Call the police," and hangs up. I hold the phone in my hand and begin to shake as the dial tone hums in my ear.

I call the police department; the information is written down with the statement, "Someone will get back to you."

There is nothing more anxiety-ridden than waiting in a silent house for a mother, who has flipped out in every meaning of the word, to come through that door. Adrenaline travels at light speed along every nerve with each passing moment; fear settles deep in my bones. The only sound is the rhythmic *tlock . . . tlock . . . tlock* of the German cuckoo clock. When the bird exits the small doorway at the top and cuckoos on the hour, it is startling. At some point in the night I descend into a kind of madness of my own. I walk to my bedroom and gather together the five music boxes I own. I wind them up, one by one, and let them play; their mismatched tones and ugly cacophony are peculiarly soothing. They fill the silence. And that's all I want.

It's amazing what can be hidden from friends, neighbors, the world. I call Dad's boss's home number, but his wife answers. She tells me that Dad is still in Minot, but didn't I have his number?

"I lost it," I lie. She gives it to me, and I scribble it. Just in case I need to get ahold of him for some reason. *Like if she dies.*

It's difficult for me to reach out. Our family has always been very private. Both of my parents dedicated themselves to keeping aloof from neighbors. "People are too damn nosy," Dad would say if someone came to the door to say, "Hi," or if they called on the phone. He didn't initiate contacts, and he didn't accept friendships. And Mom didn't show any interest in having the neighbors be anything but, well, neighbors. And neither is close with whatever remaining family they have left in Ohio. I write down the number she gives me, just in case. And I continue to behave as if everything is fine.

It's been two weeks since the police called to tell me they were still looking for Mom. One morning I am called out of my first-period aeronautics class to take a phone call. I am to meet with an officer at the police department who has turned up some information. It turns out Mom had indeed flown to Great Falls that day. Then, instead of returning home, she purchased a plane ticket to Houston. She then jetted over to Baton Rouge but returned to San Antonio, Texas, a few days later. They've established contact with officers in "San Antone" who have reported her patterns: she stays in her hotel room all day, probably sleeping. She eats breakfast in the attached restaurant, and at night she leaves and just walks around. She doesn't interact with anyone; she keeps to herself. She's not causing any trouble, the officer assures me. And I know I should be thankful she's safe, but I want her home.

A few days later I receive a phone call from Montana Power wanting me to pay a delinquent bill. Who knows how long it hasn't been paid? I explain that I have no money and my mom has left, and I didn't know when she was going to get back. "She just walked out," I tell the woman, nervous that the heat will be shut off in this early February winter. The caller says she'll make a note and keep it on file to keep the heat on. Surprisingly, I don't receive a call from the phone company or the water company, and even more surprising is the fact that nothing gets turned off. I'm not paying bills because I don't know how bills are paid.

One day Dr. Haw calls to say he just got word from the police department that Mom's been gone. He's had no idea that she wasn't living at the house. "How long has she been gone?"

"About a month."

"You've been by yourself for a month?" His voice is incredulous.

"Yeah."

"What are you doing for heat, for the utilities?"

I explain the conversation with Montana Power, but I can't explain why I've received no other phone calls, yet the utilities continued.

"What are you doing for money?"

"I have a checking account with a couple hundred dollars in it."

"What are you doing for food?"

"I shop for cans of soup, stuff like that. I'm fine."

"Do you need anything? Groceries?"

"No thank you," I say. Mom has made it clear my entire life that we are never to accept charity. We're too proud for charity. "I'm fine."

He pauses, then asks, "Will you tell me if you need anything?"

"Yes. But I'm fine."

I don't recall Dr. Haw calling me again after that.

It is a lot of work to be isolated. Especially for me, since I am an outgoing person. To hold a secret is something that doesn't come easily, unless the price to be paid is too high. This is what I know: I have no idea when, or if, Mom will come home. My life has been quiet since Dad's been living in Minot. There is no yelling, no screaming, no verbal battering, no emotional sparring. But it's so quiet, and I do anything to keep the stifling silence at bay. I turn on the radio and fall asleep to the music, or I don't fall asleep and listen to Mystery Theater late into the night. Or I read until three or four o'clock in the morning, with the light on to tell people someone lives here. Or at my worst times I wind up the music boxes. Because if I don't do these things the thoughts, the doubts, the uneasiness, the queasiness comes, and the "what ifs" start. *What if Mom doesn't return? What if someone at school finds out that I have no parents living with me? What if someone calls social services because my parents have abandoned me? Like my "real" family*, a small voice whispers. But I haven't thought about them in a long time; I've been too absorbed in worry about the family I have. Or what's left of it.

At the end of February I come home to footprints. They plod across our driveway, up the concrete stairs, through the wrought-iron gate, into the backyard, and across the unbroken field of snow. My heart pounds because two years previous someone had robbed the house while we were on vacation, walking off with our TV, my parent's silver tea set, and who knows what else. In a panic I run to the home of a close friend. "Can I stay here tonight?" I ask Danae's mother, whose mouth suddenly turns down in annoyance at my request.

"I'm sure it's nothing but the meter man," she says, brushing me off. "You'll be fine. Just go home."

Irritation floods her words, and I am embarrassed to be begging for safety. "There's nobody at home, and our house got broken into a couple of years ago. I'm really scared to be there by myself."

"Why isn't there anyone at home? Where's your mom?"

"San Antonio."

"Where's your dad?"

"North Dakota."

"Why aren't they taking care of you?" Her tone is suspicious, and I can tell she's upset that someone else's problems have landed on her doorstep. Her expensive doorstep. She lives in one of the more exclusive developments.

I have no answer for her, but I listen to her huff and puff as she pulls on her boots and her coat. "Fine," she answers, in a way that makes it clear my request has put her out. "I'll walk over with you, and you'll see it'll be fine." Her words are clipped, and her voice carries the frigidity of cracked ice.

The snow creaks beneath our boots as we walk, silent, through the cold. I struggle to keep up with her hurried pace. When we arrive at our driveway, she marches up the stairs, through the gate, and around the backyard, stopping to say, very pleased, "See? It was just the meter man. Nothing to worry about. Nothing to be afraid of." She stands with her hands on her hips, her breath rising lazily into the night air.

But I am afraid. And I'm embarrassed that I'm being made to feel ashamed of that fear, the very real fear of people breaking in, of being by myself through yet another long and painfully endless night, of the sounds that I hear and can't explain, the creaking and groaning of an older house. And those are only the fears I can openly talk about. I can't say the thing that frightens me the most: *what if Mom doesn't come back?* "Please?" I am begging now.

Danae's mother's lips grow thinner, and her eyes are like blue flint. She exhales in total frustration. "Okay," she says, "You can stay with us one night, but you'll have to figure out what to do from here on. I can't take you in."

We trudge back to her house in silence, and the way she carries herself, three steps ahead of me, her body movements jerky and abrupt, screams anger. We enter in through the side door, and she leads me to the guest room, flings open the door, and points to the bed. I am so thankful to be here that truly I don't really care how she speaks to me. I have one night that I don't have to worry.

The following day I see my best friend, Cari, between classes. "Where were you last night? I tried to call you a bunch last night but you didn't answer."

"I came home and saw footprints by my house, so I went to Danae's. I just didn't want to be by myself."

"Why would you be by yourself?" Cari asks, with a smile, as if I'm telling a joke. But I'm not, and the smile disappears when I talk about Mom leaving and how afraid I was after our house got broken into. I told her about Danae's mother's reaction and how upset it had made me. Cari looks at her hands and begins picking at the invisible hangnails that materialize anytime she gets uncomfortable in a situation. And I swallow because these days I seem to make a lot of people uncomfortable. She stays quiet for a long time and doesn't look at me, but finally she shakes her head. "That was rude," she says. I silently agree. And we don't talk any more about it.

When I arrive home from the school the following day, I am met at the door by Cari's mother, who'd pulled up in her Honda Civic and waited for me. She's holding a suitcase, and I ask her why. She smiles, the gentle smile I've always seen her wear, and says, "Let's go in and pack some clothes. You're going to be staying at our house until your mom comes back."

I'm embarrassed that I've put someone else out yet again because of my questionable welfare. "That's okay," I assure her, knowing Cari had filled her in. "I'm okay."

"I'm sure you are," she answers, as she follows me into the house. "But this is no place for a young girl to stay all by herself." She cocks her head to one side and smiles, and her bright blue eyes tell me everything is going to be fine.

"How long have you been here without your folks?"

"Since the middle of January." Well, really, since Thanksgiving, on and off, but she doesn't need to know that.

"Why didn't you tell me?"

"Because I had to take care of the house."

She laughs, an easy laugh that I haven't heard from an adult in a long time. "Well, the house will take care of itself," she says, as she goes into my room and starts opening drawers and tossing socks and underwear in the suitcase. "Go through your closet and grab whatever you want to bring with you." Shirts, pants, and dresses go first, followed by shoes and a couple of stuffed animals. "Make sure you have enough," she advises. "It may be awhile."

"But I don't even know where she is," I admit quietly, holding the lump in my throat at bay.

"Then you'll stay with us until all of this gets straightened out." She smiles again, and I hold back the tears that can come now that finally someone is in control. "This isn't up for discussion."

I live with them for perhaps two months. I live with them while snow still lies on the ground and while the sun comes out and turns the leaves green. I live with them until one day I receive a phone call from Dad, whose anger is palpable.

"How long has your mom been gone?" he demands.

I try to be as evasive as I can, but I end up telling him, "January." I don't tell him about Thanksgiving and December. He will just be angrier with me for not saying anything sooner.

"Why the hell didn't you tell me? What have you been doing all this time?"

"I've been living here, taking care of the house, going to school," I explain, irritation edging my voice.

"Well, I had to find out from one of my co-workers that you've been living by yourself, and I wished to hell you'd have told me."

I have no idea how anyone knew that. The woman who gave me his phone number? Anyway, my cover's blown. He tells me in terse tones that he'll be in Billings within the week. And I am livid and I am scared. My time with Cari's gentle, intact family will be coming to an end.

A week later Cari drives me home, and I unpack and Dad and I have stilted conversations. He makes it clear I'm going to take over Mom's duties. After school I'm to clean and vacuum the house and do laundry, iron his work clothes, and cook the meals. "What have you been living on?" he asks, as he opens the empty refrigerator.

"Soup," I reply. "And cereal."

"Well, we're going to have regular meals, starting tonight. I want you to make something."

I prepare the recipe I found on the back of a Campbell's cream-of-mushroom soup can: dilute the soup and pour it over cooked rice. Dad is furious. He tells me how to make a stew, which he wants the following night. It turns out badly. All my meals turn out badly. I don't like to cook because, although Mom did offer to teach me, I've never learned how. *And I am not going to start now*, screams my silent resistance.

On Saturday Dad wants me to cut his hair, like Mom used to do. "Just trim it over the ears and off the neck." So I do, but the line is jagged, and he's upset that I didn't do it right. In fact, nothing I do is right. It reminds me of his drinking days, even though he has been sober nearly two years. He's still a very angry, very critical, very unpredictable person, and I loathe doing these things, not for us, but for him. I don't see it as my role; I don't see it as my duty. And the resentment builds, like the pressure before an earthquake.

The next week is no better, so he decides one Saturday to lecture me on my shortcomings, which are significant. Then I begin to walk out, and he tells me to sit down and listen. So I throw myself into the La-Z-Boy and I listen. But I've learned a trick: if I stare at a spot, a picture on the wall, a ridge in the carpet, a brick on the fireplace, until it wavers and disappears, his voice disappears also. I no longer hear him. So that's what I do; I stare until his words become muffled, the vowels and consonants disappearing into the air between us. But I see movement out of the corner of my eye, and his body has risen from the couch and is striding toward me at lightning speed. His face is pulled taut, his pupils black dots, his veins stand out against his suntanned skin. Anger oozes out of him like sweat on a hot day. I don't wait to see how fast he'll reach me, but instead I jump up and bolt for the front door. The knob is immobile in my hand, and panic rises into my throat. The door is locked. And the look on his face is pure rage. I try to unlock it but my hands shake, and I realize, with a sickening feeling, escape is no longer an option.

He reaches for my arm. I fall. He grabs my leg and pulls me toward him, and I scream. I kick and I scream. And suddenly I feel the palm of his hand across my face, and the skin is hot where his hand has been. I am mute. But I'm not crying.

"What in the hell's wrong with you?" he yells. "You're a crazy person!"

I pray then, as I lie on the floor. I pray fervently, passionately. I pray as I've never prayed before for Mom to come home.

A short time later, perhaps two days, perhaps two weeks, she calls. She's bought an airline ticket to Billings. That is the one thing I do mention to Dad, because he's got to find another place to live. This house is no longer his.

It is July and Mom and I have moved to a small apartment, a vast step down from our house on the hill. She sleeps almost all the time, and I move like a ghost in her presence. Although she wasn't there to celebrate my birthday, she did attend my graduation, purchasing a set of blue Samsonite luggage for when I'd leave for college this coming fall. She also bought me a graduation dress at Sears, an empire-waist dress of white eyelet lace trimmed by black velvet.

I graduate with over seven hundred other students; you can imagine how many parents are there. I see her, though, sitting by herself on the second tier. And she smiles and waves. She tries to look happy, but she's sad. She's saying good-bye to an important role, being a mom I need.

But I wave back. I still need her.

"You know," she says to me one day as I sit with her on her bed, "when I was in San Antonio, I never felt so free. I walked around all those streets in the early morning hours, and no one ever bothered me. I was never attacked; I was never threatened. It was like the light of God kept me in a bubble. It's amazing really."

I am here beside her because this is the only time we get a chance to visit. She sleeps a lot, and when she's not sleeping she keeps to herself. Sometimes I offer to read to her, but after a few pages she covers her eyes with her arm and goes to sleep. Even when she's awake she's not fully engaged. Her eyes are no longer black; they've returned to the soft brown they've always been. But she always looks tired. I've been here only for about fifteen minutes when she lays on her back on the bed and covers her eyes with the crook of her elbow.

"You know, Jesus talked to me while I was down there." Her voice is quiet, studied. There's no awe, just a statement. I have no reply, so I'm quiet. "I was out on the eighth-story balcony, and below me was a kidney-shaped pool. 'You can fly,' his voice said. 'You can fly and I'll make sure you land in that pool. You won't get hurt.'"

She stops then and looks at me. Her face takes on the look of one who has seen Jesus, who has been saved and seen the light of his salvation.

There is veneration, a glow, a look of gentle astonishment. "I started to climb the little rail on the balcony, and I stood there. I stood there on that rail and knew that if I jumped, I would indeed fly and he would guide me all the way down to that pool that looked so small from where I stood."

She pauses, and I am suddenly aware my breathing has stopped, and a pit in my stomach has begun to pitch.

"But you know, I decided not to do that then. I climbed back down and went in and lay down on the bed." She replaces her arm over her eyes and is silent for a long time. Then, as if I am no longer in the room, she says quietly, "It's amazing to think what almost happened."

5

Sliding

Bozeman, Montana, Fall Quarter 1977.

It's been two months since Mom lay on her bed in our apartment, contemplating how close she'd come to dying. But summer is coming to an end, and Montana State University is about to begin. I'd packed the blue luggage and the bright blue trunk she'd given me as graduation presents, ready for my airline flight early the next morning. We speak little as she drives me to the airport, three miles from our home. She walks me to my gate, and as my flight is called, she hugs me, her hands shaking against my back. Although she turns quickly to walk away, I am aware of the tears that stream down her face. Within a half hour I am on the way to Bozeman, Montana, having gained last-minute admittance to Montana State University. MSU is only 150 miles away, but Mom's self-described nervous breakdown had robbed her of any sense of confidence that she could drive there and back.

A friend picks me up and drives me to the new apartment that I'll be sharing with my roommate, Collette, five years my senior. It's a two-bedroom space located just two blocks off campus. It takes me only a few hours to move in, and the end result is stark: my room is white, devoid of everything except a window, a twin bed, and a thirty-dollar unpainted white pine dresser that I'd purchased an hour earlier from Kmart. The living room has the basics, but it is brilliantly clean, having been built only a month before.

After getting settled in, I walk to the dorms and watch the students move in, their parents, the ones who drove them perhaps thousands of miles, hauling box after box of clothing, rolled up posters, lamps, chairs, cheerful bedding, everything to make their dorm room like home. I catch the lump in my throat that my family wasn't able to do that, and I feel another layer of difference.

I am uncomfortably aware of my role as a statistic: I am American Indian; I am from a "broken home"; one of my parents was an alcoholic; and one of my parents had mental-health issues. I am outside the norm in that I am going to college. But I no longer dream of going to Oregon State University and becoming a marine biologist. That dream went out like one of Dad's match flames. Because of the divorce, Dad had rescinded his offer to pay for college, arguing that now that he had his own bills to pay, he can't afford to. Now I am major-less, and I have no idea what else I will do. I have no plan B.

My nonmajor is being paid with my Individual Indian Monies. What I don't know, because no one has told me, is that I could be doing this degree for free, according to treaty agreements signed in Montana. By the time I am told this, three years later, I will have become so assimilated in the dominant, Indian-intolerant culture that I will have too much "pride" to apply for "charity." Too many people have reminded me that Indians are government subsidized. Those same people have forgotten about the blood that has soaked into the plains, the hundreds of millions of acres of land that tribes were forced to sign over, the goodwill gestures that never got delivered: the food, the clothing, the housing, the respect. But for now I don't know these things. And even if I did, I would never be confident enough to state them publicly. For now I know only that I have some tribal money and no direction.

Collette, my roommate, is in her last year of architecture. She is freckle-faced, pale, with strawberry blond hair and green eyes. She is also linearly brilliant, focused, and self-confident. I imagine she probably acted like a grown-up since she was five. Her frustration at my immaturity is audible, her questions asked in a lispy, judgmental tone. "What time did you drag in? And who'd you bring with you?"

I should have said, "It's none of your fucking business." But I am the mouse caught in her feline gaze. Like the queen of hearts, she demands submission and I give it to her. Within a few weeks we actively avoid each other.

There are fifteen thousand students at MSU, and they wander like ants across campus, into and out of buildings, of classrooms. It is so easy to fall between the cracks, and I've become invisible in the falling. I don't show up for class, and no one cares; maybe they aren't even aware that I'm absent. I am uneasy and unprepared for this foreign and competitive environment. In high school I didn't have to be competitive. My grades had been above average. I scored well in English, reading and writing voraciously; I scored badly in math. I inhaled my social studies and anthropology classes.

Anthropology, in particular, talked about other brown people who lived seemingly forgotten lives, but in modern-day times. As I moved through textbooks, watched videos, or looked at artwork, I saw living human beings. In a video about the Yanomami of the Amazon rainforest, I watched as a man, dressed in a red loincloth, poled his boat up the Amazon River, his black hair cut blunt above his ears and eyebrows, a ring through his nose. A page in the book I purchased for my Introduction to Anthropology class showed a woman wrapped in brightly colored cloth, her neck elongated by gold rings, smiling at the camera, her hair tight against her scalp. Kodachrome made all the difference. These people weren't living lives in shades of gray, forgotten, like in the black-and-white photos I was used to seeing, the ones that hung in history museums. Those photos showed people hunting with bows and arrows or sitting, unsmiling, in front of canvas tenting, clothed in their traditional dress of leather shirts and leggings with headdresses of eagle feathers, while blue-coated, mustached, and bearded soldiers stood nearby. Those people were history, long dead, nearly forgotten, except for this small window that collapsed time. But the color photos made the clear distinction between alive and dead, remembered and forgotten. Most important, when I looked at color photos, I was reminded of what I was: not white.

Although anthropology drew my attention, music drew my heart; that was where my talent lay. I had played violin in orchestra, sang second alto in choir, and tried out for background roles in musicals. Science, however, seemed the best path, if I were to follow Dad's footsteps. It was a discipline I understood, especially biology; it had defined so much of my world growing up on wildlife refuges.

But here, at Montana State University, I am in a special level of hell. I'd never learned how to study. In high school I could scan the reading material quickly, but here my textbooks are written as if I've paid by the word, their fonts small and crammed together, filling sentences, paragraphs, pages, chapters, and sections, marching endlessly before my eyes until they become blurred and nonsensical. Too many words place ideas high above my head, out of reach and vaporous, and I feel their concepts float away, unmoored and lifeless.

Parties are my saving grace; these I can understand. And there are tons of them: the prefootball parties, the football parties, the postfootball parties. And then basketball season will start. I join these parties, in the dorms, in people's houses, and drink Rum and Cokes, 7 and 7s, peppermint schnapps, and straight shots of tequila chased with salt and lime and cheap beer. The more I party, the more lifeless the concepts become.

But then I don't care about concepts, because I've found the bars. The disco bars with their migraine-producing concoctions of blaring music and flashing lights that shudder and dance beneath my feet. Or the cowboy bars, where I two-step or country swing to the twangy sounds of Waylon and Willie. These experiences, dark and smoky, are served up in equal parts frenetic energy and numbing alcohol and chased with more shots of tequila. All seem to wear away the sharp edges of living in a chaotic world where families disintegrate and people judge; the quiet kind of judgment, the no-dates-until-I-was-a-senior kind of judgment. I know mothers are uncomfortable with their sons dating American Indian girls. We're seen as kind of trashy. And no matter how white I was raised, the color of my skin always seemed to warn that I could be one of those trashy girls. These were the pains I sought to numb, but I misjudged the medicine. It doesn't completely take it away. In fact, it allows newer, sharper edges to be cut. So the dancing becomes frenzied, the shots are tossed back in increasing proportions, and the edges grow rawer. Here with the lights flaming into my vision, I don't have to deal with Dad's alcoholism or his anger that always boils just below the surface. In fact, I don't have to deal with him at all. A toast!

Here with the drums pounding a tattoo in my chest, I don't have to think about Mom or her undiagnosed bipolar antics (Dr. Haw had diagnosed her as having a fear psychosis) and her escape from reality, leaving me to experience the fallout. In fact, I don't have to think about her at all. A toast!

Here, among the dozens of sweating bodies, eyes closed to let the music take me to my caves of unconsciousness, I don't have to be an outsider. I am drinking and dancing with a crowd of people who don't seem to care who or what I am. A toast!

Rebellion, angry and rapacious, rules my world. But unlike my friends who have experimented with this under the roofs of their parents, I have no safety net. There is no one to catch me when I fall, and the falling is dangerously self-destructive. I am no longer a "nice girl," I no longer care about doing the "right thing," and I throw off responsibility like a hair shirt that's grown too small.

Because I just don't care.

A toast!

The phone rings. There's a party. It's well underway when I arrive. I am handed a rum and coke and watch people drift in and out of the room the same way they seem to drift in and out of my life. I look at the guy sitting next to me, to my left, older, clean-cut in a preppy sort of way.

"Who is he?" I ask the person to my right.

"He's the RA. It's weird he's here. He's not supposed to be; he's supposed to break the party up." He throws me a lopsided, drunken smile and reignites the conversation with the girl sitting next to him.

Preppy looks at me, a smile leftover from the conversation he has just exited still on his lips. His eyes are blue, and I can tell, although he looks at me, directly looks at me, he doesn't see me. In fact, I do not exist until I ask where he's from. Then his smile crawls away, and he leans toward me, his gaze withering and sacrosanct. "Don't talk to me," he says quietly, for my ears only. "I hate Indians."

I pass Fall quarter, barely.

At night, after the bars close, I walk. It is winter and the snow dances on the briefest of air currents, lifting itself high, threatening never to return to earth. The vapor from my breath escapes through my nose, crinkling the membranes that crack as if they are nearly frozen, and becomes a column beneath the conical light of the streetlamp. The breath disappears when I sidestep out of the light and into the cloaking darkness.

Tonight I am with Jon. He is engaged, but I'm not interested in his engagement. I'm interested in his warmth. We hold hands in his pocket, our fingers intertwined like a Celtic knot. For miles we walk on the sidewalks of town, the snow creaking beneath our boots. It is so cold our voices are muted, frozen in place while we talk about our high schools, our classes, the relationships we had or are trying to have, or the relationships we are leaving or trying to leave. We bury our chins deep into the down collars of our coats as we caution ourselves and each other about the invisible bumps that lie in the road ahead. The sky overhead is navy blue, almost black, broken only by the stars that shimmer like a million grains of glass that have been shattered on a velvet sky. We pull our hands apart and shove them deep in our own pockets, moving platonically in the easy companionship of lost souls in search of illumination.

Jon and I never go to the hot pots together, those hot springs located on the Gardiner River, just inside of Yellowstone National Park; he is engaged. So I go with other people. It doesn't matter if I've known them for years or minutes. And we go only after midnight, most often after the bars close their doors. I catch a ride several times a month to those sacred pools that slough away the heavy weight of my world. We travel over Bozeman Pass, down through Paradise Valley, until we arrive at the forty-ninth parallel that intersects with the Gardiner River and the geothermally heated water it contains.

Standing in the thin veil of steam, I strip down as fast as possible to keep the frigid air from entering my ever-constricting pores. I alternately jump from one foot to the other as my feet freeze on the rock-hard soil. I cover my nakedness with thin arms as I pick my way carefully to an area that allows me to slide into the water. The intense heat opens my pores, now confused and tingling to the point of pain.

Soon a doobie is passed, held above the water as it makes the rounds, its sweet smoke inhaled and held in lungs already at capacity at nearly seven-thousand-feet elevation. As the stars become brighter and the world stops spinning, our talk becomes whispers carried away by the rushing water just a few feet away. A man screams; the spell is broken.

"You scream like a girl," someone yells, and laughter erupts. Evidently a male has decided to prove his masculinity by swimming across the river, its frothy rapids ice cold. His movements are frantic and jagged in this narrow river, where the water runs fast. The night is split with the booming voice of another person: "I imagine his balls are up near his ribcage right now." The roars of laughter eventually fall off as the man completes his mission, and the world slows down just a bit more.

I slide over to the lap of Andrew, unknown before this evening, and wrap my arms around his neck. I shut my eyes and savor in the joy of being held, of feeling someone's arms around me, of skin touching skin, of connection.

As people drift away, their cars growling their departure in the pre-dawn hours, Andrew and I stay. Maybe it is the dawn, maybe it is sleep deprivation, maybe it is the heat that has entered our bodies and changed the chemistry of how we see the world, like in an oversized sweat lodge. But what we see is magic, the Disney film kind of magic of a plant emerging from dark soil, and a flower unfolding from the slender stem. What we see is a dark-blue dawn quietly replacing the black-velvet night, and the seam, that boundary that separates land and sky, glowing gold in the rising sun. We watch as formless shapes come out of the darkness and take form, sagebrush, healthy and large, and deer grazing the trampled grass beneath the snow. The same happens for us, to us, as the veil of steam lifts, and suddenly there is no hiding place and our bodies become illuminated and visible. Self-conscious, we are efficient in our dressing, finding ways to give each other privacy, looking to the sky, the ground, in opposite directions. I shiver and suck the iced air, sharp and bitter, between my teeth, while my fingers, shriveled and clumsy, button my jeans and zip up my coat. I climb into Andrew's red Mustang, knowing that when I get back I will have enough time to grab breakfast, catch a couple hours of sleep, and start all over again. I will also probably never see Andrew again.

I fail Winter quarter.

It is March, and I've taken a job at the student union, serving up lengths of a three-foot-long submarine sandwich, fifty cents an inch. This allows me, absent of alcohol or other substances, to watch the people around me, the people I come into contact with. To most people I'm on the edge of invisibility, just the girl who hands them their food. To me, their choices reveal much. There are the boys, young, typically good-looking, and clean-cut and dressed in nice shirts and jeans—the engineers; they order three or four inches. There are the typically blond sorority sisters, hair and makeup always in place; they order one to two inches, because they have to watch their figures. There are the jocks, taller and bigger than anyone else, bigger than life. If they're together they jostle one another, calling attention to themselves, laughing loudly; if they are alone they are introverted, barely meeting my gaze. They always order six inches and up.

One day a man comes through, red haired, fine boned, a trimmed beard. His voice is soft yet defined. And he smiles. Every day he smiles at me, and he watches me the same way I'm watching everyone else, but more overtly. Last week he told me he is studying film and photography and wants to be a director. That seems a good choice for him, and I see him as such. Today his request for three inches is followed by an invitation: "Do you want to go out this Friday?"

I'm not sure how to respond. This question is so formal, so gentle, so unlike anything I've experienced since high school, which by now seems like a lifetime ago. There is no suggestion to go to the bar, to join a party. Rather it will be dinner: his place. I'm shy, without an agenda of friendly chat about sandwich sales, so my answer is a quiet, "Yes."

I wish I could say it works out, but it doesn't. It is awkward for me, and being awkward for me makes it awkward for him. Our ages are too different—he is twenty-seven; I will be nineteen next week. He is old; I am immature. The dinner is good, but I don't like wine. I don't like kissing, and our conversation is stilted in stops and starts of inadequate beginnings and unfinished endings. I leave, knowing I won't see him again. And I don't. He finds another kind of lunch to have from that point on.

Or there is the thirty-year-old guy who washes dishes in the kitchen behind the counter where I work. He's friendly, efficient, perhaps a little off-kilter, but I can't place why. The chatter is easy, but then one day he's gone. I will see him in a few years at a convenience store–gas station, where he is the manager. We will recognize each other and catch up, just like old times. And I think for him he feels a sense of achievement.

Or there is the biology-lab teaching assistant, who looks exactly like Gen. George Armstrong Custer, who sweeps his silky blond hair off his temples, gelling it into place, letting his curls fall gently to his shoulders. His Van Dyke beard and mustache are always extraordinarily trimmed and never look scruffy, a tip of the hat to the man he emulates. As I talk with him, as I tell him about growing up in Red Rock and the trumpeter swans that my dad brought back from near extinction; as we discuss the east-west direction of the Centennial Range and its role as a fault line that transfers heat, keeping the lakes warm enough for the swans to live year-round; as we speak of so many things, I can't help but wonder if he sees the irony. That he, who goes out of his way to look like General Custer, finds it odd that I, an American Indian girl, is talking with him at all.

The gale-force winds of March and April commence. I am restless. I move from group to group without staying long in any one place. Now it's old high school friends; now it's people from the rival school; now it's guys who do five-finger discounts, who lift leather jackets from expensive stores and drive Jaguars and Peugeots. I don't know if I'm doing the moving, or if I am being forced to move because I won't give up the party lifestyle. Either way I don't last very long in any one place.

I fail Spring quarter.

Two weeks into June I receive a very official letter from the dean, who without preamble states that I am now on academic probation. I would, he explains, be given one more quarter with which to apply myself to prove my abilities. In the meantime, he suggests, I should take the summer to seriously think about my interest in further pursuing a college education. I'm so happy my parents will not be informed of my errors in judgment, especially my dad. Because somewhere along the line I have become a "goddamn-crazy-drunken-war-whoop."

In June, within the week after school ends, I pound the sidewalks of Bozeman with the briefest of resumes, having almost no job experience.

I am shocked when I land an interview and even more so when I am hired within fifteen minutes. My job will be to sell jewelry in a store that deals in "fine" American Indian jewelry and assorted gems.

The store is small and on the far edge of Main Street. Inside two glass cases stand apart, segregated. One case is filled with boxes lined with black velvet, showing off the traditional jewelry of the southwest: Navajo, Hopi, and Zuni silver hold colorful stones of turquoise, coral, mother of pearl, and abalone. There are necklaces, rings, watchbands, and bolo ties, along with earrings sitting in perfect rows, their bright, multicolored designs gleaming under the daylight lamps. The other case holds precious gems, their colors exploding in the real sunlight that pours through the store's windows. I am told to tell people that the cut is the most important aspect of gems. That will determine how it throws and refracts light. I have no illusions as to why I've been hired. What could be more compelling than to buy American Indian jewelry from a real American Indian? If my boss only knew.

But I am not compelling. I am shy. Painfully so. And the symptoms begin as soon as a customer walks in. I blush with their first "hello," and my replies are jagged and filled with stutters, if they are audible at all. To make it more comfortable for all of us, I begin to ignore people, allowing them to peruse in silence. This works great for me, just not for the store owner—they rarely walk away with an item purchased from the store. At month's end the owner hands me a check and says, almost apologetically, "This isn't working out well for either one of us. Best of luck in whatever you decide to do next."

However, I don't do anything next. I just do more of the same.

In July I land with a group of people who change the course of my life. Two of them have names of the ancient Greeks: Cornelius and Thaddeus. Marty becomes known as Illius so he won't feel left out. And then there is Herb; yes, it's drug related. Evidently, Herb had been on the two-strike rule, which had landed him in this town. His first strike was being angry with his folks for denying him access to a concert and then accidentally driving his car into a tree at a relatively high rate of speed, breaking his jaw in three places. His second strike was getting caught selling pot at his high school. Tempers flared; a break was needed. He would, his parents decided, leave his California home to live with his brother, who attended college in Montana. As his mom walked him to the airline gate, she whispered in his ear, "I know you're going up there for the summer. Why don't you just plan on staying there." That last sentence was a statement, not a question.

This group is not a bar-crowd group, unless the bar includes a pool table. Outdoorsy and active, they race bicycles, run marathons, climb both bare and iced rocks, and cross-country ski. They are musical and like to cook fresh foods, regularly imbibe, smoke pot, and drop acid. I learn to do a lot of these things, except the last. I have no doubt acid would land me in the psychiatric hospital. I do know my limits, although they seem pretty expansive.

And I discover important information along the way. I discover that smoking hash causes me to ride my bike erratically. I can stay in the middle of the street only if I bounce off the cars on either side. This lasts several blocks, and then I'm fine. I discover that sleeping with a lot of men has consequences beyond babies. One night after the bars close, I run into Meredith, a quasi-friend of several people in the group. She's eighteen and has been having sex since she was fourteen. She's lost count of the number of boys she's slept with. Today was her third and final cervical cancer treatment: a strong treatment of liquid nitrogen, which burns the cancer cells off her cervix. She will need to have regular checkups for the next three years. "Does it hurt when they burn it?" I ask. "Not much," she says, shrugging her shoulders. "But I've made a lot of changes. I stopped drinking, and I don't have sex with anybody now."

I discover that Strawberry Hill does not have a road that crosses the Bridger Mountain Range. But it looks like it does from afar. So Herb and I try to locate the mythical road after a particularly solid night of drinking beer with a pot chaser. The two-track we follow is barely visible as we climb his Chevy Nova high into the darkness, far away from the city lights, far away from the moon. The suspension no longer protects us from the jolts of a disintegrating road. But it is the mud pond that gets us, the one we see in our headlights. Herb hits the gas, hoping for speed to carry us to the other side, but it doesn't. We come to an abrupt halt in the bumper-deep slime. I open the door and the slime sits just below the running board. So we sit and drink what is left of our beer, listen to Meatloaf's "Paradise by the Dashboard Lights" on the college radio station, and talk, waiting for the sun to rise over the valley. We get out when the hillside becomes visible. Herb's long legs are able to reach the hood, and he jumps to safety. My legs are not so long, so I jump to the edge of the pond and mud oozes around my ankles. Tired, defeated, we walk down the hill, catching the attention of an old rancher, who listens to our story with a twinkle in his blue eyes. "Well," he offers, "if you kids can wait until tomorrow, I can get my truck with the winch on it and haul you out, but I can't do it before tomorrow." He writes his number on a small piece of paper and tells us to call the next day before noon. He then drops us off near the interstate, and we walk the rest of the way to town. Herb's brother blows a gasket when we ask for a ride back out there and tells us to find another sucker. He isn't going to pull us out of our stupidity. But our sometimes friend, D.W., does, after a promised six-pack.

I discover that hypothermia is probably the best way to die if you have an option. Cross-country skiing has not been an easy sport for me to pick up. When the snow is good, I am not bad. When the snow is bad, there are few worse. We ski on a spring day when the overnight snow has accumulated significantly and piles heavily on the shaded trail. In the morning the twelve-mile trail is easy; by two in the afternoon it starts to melt; by three the wax no longer works. I put on the red wax, but now I'm tired. By four the sun lies low on the horizon, and the top layer of the trail turns to ice. Suddenly, I can't stay upright; the skis keep flying out from under me, and with each fall I land harder on the packed surface until, three miles from the car, I lay down bruised, battered, and exhausted. I am numb and my senses are no longer accepting new information, or at least interpreting it. I watch Herb ski off easily in the distance, his slushing growing quieter. In fact, everything is quiet. I look above me at the cerulean sky, and it seems endless. I am so tired. And the shivering that started a couple of miles back is worse. And my eyes close of their own accord. Sleep threatens to drag me under, and I'm vaguely aware the shivering has stopped.

"What are you doing?" That's Herb's voice. I can't tell if it's near or far. It sounds far, but it's too much work to open my eyes. But I force them open anyway and am surprised that he's standing directly over me.

"Just resting for a few minutes," I say. My thick tongue wraps around my words, making it difficult for them to come out. I close my eyes again without meaning to.

"Well, you can't rest here; you've got to get back to the car." I knit my eyebrows; his voice is surprisingly authoritative. I've never heard this voice before.

"I'm really tired. I just need to sleep before I get back to the car."

"That's not a choice," Herb insists, and he puts his arms beneath my armpits and helps me up. The skis shift beneath my feet, sliding dangerously over the snow, and all I want to do is lie back down. The shivering is back with a vengeance, and I shake uncontrollably all the way to the car and all the way home, even with the heat turned on full blast. When we get to the house, Herb pulls a hot bath for me, and only then, after what seems like a long time, I stop shivering. Hypothermia is uncomfortable, but it doesn't hurt. You just fall asleep. Yep, that is the way to go.

But probably my most profound self-discovery is that even a boyfriend can't protect me from myself, as I, one night in a drunken craze, dance into a polka band. Thaddeus immediately takes me outside, and we stand quietly for a moment. And he looks at me with his hazel eyes, the color of aspen leaves in August, and his golden hair fringes beneath his ski cap. And he says, gently, but with a certain forcefulness I can't disregard, "You know, not everyone drinks to the point you do." He pauses then, his eyes never leaving mine. There is no judgment; it is just a statement. But I'm too embarrassed to thank him for his caring. I look at the ground and nod. I hear him say, "Just think about it," before I hear his footsteps walk away.

In December, during Winter quarter, I receive a letter from the dean informing me that I am now on academic leave. I am not able to return to school for a full year.

6

Fort Laramie

Fort Laramie National Monument, Wyoming, Summer 1979.

After having been put on academic probation by Montana State University the quarter before, I get a job with the Young Adult Conservation Corps (YACC) in Yellowstone National Park. It is the older sister program to the Youth Conservation Corps that I worked for in Glacier four years ago. During the winter months it's a group like me—people who, for one reason or another, have nowhere else to go. During the summer months, the YACC employs a lot of students in transition, to college, summer break, after college. So far I've worked as a teacher's aide, a secretary, and a custodian, and I am now in purchasing. The purpose of the program is to help young adults, ages eighteen to twenty-four, gain important job skills. I don't get the skills so much as I get a paycheck. In two months I will attend the University of Montana, where I've applied to and been accepted. I've learned an important lesson from the last educational fiasco; school will need to come first.

But now it is July, and I, along with five other people, have been chosen to drive six twelve-passenger vans to an event being held at Fort Laramie, a National Historic Site. I don't know anything about

Fort Laramie. I don't even know where it is. After six hours of driving beneath the searing Wyoming sun, I find out it is in eastern Wyoming, near the Nebraska border.

At the time I had no idea of the history behind Fort Laramie, other than a bit that I'd read in James Michener's *Centennial*, mainly because high school history classes were more concerned about names and dates than about events that tumbled and cascaded into one other like dominoes. Fort Laramie was the symbol of untrustworthiness, especially in terms of American Indian treaty law. For American Indian tribes, treaties with the federal government were a fact of life. Francis Paul Prucha writes in *American Indian Treaties: A History of Political Anomaly*, "Between 1778, when the first treaty was signed with the Delawares, and 1868, when the final one was completed with the Nez Perces, there were 367 ratified Indian treaties and 6 more whose status is questionable."

The Treaty of Fort Laramie of 1851 was one of the six questionable treaties. That treaty had been attended by ten thousand members of the Sioux, Cheyennes, Arapahos, Crows, Assiniboines, Gros Ventres, Mandans, and Arikaras. Each tribe was to appoint one chief to speak for every member of that tribe; that one chief would also be the one to sign the treaty. The 1851 treaty required that tribes would agree to get along; they would agree to one another's territorial boundaries; they would allow the U.S. government to build roads and military posts within those boundaries; and they would make reparation for any harm caused to whites who crossed their lands lawfully. In return, they would receive protection from harm caused them from white settlers, as well as an annuity of $50,000 paid each year for fifty years. The annuity would take the form of merchandise, food, domestic stock, and farm implements.

The problem was that when the treaty was submitted to the Senate by President Millard Fillmore, it was amended without the tribes' knowledge. The discussion centered on the length of time the annuity would be paid. After many back-and-forth arguments, it was decided that the annuity payment would be decreased from fifty years to ten, with the option of the president to continue payment for no more than five years after that. As amended, the treaty was approved by a vote of forty-four to seven, all without the tribes' knowledge or consent. As far as they were concerned, tribal representatives had signed their names to $2.5 million rather than the $500,000 to $750,000, the annuity had become.

Prucha explains the change from the senators' point of view: "No doubt [the Senate] felt that $2.5 million over fifty years was too much for a treaty in which no land cessions were made, and the new policy of strictly limiting the duration of annuities ran counter to a term as long as fifty years. It was hoped the civilizing provisions would have taken effect sooner than that."

Representatives began to obtain consent, but by 1854 only three tribes had given theirs. No other approvals were sought. As a result, the treaty never was officially proclaimed by the then president Franklin Pierce, although annuities were paid over a period of fifteen years. In the 1920s the Department of the Interior attempted to get the Fort Laramie Treaty of 1851 proclaimed, but the secretary of state argued that the Act of 1871 forbade further treaties; therefore, ratification of the treaty came to a halt.

In the tribes' eyes, this was a broken treaty. Fort Laramie was also known for the Fort Laramie Treaty of 1868, which, in some ways, was more nefarious, though legally ratified. The idea of assimilation through civilization became apparent in the types of provisions, goods, and equipment that the U.S. government would provide American Indian people. It also became clear, through the treaty's language, how Indians should use their land: like white farmers. Indians would willingly make the reservation their home, land that would be described as arable. Trade buildings would be constructed and the education of Indian children would be compulsory. The treaty required that Indians' leather clothing would be replaced by garments made from wool and flannel and calico. In addition, the U.S. government would determine the property, the government, and the workings of the reservation.

Not all the Sioux agreed to these terms, and the terms of the treaty were not all met. Promised provisions of clothing and food were interrupted, if not altogether halted. White settlers crossed Indian lands without permission, and the so-called arable land was eaten up by buildings, roads, and railroads that tribal members had no intention of using.

As the agreements, outlined by the treaties, deteriorated, so did the tribes' patience. Brutal wars erupted, including the Great Sioux War of 1876–77 and the Battle of the Little Bighorn. In retaliation, the U.S. government launched massacres, including the Wounded Knee Massacre, where more than two hundred men, women, and children of the Lakotas had been killed.

I had no idea, when I worked at Fort Laramie for those five days, that these were the issues that fueled the Occupation of Wounded Knee in 1973, which my father and I never discussed that summer in 1974.

On our first day of work we shuttle people a quarter mile from the parking lot to the fort and back to their cars. The temperature is already in the mideighties by eight o'clock, and I know by three it will hover near a hundred. We drive all day, back and forth, between the dust-choked parking lot and the fort itself, making four runs an hour. Tiny particles of grit coat our noses and choke the van's vents and blankets seats. We are encouraged to wear watered-down handkerchief masks, but it feels too suffocating, so I decline, not thinking about the finely ground soil now settling deep into my lungs. It is the same dust that obscures the parking lot, all but the cars whose windshields reflect the fierce midday sun. The vans run constantly and so do their air conditioners; the cool air is the only thing that keeps us sane. We live for evening, when we can shower and wash the day's accumulation of sweat and grime from our bodies, drink a beer, and poke fun at the clientele.

For five days we drive. There is no time to walk among the buildings, so I study them from a distance as I commute back and forth on my route. The site consists of a spread-out collection of restored officers' homes, army barracks, stables, mess halls, and supply posts, all surrounding the parade grounds. The structures, with their freshly painted white exteriors, sit harsh against the golden-brown backdrop of the American prairie and waver in the brutal heat. I watch as a small breeze spawns a dust devil, sending it scurrying across the landscape. It is easy to see how an upper-class officer's wife from the East would find these surroundings repugnant.

At the age of twenty, I am not only innocent; I am unaware. I don't know this place's significance, or my heritage as an American Indian within it. To me, it isn't much different from the other forts that rest on the western landscapes, reminders of a fractious history, that the enemy had been conquered. It will take years for me to fully accept that the enemy that white America is talking about is me. In movies, in textbooks, in literature, we were "savage warriors" who attacked innocent settlers as they caravanned their wagons across the vast prairies of the United States, looking for free land to make their own. The Indians' price for their savagery was to be rounded up and placed on reservations. Like many people, I didn't question where that "savagery," that anger came from.

In years to come I will be shocked to find out that more than one thousand wars were declared on tribes by the U.S. military; that President Andrew Jackson considered treaties to be nonbinding, empty gestures to placate Indian "vanity"; or that the largest mass execution in U.S. history occurred the day after Christmas in 1862, when thirty-eight Indian men were hung in Mankato, Minnesota, for their role in the Great Sioux Uprising, a protest of their starvation and death due to illness, lack of provisions, and exposure.

But now, at this stage in my life, I'm not sure of what it means to be Indian. And one look at my brown skin, burnished beneath an unforgiving sun, says I'm not white. For now I don't think about these things; I push them to the back of my mind because they make me uncomfortable, and I sense they make others uncomfortable as well. So I drive the mind-numbing and repetitive route and grow quieter each day, no longer chatting with people who get in, get out, get in, get out. I am tired. I am tired of the endless hot days that have taken my good nature and tossed it to the afternoon winds that gust across the empty landscape. I am tired of people complaining about the weather, the heat, and the dust on the seats, on their faces, in their mouths. I am tired of making small talk about where I'm from, where they're from, when they're going home, when I'm going home.

I don't think about what it means to be Indian until I get ready to pull away from the fort and see a man flagging me down, holding up one hand to indicate his interest in getting on this van. He lopes easily toward me, as he holds his white straw cowboy hat in place against a breeze that has begun to stir. As he jogs in front of my grill, I see he is tall and slim. A moment later he climbs in, grabbing the back of my seat as he does so, jarring me into yet another level of annoyance. I study the rearview mirror to make sure he's seated before pulling the automatic gearshift into drive and starting forward. He catches my gaze and grins, showing long, white teeth that nestle in his chiseled jaw.

"Well, that's quite the place!" Cowboy says, his voice booming in my ear. I look at him, nod and smile. I have to. It is a requirement of my job, outlined the first day we arrived. The others in the van remain silent, gazing out the window and fanning themselves in the stifling heat, probably wondering if the weather is going to follow them to Kansas or Montana or Colorado or wherever their next stopping point is. "Yes sir," Cowboy continues, "that is quite the history."

"Where are you from?" I ask. He has to be local.

"Cody, Wyoming. What about you?"

"Montana," I answer. My annoyance grows at the aviator sunglasses that hide his eyes. I watch people's eyes because they tell me what words don't.

"Well," he says, as he looks out the window and mulls over the landscape, his arm thrown lazily across the back of the bench seat, "I don't care what they say about you people; you're okay." And he laughs, a big rolling laugh that takes me off guard. He's still chuckling when I leave him off at the parking lot. As he exits, he turns around, touches his finger to the brim of his hat, and saunters away, the grin still on his face.

You people? You're okay?

The laughter is meant to make it seem like an inside joke, but the meaning is unmistakable. As an Indian, I'm different from him, but not in a good way. He has to tell me we're okay. He gets to decide whether or not we're worthy. And that's when the discomfort settles in. I'm Indian, but I'm as white as he is. I've gone to the same schools, schools filled with people who look like him. I've had the same classes, the ones that tell me about our savage history. Hell, all the men I've dated look like him, with their brownish blonde hair, their blue/green eyes, their tan that evaporates in the winter. So where does he get off telling me that I'm "okay"?

When I tell this story to different people, over the next days, weeks, months, years, I realize many of them are fine with his statement. He probably didn't mean anything by it. He laughed, right? It was a joke. But I'm familiar enough with the lingo of the West to know that even though statements like his sound fine, beneath the surface they're meant to keep me one notch down, a member of a conquered and forgotten race.

And I then have two choices: let it slide because I don't want to get into a heated argument, which then translates to, "You are passive; you know your place"; or I can get angry, in which case I'm told I'm overly sensitive, too ready to take offense. I have a chip on my shoulder. If that wasn't true, people reason, others would be getting excited about the conversation. The thing is, I might have heard the same slur, in different words, ten times that month.

But in the summer of 1979, I didn't know the history of the ways non-Indians perceived American Indians. I didn't understand the anger and animosity that each group felt for the other. All I knew was what I experienced, my perceptions filtered through the eyes and knowledge of white America. Is it, then, any wonder that I felt confusion at being me?

7

Institutions of Higher Learning

University of Montana, Missoula, 1979–83.

After Yellowstone I landed on campus once more: Dad's alma mater, the University of Montana. I've chosen to begin anew, tabula rasa. At the end of my first quarter in 1979, I received a letter congratulating me for making the Dean's List. The parchment-colored paper sported an official gold emblem in the upper right corner. It accomplished two things immediately: it brought tears of joy to my eyes and restored some of my lost confidence. I don't believe I received that letter because I was super smart. I received it because I was isolated. By choice. I knew only Herb, who had moved here with me and was majoring in geology. Distractions were at a minimum; class effort and output were at a maximum. And it paid off.

At the end of the quarter I'd caught the attention of a biology professor. My first few tests didn't go well, and I was pulling a D. Herb made me go to IHOP the night before the final exam to pull an all-nighter. He quizzed and requizzed me on all aspects of the Krebs cycle. Who knew there were so many steps? In high school biology I'd had to know only six. I hadn't realized how easy high school had been. After finals the professor contacted me and asked me to come talk with him.

"I checked for cheating, but found not only were your answers different from those around you; they were right! You have worked hard to bring your grade up, harder than anyone I've ever seen." He handed me the test. I'd missed two questions on the hundred-point exam, the second-highest score in the class. "This exam was weighted pretty heavy. As a result this brought your quarter grade to a B; I gave you a B+. I've never seen anything like that. Congratulations!"

Life was good.

Well, life was better than it had been two years before. But now I'm in my second quarter, and I'm slipping. The problem is I've made friends; I've found groups to hang with. Distractions abound.

I want to major in anthropology, a forbidden discipline among Natives. I know this because in Bozeman I attended a lecture by a young Inupiat man, who talked about the Native economy in Alaska. Afterward I approached him and introduced myself as a Salish woman, telling him that I was majoring in anthropology. His smile was contemptuous, as he said, "Oh, I know all about anthropologists. They study us like we're bugs under the microscope, talking about us like they know us, making up lies about our culture, fascinated by our primitivism. Every summer anthropologists come up to our village and walk the riverbank. They'll see something in the rocks, bend down, and pick it up. They'll hold it up in the air and turn it this way and then that, and say, 'Oh, this must be a very powerful spiritual symbol.' Ha! We laugh then. It's a fishhook!" And just like that he turned away, and I was dismissed.

To be an anthropologist is to be a traitor. But I have a secret. I believe this is the only way I'm going to ever learn about Indians, about being an Indian: this discipline and the books I read. So I take my classes, and by the time I graduate from the University of Montana, in 1983, I have learned so many lessons.

Lesson 1: Indians Don't Go to College—They Go to Vo-Tech.

It is September 1979, and as a newcomer to the university, I've been assigned an adviser in the Economics Department, a balding professor who rises from his chair as I walk in the door. We shake hands. Being a mathphobe, this department makes me anxious, and the perspiration begins. He is a serious, forty-something man who wears glasses as well as a touch of arrogance.

After our introductions he motions me to take the seat opposite him. My transcript file lies unopened on his desk. Seeing the direction of my gaze, he explains it away, saying, "I never like looking at those things. People just talking to me helps me understand their goals so much better." He leans back in his chair, at ease, and crosses his fingers over his stomach. "So, what's your major?"

"I haven't chosen one," I reply. "I'm not sure what I want to major in."

"Well, what are you interested in?"

"I'm interested in a lot of things. I love writing; I like anthropology; I enjoy science and music."

"Hmmm," he says, nodding; he studies a spot on the wall to the left of my head. "That's pretty broad. Is there any particular direction you're leaning?"

"Toward science. The problem is," I confide, my voice dropping, "whatever I choose can't have a lot of math in it. I can't do math."

"Why is that?" The confusion on his face is clear.

I shrug; my cheeks warming in embarrassment. I have no idea why I can't do math. I have no idea why I could get As and Bs in all my classes in high school and get Ds in math. I have no idea why I could get the concepts of chemistry and physics but be unable to prove my understanding of them by running the numbers. As a junior I was encouraged by my chemistry teacher to take physics my senior year. In early November, in the midst of Mom's bipolarities, the physics teacher laid it out: "If you quit now, before the end of the semester, I can guarantee you a D. If you stay, I can't guarantee you'll pass at all, and I would hate to see you fail so close to graduation."

I have no idea why no one thought to explore the disparities in my abilities, or why Mom would look at those grades year after year after year and not do anything. Years from now when I tell her this, she will look at me with a certain amount of guilt, and she will say, "Your home life was so chaotic, I didn't think you needed additional pressure to get through your day. And by the time I realized how important it was and enrolled you in remedial math, you joined the swimming team instead."

"Mom," I will say, "I was a senior in high school! There was no way I was going to go to dumb math!"

The economics professor looks at me and lays the unopened file aside. "I'll be honest. I don't think college is a good place for you. With your skills I think you should check out the vo-tech program. I really do." He says this, not with sincerity, but with the sound of proclamation.

I thank him for his time and leave, thinking, *You son of a bitch, you watch me graduate with a degree.*

Lesson 2: Don't Expect Every Professor to Be Happy You Are in Their Class.

It is Spring quarter of 1981, and I'm looking into the ice-blue eyes of the cultural anthropology professor, a woman who has extensive experience researching the American Indians of the Great Basin. After she hands back our midterm exams, she asks me to go directly to her office. She has something important to discuss with me. When we leave she, birdlike, flutters her way out of the classroom and down the hall.

I arrive and survey the room as I'm taking a seat. She is already sitting at her desk, her aqua-blue shirt illuminating her silver hair, which has been styled in an abrupt blunt cut that sways above her shoulders. Her desk is messy, but my guess is she knows where everything is. She is surrounded by books, standing upright, laying down, leaning against one another, lazy and resigned to being forgotten.

As soon as I take my seat, I see her annoyance. Her already thin lips stretch even thinner as she contemplates what she'll say. She crosses her arms in front of her skinny chest, and as I focus on her words, I realize she's telling me that my work, my average "C-level" work, is inadequate.

"I have higher expectations of students in my class," she says, releasing one of her chest-hugging arms and pointing a slender finger in my direction, its broadening knuckle revealing her fifty-plus years. "You're not doing well, and I believe anthropology isn't a discipline you should even be involved in. I don't think it's an interest of yours, and I don't see you applying yourself in any way."

What she may or may not know is that those classes, of which I've had several, in which I don't apply myself aren't C classes. They are Ds and lower.

"Find yourself another major," she says, dismissing me from her light-blue office. "This one isn't working out for you."

My blood pulses angrily in my ears and along my wrists. In the seven weeks I've been in her class, we've had no conversations about my interest, my work, or my abilities. I have no idea why the sneak attack just happened now.

"I'll tell you why," says Carl, a graduate archaeology student who I can usually find in the lab, and today is no different. He is doing paperwork resulting from last summer's field school. When he looks at me, his blue eyes sparkle, but his gaze is serious. "She hates Indians."

I laugh. "What do you mean she hates Indians? That's all she studies."

"Yeah," he says, returning his attention to the forms in front of him. "But from her perspective, Indians are great to study. They're just not much good for anything else."

Lesson 3: "Apple of My Eye" Has a Whole New Meaning in Indian Country.

Later, that same quarter, I'm standing in what used to be the living room of a small turn-of-the-century house, but what is now Native American Student Services. My attempt at invisibility is successful. Since I came here no one has talked to me, nor has anyone shown any interest in me whatsoever; no one has even turned their attention in my direction. But that's okay; for once I'm surrounded by people who look like me—with their brown skin, their black hair, their dark eyes, and round cheeks. I watch as they talk with one another, girls behind curved palms, boys in good-humored conversational one-upmanship. They never act like this outside of these four walls but rather sit quietly in their seats, mute to participating in the education around them. Just like me.

I so badly want to belong here.

And within a couple of weeks of hanging out, I finally get my invitation. They're meeting up at the Trading Post, a local bar. Did I want to come along? I do, but I'm nervous. Because I was actively raised not to "be" Indian; I am not supposed to act like them (whatever that means), dress like them (with their ribbon shirts and cowboy hats), talk like them (that rez dialect drives my dad nuts), and most of all date them. I don't know anything about them, except that I look like them. Outside of the bar I am joined by a group of eight or so Native students, who immediately surround me and crowd inward. Out of nowhere, one asks, "What are you?"

The question, forthright and demanding, takes me by surprise. Before I can answer, another question is tossed out. "Are you Indian?"

And another: "Are you a skin?"

And yet another: "Are you a breed?"

Redskin. Half breed. Their questions are rude, but I want to belong, so I listen and remind myself their questions are not much different from the questions I get asked by whites on a nearly daily basis. But here among this group it is somehow more painful, more cutting. But it is nothing compared to what comes next.

"Naw," comes the answer from one of the young men who stands off to the side, the sneer barely hidden on his face. "She's an apple."

Their laughter, raucous and filled with contempt, interrupts the night, and they turn their back on me and wander inside, their talk soaked up by the music drifting through the opened doors. I'm stunned. I don't know what to do. The verbal slap stings to the core of who I thought I was, a physical assault on my psyche. So I hang back. Alone. Soon I am joined by a short, slender brown man, whose face is pocked with acne scars and whose ponytail twists uncontrollably down his back. He gives me an apologetic, but sad, smile and remains silent.

"What's an apple?" I ask.

"Red on the outside, white on the inside," he answers, then holds the door open for me so we could join the group.

That thud? That was me hitting the boundary of what it is to be Indian.

Lesson 4: Everyone Knows More about What It Means to Be Indian Than I Do.

It is October 1981, and I am standing in the middle of a snowstorm near Wibaux, Montana, a dying little town that sits on the border of Montana and North Dakota. I am part of an archaeological fieldwork–survey course scheduled to walk the private ranch today looking for sites under the three inches of accumulated snow. I'm cold and even the hot breakfast and hotter tea isn't warming me up. It's twenty-something degrees, and I had no idea how to work the ancient steam-heat register in my room, and the bed had only a sheet and a medium-weight cotton blanket. So since arriving here, I've never been warm.

"Ready?" asks Will, a fellow classmate and an ex-biker from South Carolina. He looks at me while he lifts his backpack over his shoulder and lights a cigarette, protecting the flame of the match behind a cupped palm.

I sigh and nod, as the cold air sears my lungs. We begin the walk of futility, holding our coats close against our bodies and pulling our hats low over our ears, as the wind seems to divide the cells of my body. The author James Herriot referred to this kind of wind as a "lazy wind," blowing through bodies instead of around them.

Will is an easy guy to survey with, and I've gotten to know him well over the past two years that we've been students together. Our conversations have covered a wide range of topics. So while the wind threatens to take our words and blow them away, he asks, "What tribe are you?"

"Why, you want me to build you a fire?" I smile and wait for his reply.

I am suddenly in unfamiliar territory. No subject has been off-limits in our conversations, but we've never talked about me being Indian. But for me humor is the easiest way to discuss the elephant in the room. It allows me a certain amount of control in the conversation: if I make fun of it, I won't be taken off guard if someone else does.

He throws me a lopsided grin, but he is more serious, and I'm not sure where to go with this. "I'm Salish." I add no other descriptors. I don't know any.

The snow lies lifeless and silent beneath our feet, and when I look up the sky shows signs that the weather will break; chances are the snow will be melted by the middle of the afternoon. "Why don't you sound like an Indian?" he presses. "You know how Indians talk in that dialect, that reservation dialect?"

I didn't use to mind these kinds of questions, but lately this topic has a certain edge to it, a discomfort that slides beneath my skin like a surgical knife. Now it seems that every time it comes up, it cuts away a little piece of me. "I wasn't raised on the reservation," I explain. "I was adopted by a white couple." I am beginning to hate that explanation.

He turns his head and studies me for a long time, his green eyes sizing me up. Then we continue to walk, in silence. That afternoon, when the sun comes out, Will resurrects the conversation.

"You know, you're lucky," he says, squatting down to light another cigarette. This time the wind is gone, and he doesn't need to shelter the flame. He inhales deep and, throwing his head back, exhales long and slow. "You've got this great Indian heritage, but then you've also got this ability to walk in the white man's world—it doesn't get any better than that." His voice is slow and melodious, almost soothing, and his South Carolina accent draws out his words so they pour thick and warm, like honey on an early spring day. He squints against the smoke as the breeze changes direction. Then something on the ground catches his attention, and he runs his index finger lightly into the black soil.

After a few moments he pulls out a broken obsidian scraper. I write the description and mark its placement on the map.

"Why do you say that?" I hear the defensiveness creep into my voice, and I know where it comes from. Me against the world. Me pitted against the "other." The Indians don't want me; the whites don't accept me. They push me into each other's court, always away from them. I am isolated; I am in-between. But this, this thing he says, suddenly feels like a lifeline. No one has ever said I was lucky. My tone changes to one of curiosity. "What do you mean?"

"You can live anywhere," Will continues, moving his hand to take in the world around us. "You act white and can move around this world really easy, but you're a tribal member. You can go back anytime you want. They have to take you back."

"Who says?" He is naive, and I can't help but laugh.

"Just the way it is." He pauses and kneels down, scratching the surface of the dirt with his fingernail, exposing a small broken piece of worked chalcedony. "Doesn't your real family live up there somewhere?"

Now I'm really uncomfortable. "I dunno. Maybe."

"Contact an elder," Will says, drawing hard on the last of his cigarette, making it all sound so easy. "The role of elders is to help people in need. Contact one, and they've got to help you."

I'm hopeful and reluctant. I'm curious and resentful—right now, mostly the latter. I look at this blond-haired, green-eyed, freckle-faced ex-biker and note, with a certain amount of frustration, that he sure seems to know a lot more about being Indian than I do. He has the road map of where I should go, who I should contact, what I should do. I know he's talked to elders and played Stick Game, and suddenly I feel so inadequate. I feel so inadequate in my race being Indian.

And I wonder, how is it that he knows so much more than me?

Lesson 5: Just Because You Look Indian Doesn't Mean You Are Indian.

It is the fall of 1982, and although I'm in my senior year of college,

I've taken a graduate seminar on social theory. Twelve of us sit at the oak table, surrounded by oak bookshelves in a room that screams academia. The question is palpable: how difficult is this class going to be? We eye one another and wonder who is smarter than whom. I know there are a lot of people here far smarter than I am; I don't see myself as particularly bright.

The professor, when he walks in, seems to be a brilliant man, whose demeanor indicates he's far more uncomfortable walking around this world than I am. He sits down, shuffling his papers, and mumbles his greeting with a shy smile. His voice is soft, and he avoids lengthy, if any, eye contact. "First thing we'll do is take roll, so I can learn your names, and you can learn one another's." His voice is gentle, and there's that reassuring smile again. "Let's see . . . Anderson, Becky."

"Here."

And so it goes. My turn is coming, and my anxiety heightens. With wearisome familiarity my face grows uncomfortably warm, and my hands grow clammy. My name is the fifth one he calls.

"Devan, Susan."

I clear my throat and raise my hand, my voice not obeying my command to speak.

"Devan . . ." He peers at me over his glasses, and I feel like I'm a specimen under a microscope, illuminated, bare. "Devan," he says again, feeling it on his tongue, swishing it like a nice glass of red wine.

And I know what's coming. I close my eyes, just for a moment, and feel my heart race. When I open them all the students are looking at me to see who this creature is that has captured the professor's attention.

"That's French?" he says, not really asking. It's more of a statement.

I swallow and want to crawl away, because we have entered the "Guesses." I'm so tired of the guesses, those endless predictions of "what" I am. Usually they are based on my looks: Japanese? Korean? Hawaiian? Taiwanese? Eskimo is always the last resort. It's my Cree blood that creates those Asiatic eyes, but few guess, or perhaps want to guess, American Indian.

His guess is based on my looks as well, after taking account of the name. So many members of my tribe, as well as others along the northern boundaries, have surnames that trace the lineage of the French fur trappers and traders that roamed the vast plains and timbered areas of the northern climes. What they reveal are relationships with Native women and the children they produced. So when he guesses French, he is essentially asking whether I am Indian with a French surname.

"No," I reply. And I'm silent. Being Indian is not cool.

"Not French?" he asks, prodding in the politest manner possible.

I shake my head. Being Indian is not romantic. My face is flaming.

Silence. And stares. And shame. Because I'm beginning to fully appreciate the burden of my skin and the assumptions that are made.

"Can I ask you what nationality your name is?"

People giggle at my insistence at anonymity. His insistence at knowledge wins.

"It's Czechoslovakian."

His eyebrows rise to the crown of his head, and I'm silently angry. Not a single person in this class or any others have been asked their heritage, based on name, based on skin, based on anything. Once again I am singled out. And now, in my set-apart role, I refuse to tell him I'm Indian. And I refuse to say I'm adopted. I refuse to explain my in-between status, because I can't explain it.

Lesson 6: Just Because You Act White Doesn't Mean You Are White.

The most powerful lesson I learn, the one that stays with me the longest, happens in the winter of 1979, when I returned to Montana State University to visit friends. We are standing on the downtown sidewalk. The bars have closed, and a stiff spring breeze starts us thinking about what we want to do next. But we stand around, like we have before, with our hands in our pockets, shooting the shit, telling stories, and laughing at antics, our own or someone else's. The familiar lull in the conversation makes time for the jokes, and they are pulled out of our memory like stuffing from a favorite toy.

There're the eastern European jokes, the Scandinavian jokes, the Irish jokes, the Asian jokes, the Mexican jokes. But then someone starts telling an Indian joke. And it's not as if I haven't heard a million of these. I have. From just about everyone around me. And I laugh, just like everyone around me. I don't want to make waves. I suck it up and take it; I know the rules. So I listen and the joke continues.

And everyone's laughing, and I'm laughing too, but then suddenly, without my permission, my laughter turns into something else. It turns into sobs caught in my throat, and tears begin to fall, large tears, heavy tears, tears that I've held onto my whole life so people wouldn't know how bad all this hurts. . . . It hurts that that they don't see me as the butt of the joke but rather as one of them, pale skinned and golden haired, but I'm not. . . . I see the world in shades of red, angry, angry shades of red. Someone catches sight of me, because now I'm turned away, and my shoulders shake of their own accord, and I'm so, so embarrassed. That person says, "Oh my God, what's wrong?" and I can't talk because my throat is closed, an allergy to shame, because if I let loose the sobs, they will be loud and endless until I'll want to scream.

Then I feel arms around me, hugging my shoulders, pulling me close, and I want to bury my face in the jacket, the wool jacket that scratches my skin, now wet and delicate. Then I notice that the voices have stopped, the Indian joke has stopped, and someone, a male, takes my face in his hands, cradles my cheeks in warm, soft palms, and gently forces my face up, forcing me to look at him, his eyes wide, his brows pulled together in concern for me, this friend who suddenly seems like an unknown. He says, through the storm in my ears, through the storm in my head, he says, almost in a whisper, his lips very close, "Why are you crying?"

I feel his breath, gentle and quiet, and I answer through a clenched jaw that suddenly starts shaking when I've relaxed it enough to allow words through; it shakes uncontrollably, like me, like my words as they spill out of the mouth I can't close, and I answer, "I don't know, it just started." . . . As if "it" was a mound of cans in grocery aisle number three that has fallen, and everyone has stepped out of the way except for me. . . . But the tears don't stop; they continue, they continue to come up from the depths of my soul and empty out onto the earth, splashing on my clothes and my shoes, one after another until they run together, united . . . and I cover my mouth with my hand to stop the words, the words I can no longer hold safely behind closed lips, and I so badly want to reintegrate my disintegrated self, a self that is like a sugar cube coming apart under a stream of water, but I can't do that. . . . I can't do that with people here, with people watching, a game tied in overtime. . . . I want to be who I was just moments ago, before the joke; I want the lips to go away, the hands to go away, the coat to go away, the people to go away and leave me here alone and frozen and isolated in my shame, but they don't. . . .

"Was it the joke?" another voice asks, as soft as the first . . . and I gulp air and wonder in horror, why I can't just seem to just let it be okay. . . . I don't know why, but I can't, and I find myself nodding, unable to look at anyone. I close my eyes to the man who holds my face. . . . "I'm sorry," he says, and I can hear his words, but I can't see his lips move. "I'm so sorry. I had no idea you felt this this way. I wasn't thinking." When I look up, I want to smile; I want to put him at ease, want to be okay with being the butt of yet another joke, but I can't . . . and the disintegration continues, and they're watching; they're all watching, and the man once more takes my face into his hands, and my chest feels like it will explode with the anger and the shame I have boiling up inside of me, a geyser that has become tapped. "You know," he says, looking deep into my eyes, "you have the right. You have the right to say 'stop,' to tell people when something hurts or when you feel uncomfortable with what's being said to you or done to you." He pauses and the geyser is dangerously close to the surface. "Do you understand you have that right?"

Oh God, the tears come, new rivers of tears; my chest heaves, and I fall forward, hands on my knees, unable to stand straight any longer, and the tears have less distance to fall. I can't move because I am lead, and as I bend over myself, into myself, I curl my fists into balls, and what is left of my badly bitten fingernails bites into the softness of my palms. His words make it through the storm in my head, the storm in my ears, and I realize finally, finally, I have permission. I have finally been given permission to say, *I have the right to say how much it hurts to be Indian in the world in which I live.*

8

Coyote

University of Montana, Missoula, Autumn 1981.

He is beautiful, this brown boy whose skin is the shade of well-baked bread. His hair, which lies fringed around his youthful face, is the color of amber honey. Golden-brown eyes peer from beneath that fringe, playfully, their corners creased. Although his cheeks are round, they are thinning, allowing me to see the young man he will become in the not-too-distant future.

He draws me like a magnet when he walks into the room on a carpet of energy, his body slender, moving with purpose. I've never seen him here, in this remodeled living room that is now the Native American Student Services building. Although I am fascinated, I don't speak to him; I am too shy and awkward. I am waiting for the secretary to return, a woman I've made friends with, a white woman who, among all these brown faces, is most familiar to me. Working here, she is a stepping stone, a bridge between who I am and who I want to be. But the cultural creek is wider than I thought. After several months the Native students still look at me as an outsider, their eyes judging who I am, what I am doing here.

I don't know what I'm doing here; I'm still a foreigner in my own land, and as a foreigner I stand at the edge of the group, trying to be invisible. At some point I hope to leave my in-between cocoon behind, ugly and empty, and become the butterfly that moves easily in this world. I feel such an ache to be one of them, this group of young men and women who share their laughter and tell their secrets to one another.

It is with this awareness of otherness that I study the man-boy who walks in with his energy encasing him like a blanket, and I wonder if he sees this thing that still hangs off me. His gaze, soft and direct, tells me he doesn't. His smile is both gentle and shrewd as he silently and openly observes me. This action makes me nervous. He moves quickly to the adjacent vacant office desk and hops up, sitting on the edge, swinging his legs back and forth, tapping the front of the desk with each pendulum swing. The smile remains.

I smile hesitantly, he knowingly.

Does he know that I am not like him? That I am not like anyone else in this room? Probably not—I haven't yet opened my mouth, allowing my white words to slip out. Does he know that I am aware of the brutal histories, the stereotypes of his people? Our people? Does he know that I am well aware of those things, that those are the things I think about when I sit on the highest point of the Bison Range and look down at the Mission Valley, blanketed with bright green irrigated fields that look like squares in a homesteader's quilt, because, really, that's what they are? Does he know that I've journeyed to the Medicine Tree, not with the elders who migrate there each year, but by myself because I have no elders? Does he know that I've held the pink bitterroot, dainty and sacred in my hands, on the late days of springtime before putting it back in the ground from which it came? Does he know that I've done everything I can think of to become one of them, to become Indian, and that I'm still not, even though I have a Bureau of Indian Affairs card that says I am?

His words are electric. "What's your name?"

I guard the smile that begins to emerge. "Sue."

"What's your last name?"

"Devan."

I scan his face for some flicker of recognition, as he pauses, thinking. Does he know me? I shake my memory like a box. Do I know him? Have I seen him somewhere before? Any of my classes? The bars? A powwow? I shake and shake and shake. Nothing.

The boy shifts his attention to the scene outside the large picture window, now shaded by eighty-year-old maples. When he looks back, his gaze is penetrating, the half smile still there. "What reservation are you from?"

"Flathead."

I feel as if I'm being grilled, that if I answer this barrage of authenticity questions correctly, I will be allowed to cross the bridge.

"What tribe?"

"Salish." I am able to breathe a sigh of relief. I have a tribe; I have a homeland. I wonder then if I am finally "Indian" enough; if this knowledge, supported by the Bureau of Indian Affairs card, erases the quasi descriptions of "skin" and "breed"; if it means I no longer have to be an "apple."

"Who's your family?"

Snap. I stop breathing. He is asking about my reservation family, the family with whom I've had no contact, no details since my adoption. The family who has been severed from me as neatly as a sword severs the head from the heart. The family I do have, the ones who raised me, is no one he would know. With this realization I feel the key, that beautiful golden key to being "one of," "part of," slip through my fingers like heavy silk. With these words the boy has reminded me who I truly am and, in the darkest of ways, why I will never be anything but.

"I don't know," I reply, my voice soft, my throat tight. That smile, the one I've been holding in, comes out now, apologetic, begging for understanding.

The boy laughs then, throws back his head and laughs in a way that makes his golden eyes dance, crinkling at their edges, and the dimples along his smooth cheek crease and deepen. Soon his laughter calms to a chuckle, and soon after that it stops entirely. He once more shifts his enigmatic gaze to me, that half smile, and he tilts his head. "What do you mean you don't know?" Moments slip by; I have no answer. "You have to know. Everyone knows who their family is." His smile is generous, inviting. *If I just thought harder*, it seems to say, *I would know*.

"I don't."

I feel the familiar warmth slip across my face and down my neck, and I look away, no longer able to meet that gaze of those golden-brown eyes.

"Why don't you know?"

"I'm adopted." I look up again, and he is still watching me.

Electricity dances in the emptiness around me, except I'm not sure whom it belongs to, him or me. I look away again, trying to hide myself, my soul, from his scrutiny, but I still feel his gaze, sharp and penetrating. I look up in time to see him push off the desk, his face wearing a jaunty grin. He crosses the carpet once more, and before heading out the door he says, his smile large, "Okay. See you around."

But I don't see him around. A week later I ask the white secretary who he was and give her a description. She has no idea. She's never seen him. I ask the few people I talk with here and am met with blank faces and shaking heads. "No," they say, after considering my verbal sketch, "I've never seen anyone like that here. Doesn't sound familiar." Over the next few weeks I think about him, about his half smile, his golden-eyed contemplation as his questions bared my soul, to me, if no one else. I turn his memory, his words, his questions, over and over in my mind like a quarter spinning through space on a flip.

Then one day the quarter lands, and I am aware of who he is. He is Coyote, the trickster. Who else would ask the pointed questions I no longer asked? Who else would push for answers about searching through the unknowable about my family? Who else would look as beautiful as he did, smiling with enigmatic charm, knowing an attraction would follow? Who else would make me begin to think: *Is this my brother? Have I been attracted to my brother?* Within minutes I scour my memory of every Indian I've known here, met here, contemplating their possible relationship to me. *Are these my sisters? My cousins? My aunts and uncles?*

I've been reminded how important it is to find my birth family. But I won't get up the nerve to look for them for another year.

Helena, Montana, March 1982.

I'm sitting in the reception area of the Montana State Social Services building in Helena. The secretary asks if I want tea or hot cider and points to the cart across the room. I'm nervous, so I take her up on her offer just to give my hands and my mind something to do. My hands shake as I stir in the sugar. I've driven 120 miles to meet this woman, a stranger with whom I've corresponded through letters and, more recently, phone calls. I hope, more than anything, I hope she will be able to give me information that leads me to my birth family. So I stir and look out the window and try not to feel the pressure with which my heart is pounding.

So much has happened within the last year that helped propel this meeting, including meeting Rick, the man who would become my husband. I'd met Rick the summer before, when both of us worked as seasonal park rangers at Carlsbad Caverns National Park, New Mexico, a park located in the far reaches of my known universe. Having grown up a navy brat, Rick had lived throughout the world, the United States, Spain, Japan; this was his first trip out west. He told me that the only education of New Mexico he'd been given was a friend's story of how they'd come back to their car after eating in a restaurant to find all four tires had been slashed.

I was drawn to him from the beginning; he was everything I wasn't. Where he was confident, strategic, and focused, I was uncertain, impulsive, living life in the moment. While he worked through a problem, I danced around it trying to find a different route. But even with all these profound differences, we were curious together, exploring the arid and alien country we found ourselves living in. We hiked dry streambeds filled with unstable cobbles, as we scanned the canyon walls for ancient Native pictographs; we spelunked the lower depths of caverns, amazed at the pristine crystals that grew from the limestone; we danced, we told stories of our complicated lives, we lived in each other's sphere for four months.

But one day, with just three words, Rick revealed the protective space I kept between me and others, a space unknown to me. A month after meeting he said, "I love you." There was no preamble, no uncomfortable nervousness—just a calm statement. As if he said that every day.

Disconcerted, I replied, "Thanks."

A phone jangled in the background, pulling me once more into the present. The person I'm waiting to see in the social services office is Helen Childs. She's the one who has helped me with my Individual Indian Monies account, an account that the Bureau of Indian Affairs oversees for tribal members. Money in my IIM account comes from the Treaty of Hellgate, a signed agreement between President James Buchanan and the Confederated chiefs on July 16, 1855, although there are discrepancies as to whether Chief Charlo actually signed the treaty, or if it was signed for him in his absence. The Treaty of Hellgate was ratified March 8, 1859, nearly a hundred years before I was born. One of the requirements of the treaty stated that whites would not be allowed to live on the land without the expressed permission of the chiefs as well as the Indian agent. The Allotment Act (also known as the Dawes Act) changed that, and white homesteaders flooded into the boundaries of the Flathead Indian Reservation. The U.S. government was found guilty of breaking the treaty in 1971.

The IIM account and my tribal account (monies collected from land, water, and timber leases) were kept for me untouched until I turned eighteen. Unlike foster families, adoptive families do not receive money from the state or any other agency to raise their adopted children, unless that child is a special needs child, which I wasn't. Therefore, these funds were held in trust for me and administered by Montana State Social Services, who acted as a go-between, between the tribe and me, originally to veil my identity.

When I turned eighteen, the bureau gave me a choice: keep the account in my birth name and continue to allow social services to administer the account, which meant I needed to request money in writing; or change my name legally to my adopted name and have direct access to the monies themselves. There were costs and benefits to such a name change. The benefits would be that I would no longer require a go-between to access tribal disbursements. The costs had been well laid out by Dad over the years: my name would be a matter of public record and any one of my deadbeat relatives could look me up. "You'll have family crawling out of every space to find you," he warned. "They'll camp out on your doorstep, and you'll never get rid of them. Indians are notorious for mooching off anyone, especially if they're family. They'll suck you dry." Dad wasn't saying anything I hadn't heard many non-Native people say. Given those options and no fair hearing for the Indian side, I decided to keep my legal name off the documents and to request, in writing, the funds I needed to cover my school and living expenses.

These were the requests that helped establish a long-distance friendship with Helen Childs. And the requests, formal and stilted written letters, all said essentially the same thing: "Mrs. Childs, my name is Susan Devan. My birth name was Vicki Charmain Rowan. I would like to request (some amount of money) to cover school expenses. Please send it to the following address. Sincerely, Susan Devan." After a few years I relaxed and they became "Dear Mrs. Childs" and later "Dear Helen." At some point we began sharing small, chatty details about our lives.

"Oh, you're down in New Mexico," she'd written after receiving one of my requests from Carlsbad Caverns. "New Mexico is such a beautiful state. What are you doing there? I've processed your request, and you should receive it within a week. Warmest regards, Helen."

By July I knew I loved being a park ranger, and I began considering the Park Service as a career. Rick, however, continued making his plans to go to Pensacola, Florida. He'd applied for, and been accepted into, the Naval Flight Program, and there was still paperwork for him to complete, but he had to go to El Paso to do it.

"Do you want to go to El Paso with me?" he asked.

The drive was empty of interesting landscape, but Rick filled me with stories of his adventures, taken with other park rangers. He pointed out Guadalupe National Monument, the sister park to Carlsbad Caverns, where he'd hiked several times with friends. After a particularly challenging hike, he and a colleague from New York stopped at the little restaurant-bar-garage ten miles down the road to have a beer. They sat on their stools, watching a Mexican man, with broken but intelligible English, inquire about a fan belt for his model of car. The ancient white woman behind the counter told him she didn't speak Mexican. He asked again, slower. She interrupted him, again saying she didn't speak Mexican. Two other patrons looked on in amusement. Finally, Rick stepped in and said he would act as an interpreter, although, he confided to me, the only Spanish he knew was *cerveza* and *baño*. I could only imagine the indignation and humiliation the Mexican man felt as he turned to Rick, asking him in perfectly understandable English if the garage had a fan belt for his make of car. Rick turned to the ancient woman and repeated the question, word for word. She went to the garage and pulled a fan belt off the wall, then handed it to the man. He turned to Rick once more and asked, "How much?" Rick asked the ancient woman, "How much?" The woman gave an amount that was twice what the fan belt was worth; Rick saw the price before she scratched the tag off the cardboard cover. The man paid the stated amount without question.

Rick said the experience was hysterical and surreal. I didn't say anything. As we drove through the empty miles of lechuguilla and creosote bush, I wondered how that old woman lived with herself as she conducted commerce with someone she obviously loathed while ensuring a loss of his dignity. But some white people are like that. I remember being five years old, standing in line at a tourist shop in Yellowstone, cradling an Indian doll in my hand, waiting to purchase it, while the woman behind the counter waved everyone else ahead of me. "You wait on her," Mom demanded as she came into the store, wondering what was taking so long. "Her money is just as good as anyone else's." The woman did so with an abrupt transaction, which caused her to slam the cash drawer. She threw me an angry look; evidently, her smiles were saved for those people before and after me.

I had an idea of how that Mexican man might have felt.

After Carlsbad, when I'd returned to Montana, each of my letters written to Helen involved either asking for money or my account balance. Finally, I called her, under the pretense of finding out information about my account, after which I blurted, "Do you have any information about my family?"

Silence. I cringed, aware that I had overstepped an important boundary. I immediately tried to alleviate discomfort, saying, "It's okay if you don't. I'm just always curious."

The silence continued for a few more moments while the familiar adrenaline pumped through my body. My fingertips felt like they were burning with lightning.

Helen answered, her voice quiet and somber. "What is it that you know?"

I breathed. At least she'd answered.

"Not much. Just that I was adopted when my parents died in a car accident, and that my birth name is Vicki Charmain Rowan. That's all I know."

I let the silence ride.

"I'll tell you what, why don't you plan on coming over to see me in my office in about ten days. Perhaps by that time I'll have some information for you."

So now it's ten days later, and I'm sitting in the Montana State Social Services office waiting for Helen Childs. It's March and snow settles like a down quilt on the gentle landscape. The roads, thankfully, are free of ice. I don't like winter driving in Montana on the two-lanes—I imagine myself skidding off the road or, worse, into someone else. But driving here has allowed me to consider the feelings that might arise: sheer exuberance undulated with dark and disappointing doubt. A mantra calmed the war within me, *Whatever happens is whatever happens. Don't make it bigger or smaller than it already is.* A few deep breaths calmed my anxiety, until I turned the car into the parking lot of the social services building. That's when my hands began shaking.

The office had been built in the 1970s, evident by its architecture, the color scheme, and the brick on the outside of the building. Inside, gold carpet dominated the flooring, and the room was tastefully decorated, so unlike the 1950s Cold War theme of Dad's federal building. The secretary took my name and disappeared down the carpeted hall, reappearing a few minutes later to announce, "Mrs. Childs will be with you in about five minutes. Have a seat. Do you want tea or hot cider?" She motioned to the serve-yourself cart across the room. I took her up on her offer and poured some bubbling water over a tea bag and stirred in some sugar, then settled down to pretend this wasn't my life I was interested in. It was a friend's.

"Susan?"

I look up, and my gaze lands on the smiling face of a tall, blond woman, who says, "It's so good to finally meet you." I extend my hand for a handshake and am surprised when she reaches out and wraps me in a hug. So uncomfortable. That's something we don't do in our family. She steps back and smiles, "I'm so glad you were able to get here. How was the drive?" I follow her down the short labyrinth to her office.

"It was fine." I can feel the coldness of my hands through my pants pockets. Nerves. Suddenly, I am a rabbit, ready to bolt if anything begins to go wrong. That's when the words I've held at bay take shape in my brain: *This is a bad idea. This is a bad idea. I shouldn't have come here; this is not going to go well. This is a bad idea.* Although I try to push the words aside, they beat harder and harder until I breathe, until I draw a breath so deep in my lungs they drown in the air. I remind myself that it's better to have an answer, whatever that might be, than to know nothing.

It is evident from the title on her door that she is more important that just the person who directs my disbursements. The nerves start bouncing again. She unlocks the door, but instead of entering and taking a seat behind her desk, Helen glances at her watch and winces apologetically. "I hate to say this, but I got called in to a last-minute meeting this morning, and I didn't have time to change our appointment." She gestures to the chair behind her desk. "So why don't you come in and have a seat, and I'll come back when the meeting's done. Then we can talk."

I am uncomfortable with the chair behind the desk; its feeling of importance sifts throughout the room. Instead I sit in the armless chair by the door. She laughs. "Why don't you go sit on my chair behind the desk? It's a lot more comfortable, and I'll be honest, I don't know how long I'll be."

"That's fine," I answer. "I don't mind sitting here."

"No, really. I insist." Smiling, Helen maneuvers me gently out of the chair and propels me to the large leather executive chair behind her desk. When I'm safely seated, she says, "I'll try to be back in a half an hour, forty-five minutes. Until then make yourself at home. I'll lock the door, so no one bothers you."

She exits and I hear the lock click into place. The chair is posh, and the desk large, cluttered with files. I've deferred to authority in sitting in this chair, which is too swanky for my taste. I always defer to authority. Maybe it's an adoption thing. Maybe it's a Dad thing. Maybe it's just me.

This room does not say "government office" with its leather chair, the massive oak desk, the wall-to-wall carpet in soft gold. Two large philodendrons guard the narrow, vertical windows, and they seem happy enough, tall and lush. The federal building in Billings provides a harsh contrast with its yellowed linoleum, cracks running along its worn surface. In that building every wall is painted a sensory-numbing green and acts as a backdrop to the heavy metal furniture, gray and unimaginative.

My heart begins speeding again. I have no idea what I'm going to do here for the next half hour. I walk around the room, eyeing the books in Helen's bookcases, which consist of case studies and legal tomes. I look out each of her two windows at the snow, already melting quickly under the early spring sun. I glance at the clock on the wall. Five minutes have passed. I wish her meeting had been rescheduled; I don't know what to do in this room. I make my way back to her chair and twirl slowly in circles in the revolving seat.

A woman stops by the door and glances in the narrow vertical window, leaving quickly when I see her. In looking away, my eyes catch something familiar on the top of Helen's desk, but I quickly avert my gaze. Whatever is on her desk is none of my business. So I try to find somewhere else to look: out the tall window to the grassland below and once more out the other window to the railroad tracks. I glance at the door, expecting to see the face again at any moment. Again my gaze skims across her desk and stops. It is a file with my name on it. "Susan Jean Devan" is typed on the index tab of the file on top of the clutter. My heart beats against my chest, and I fight my urge to lean forward and look. These are confidential files, open only to the people who need to see them. My gaze slides away, but it slides back, magnetized by what those files might contain. I reach out, stroking the tips of my fingers gently over the manila folder. I can't breathe, as I inch the file closer to me. Guilty, I glance at the door. No one can see me doing this. I shouldn't be doing this, but whatever is contained in that file is about me. About my family. About my life. How is it that I shouldn't know information about me?

I open the file gingerly. It contains several pages filled with names, notes, letters, and memos, some typed, some handwritten. Paragraphs outline social workers' visits, while one page describes in detail the condition in which they found me: infected mosquito bites covered my arms and legs, my whole body, my buttocks raw with open sores. There was a question of how long I remained in an unchanged diaper—hours or days? Another page notes that social services had been called because the mother had left me; my sister, who was three at the time; and an infant brother in the care of our six-year-old sister. Our mother hadn't been seen in several days. "The girl tried the best she could," someone had written, "but was not prepared to take care of three babies for that length of time." Our grandmother was quoted as saying she herself was too old to take care of that many infants and toddlers. According to another page in the file, our mother had been given a court date. If she wanted her children returned to her, the memo said, she needed to be present in court on that date. A hand-scrawled note on the following page reads that she never made it to the court date; she'd been located at a nearby bar. As a result, she'd lost custody of three of her five children.

One page lists the names of all my primary relatives: my birth mom, her husband, my siblings, both full and half. I grab the nearby pencil and copy these quickly onto a yellow legal pad. The file also reads that I'm part Blackfeet. It reads that my father is a "dark, swarthy man" from Minnesota, "perhaps Norwegian," although ethnicity remained undetermined. It reads he died of a drowning accident in Washington State when I was five. It reads my birth mother, Clara Victoria Plant, followed by three other names, lives on the Flathead Reservation. The note also adds that she goes by the name Victoria. I stop and process that information. My birth mother, Victoria, *lives*—present tense—on the Flathead Reservation! She lives only thirty miles away from me! My thoughts churn around the stories I'd been told since I was six, about her dying in a car accident. But according to this file, there was no car accident. There had never been a car accident. I stare out the window at the melting snow while emotions swirl, coiling around one another: happiness and possibility, anger and betrayal, hope and curiosity, fear and uncertainty. I can't seem to fully catch my breath; I can't seem to catch my thoughts.

I scribble as much of this information as I can and commit the rest to memory. I read, reread, and reread again the words and descriptions that burst from the page. I'm so involved that when Helen knocks at the door I jump. Her keys release the lock. The look, when she enters, is a mixture of intensity and trepidation. She shuts the door, puts the lock back into place, and leans with her back against it, saying in a low, powerful voice, "You must never, ever tell anyone I showed you these. What I'm doing is illegal. I could lose my job. But I have difficulty saying the information in this file is not yours to know. This is your life we're talking about. That's why I'm showing you these, but I am deadly serious. I could lose my job for that." I nod in understanding.

"Now, do you have any questions?" She takes a seat in the chair by the door. I shake my head, overwhelmed at the danger she's put herself in, overwhelmed with this newfound knowledge, and overwhelmed at my life—the life my dad had worked so hard to keep from me with his lies and misinformation.

"Plant," she says, "is a very common name on the Blackfeet Reservation."

I nod. There is nothing to say; I have nothing to add to this conversation. I thank her, and the words come out stilted. My world has been turned, and I'm no longer sure if it's upside down or right-side up; it's like a rollover accident where the landscape outside the window keeps shifting perspective. How can I ever say thank you? How do you say thank you to someone that you're not even supposed to know or who gives you information you're not supposed to have?

At the end of summer Rick and I had taken one last trip before he went to Pensacola and I returned to the University of Montana to finish my studies: a tour of the Four Corners region, which included the Grand Canyon, Havasupai Falls, and Mesa Verde. When Rick dropped me off at Stapleton Airport in Denver, I cried, although we planned to see each other once his training ended, sometime in March. The elderly woman who sat next to me on the plane gave me a gentle smile. She knew.

Although Rick and I spoke by phone over the following month, those calls became terse and short; he was beginning to embrace the military mentality. One night he called to say he wasn't going to be able to talk to me for sixteen weeks.

"Why?" I asked.

"Because that's just the way it is. Didn't you just hear what I said? I'm not going to be able to call you for sixteen weeks!" *Only the facts, ma'am, and when I want you to know more, I'll tell you,* he seemed to say in our last phone call. I ended the conversation soon after that.

Four days later the phone rang. Rick was in Mobile.

"They've stationed you in Mobile?" I asked, thoroughly confused now.

"No, just passing through."

"What do you mean?"

"I'm coming home."

"Back to Virginia?"

"No, out to Missoula."

Evidently, Rick realized this dream wasn't entirely his but rather a way of making his dad, who was a carrier pilot during the Korean War, proud of him. That's when he hit the bell, announced, "DOR" (drop on request), took his honorable discharge, and followed me to Montana.

Three months after our initial meeting in Helena, I call Helen and ask for my birth mother's address. I hear the quiet fury in her voice. "You cannot call me again," she states, quietly, vehemently. "I will not lose my job for you. I don't have any information other than what you've found."

"I just want to find them." Why am I begging for something that is rightfully mine?

"Why? You can't go home," she says. "Kids who have done that, who have been raised in this society and try to go back, can't. They have a really rough time of it because the cultures are so different; the expectations are too high. It's heartbreaking to watch. You must know that."

"I don't care. I just want to know them," I state. "I just want to know who I'm related to. I just want to find out if anyone looks like me. I'm so tired of being the only person with dark skin in my family, among my friends, in my classes. No one looks like me. I want to see if they look like me."

I hear the resignation in her voice. "I will arrange to have you talk with a social worker who can tell you what to expect. But you are not to call me again. And if you tell anyone about these conversations, I'll lie. So this will have to be the last contact we have. Clear?"

"Yes."

The line clicks and tears threaten. In the three years that I've come to know her, she'd become a friend, an ally. But each of us were willing to put this friendship on the line as I sought the truth to my heritage.

She's arranged for me to meet Judy, a tribal social worker. We sit in a local restaurant, drinking tea and eating pie. She is dark skinned and laughs easily, her beautiful smile dimpling her cheeks. "So you want to meet your family?" she says as she slices the fork into her crust.

I nod.

"How do you expect they're going to react when they see you?" This sounds like a predatory question.

"Happy? I don't know."

Judy stares at me, her black eyes piercing. "What if they're not? What if they're angry that you showed up at their door? You know," she continues, sipping her coffee, "there was a little gal who lived in Billings. She tracked down her family in Browning and decided to meet them after high school ended." She takes a bit of pie. "And she took her cute clothes, her tennis racquet, and her novels." Moving the cup to her lips, she looks at me. "How do you think that went?"

I shrug and look out the window at the cars zooming by, the sun glinting off their metal. Suddenly, I want to be in one of those cars, not here, getting grilled, feeling guilty for the feelings I have. Her smile is now ugly, her words offensive. Her voice pulls me back to the one-way conversation.

"Well, it didn't go well. Her siblings didn't have high reading levels, and no one plays tennis on the rez. And those cute clothes? Most everything in Indian families is bought from Kmart. These kids like you, who are adopted, don't have anything in common with their families."

My heels dig in. "I still want to meet them," I say. We are no longer smiling.

"What do you hope to gain from it?"

"To find people who look like me."

"That's not a good enough reason."

I could feel my anxiety rise. "If they don't want me to hang around, fine, I won't. I'm not asking anything of them. I just want to meet them."

She pulls her face into a wincing smile and crosses her arms in front of her chest. "But what if they don't want to meet you?" Her question feels like a physical slap. "What if, when you walk back into their lives, they reexperience the pain, the trauma, of having you taken from their home? It will be like seeing a ghost if you walk back into their lives twenty years later. You'll resurrect all those bad memories for them, memories they've been able to let slide by the wayside as they've moved on. But if you come into their home, how do you think they'll react? You've been dead to them all this time."

What she says both angers and chills me to the core. That night I replay her words, her reasons, her scenarios. I hadn't counted on discomfort as one of my family's reactions. I hadn't considered that I'd be unwelcomed, unwanted, a reminder of something bad.

I decide not to contact them.

Ever.

I graduated in March 1983 with a bachelor's degree in anthropology. I chose not to participate in commencement because, as I asked Rick,

"Who would come?" I didn't see the hurt in his eyes when he replied, "I would." The problem is, I thought that commencement was for the parents who sacrificed for their kids to go to college. Commencement was their trophy for getting them there. But neither of my parents had asked about commencement or even graduation. Dad mailed me $500; Mom gave me a Yogo sapphire necklace and earring set. But I didn't experience any marking of achievement. Perhaps it was a surprise to everyone that I graduated at all.

Two months later Rick and I got married in a campground up Pattee Canyon, outside of Missoula. Mom gave me $1,000 toward the wedding, and by budgeting carefully, I paid the Methodist minister and bought the dress, flowers, cake, homemade invitations, keg of beer, and case of champagne. I didn't invite Dad. He and Mom hadn't spoken in seven years; I didn't want them to start at my wedding.

It rained that morning, stopping as people gathered in a grassy meadow. During our vows a beam of sunlight appeared through the clouds and shone on Rick and me. Mom said it was a blessing from God, high praise as she wasn't particularly religious.

Rick supported my visit with Helen Childs. He supported my wanting to stay silent. And a year later he also supported my breaking my promise never to contact my family, and he listened to me read the letter I wanted to send to my birth mom. As I read, my voice shook and my heart pounded in my chest. I had no idea how close to the surface these conflicting feelings were. But I wanted her to know that she needn't worry about me because I was fine. "I have good parents." I said, "I have a good life." I told her I missed her and wished I was able to know her. I gave her my contact information, writing my address and my phone number down in careful lettering. By the time I was finished, I'd written three full pages, front and back.

I folded the pages into thirds and placed them into a plain white envelope, printing "Victoria Plant" in ink, on the outside. I put the letter

4. Susan and Rick, wedding photo. Courtesy of the author.

aside, then wrote a second letter, addressing it to the most powerful elder I knew on the reservation, Mr. Snipe. "Please take this letter to my mother, as I have no way of knowing how to contact her. I thank you in advance for your time and look forward to hearing a reply." I placed Victoria's envelope and the letter I'd just written into a larger envelope and addressed it to his attention, care of the Longhouse Culture Center. I stamped it and put it into the mailbox, lifting the red flag.

Then I waited. I waited a year. No response ever came.

So I again decided I would stop trying.

Making that decision, I once more revisited those fifteen minutes two years ago, when I first met Coyote, the trickster, and I wondered again if he was a relative. Or if he was even real. Or why he'd chosen to talk to me.

9

How Rez Cars Are Made

Fort Collins, Colorado, May 1993.

It is midafternoon, and I'm sitting in our kitchen, skimming through the tribal newspaper, the *Charkoosta*. I get the paper weekly, but because I live in another state, my news is a week behind everyone else's. Still, I keep abreast of what is important on the rez, through the articles, the topics of discussion, the debates, the Tribal Court Judgments, and especially the letters to the editor. I look for names, familiar names, names I should know, names that no longer mean anything to me, if they ever did. This newspaper, the only remaining link to my tribe, is a golden gossamer thread. Each year the thread gets thinner, until one day, I believe, it will disappear.

Since the year I vowed not to attempt to return to the reservation or try to make contact with my birth family, I've never heard from my birth mom, Victoria. Slowly, she drifted to the edge of my thoughts, or perhaps I pushed her there, not wanting to acknowledge the seeming rejection. My focus was no longer concentrated on the family I sought, but on the family Rick and I had created. I began working at the University of Montana in 1984 as a purchasing technician. I took three months off when our first son, Christopher, was born in a snowstorm in early March 1987. I returned half-time in June. I loved those days of keeping my son near me, holding him in my arms in the middle of the night while rocking in the wicker rocker Rick had bought me prior to Chris's birth. In the springtime, when the wind blew gentle and caressed his face, I laughed as he caught his breath. His eyes were dark blue. I argued they would stay blue. The physical anthropology professor, whose classes I took whenever I could, said they would turn brown, since that is the dominant gene. But my non-Native birth father must have carried a blue gene. Chris's eyes eventually became green, the color of prairie grass on a spring day.

As summer came to a close, I was thankful I didn't have to make a choice of whether to return to work full-time or not; Rick had accepted a job in Fort Collins, Colorado. We moved and bought a house that had more rooms than furniture. One day, when Chris was eighteen months old, I watched as he picked up the black-and-white round cow from his Fisher-Price farm set and brought it over to me, placing it in my hand, his smile broad and trusting. He trusted that I would accept his gift and say a heartfelt thank you. He trusted that love would be given by everyone, and that everyone would return his smile. He trusted that I would feed him when he was hungry, hug him if he got hurt, and hold him when he was tired, rocking him gently to sleep against my chest. In his world there were no worries that we would be separated from each other.

At eighteen months of age I imagine I didn't worry about separation either, but I doubt I had the same trust that Chris did. That was the age when I was removed under the label of "neglect." In that thought, that seeming memory, I saw Chris then, as me, small and dependent on people, bigger people, for everything. And I couldn't imagine that sense of safety not being given to someone so young, so innocent, so trusting.

And that's when the tears flowed, in a way they hadn't in a long time. Chris tottered over then, making sure I was okay, and wiped one tear away with his hand, his face pulled into a look of worry. I pulled him onto my lap and hugged him so hard he wiggled, assuring him without words that I was fine. Chris relaxed then, folding himself into my body. He leaned his head on my shoulder, placed his thumb in his mouth, and shut his eyes just for a few moments as I rocked him gently back and forth. Within a moment my concern of caring for him was replaced by a wave of raw anger at Victoria.

How could anyone (she) allow one of their children (me) to be taken away? To not know where they were? To know she might never see them again? The notes scribbled in the margins of the social services records indicated they located her at a bar before the court hearing. How could she not have fought to keep me? To keep us? I looked down at the top of Chris's golden-haired head and thought about his innocence, his full-hearted awe of the world around him and his interest, deep and exciting, of showing that world to me. And I cried, because I couldn't understand, couldn't comprehend, how she could just let us, let me, go?

The same thing happened when our youngest son, Dan, turned a year and a half old, and I wondered, once more, with such heartache, *How could she have let us go, never making an attempt to keep us?* That's when I fully realized, I was not her. I couldn't imagine letting my life get to such a point of chaos where my children were threatened with removal from my home. And I couldn't imagine not doing whatever I needed to do to keep them.

So today, in early May, I read everything the tribal paper has to offer. I scan the headings, run through the news, scan the letters to the editor. Then one catches my eye. I read a few words, scan a few paragraphs, then I stop. I stop and I reread those words again, those first couple of paragraphs. Suddenly, my heart is pounding, and I can feel my face flush, but this time not out of embarrassment but out of anger.

"The time has come," the writer states, "to submit the following as an inspiration and enlightener from one who reads things for what I perceive as the real picture and is not meant to attack any one faction or person, but more to encourage you to look at things from a different perspective. However, if certain former [Indian Health Service, Bureau of Indian Affairs] and power project employees take offense, so be it." He rambles on, until he wraps up his argument by writing, "If you don't like the way your leadership is conducting themselves, run for office and make a positive contribution."

Okay, though the first portion is a bit aggressive, he has a good point in the last sentence. But the next phrase incites my ire.

"It is better," he cautions, "to remain away and have people think of you as an idiot than to return home and remove all doubt. . . . If [the tribal council] spent as much time just doing what's right as our leaders and making the best-informed decisions for us and our best interest, there is no need to give any special recognition or even acknowledge the existence of one or two tribal members who seek to tell us Indians what is best for us, whether we like it or not. Especially when in most cases, these people are the ones who never had to suffer the racial slurs, emotional and physical bruises, or character assassinations those of us of color have had to do."

What does he mean "those of us of color?" Is he implying that because I'm not living on the reservation I somehow don't know what it means to be a person of color? But the kicker, the one that hits me in the gut, is what follows next:

"Question: What is the difference between a tribal member and an Indian? Answer: A tribal member is one who claims affiliation with the tribe as long as they can benefit monetarily or personally in the material sense from claiming tribal affiliation, and who could and chose to grow up on the white side and were light enough to do so. Indians are those who, because we are darker and prouder, had to be Indian when Indian wasn't cool."

I don't remember "being Indian" when it was cool. I remember the words *squaw*, *redskins*, and *savages*; I remember eyes following me as I walked through hallways, store aisles, following me until I walked out the door. Not everyone was watched the same way I was. I was aware the people who were white received merely a glance.

When I was in ninth grade, I remember my high school friend Cari and I walking over the fields near a subdivision of expensive homes. We'd walked to a convenience store, purchased a soda, and were returning home. A police car roared up to us, its tires spitting dust. The driver and his partner asked us what we were doing, where we had been, where we were going. Then they focused on me. The driver grabbed a sheet of paper from his console and studied it, then turned his gaze on me, then returned his focus back to the sheet of paper. Three times he did this, asking my name each time. He asked who my parents were, where I lived, and how long I had lived there. The two officers conferred with each other. "Well, we could take her down to the station," one said. "She matches the description." They conferred some more, as if I no longer stood there, the object of their conversation.

"What description?" I ask.

The driver pulled down his sunglasses and stared at me. "Of a runaway."

"Let's just go," the other officer said. "I don't think it's her."

Cari and I looked at each other as they drove away. "That was weird," we said at the same time.

"Runaway?" Mom asked, anger edging her voice. I'd told her about it when I got home. "That's bullshit. There was no runaway. They stopped you because you were Indian walking by a wealthy subdivision."

No, I wanted to say to the letter writer, being Indian was never cool for me.

What this man was saying was because I walk in a white world, I was supposed have no knowledge of what it means to "be Indian"? That my experiences are somehow less than his? My hands shake as I realize this man and the words he spews echo the attitudes I'd heard from the Native community, from Native American Student Services and the Kyi-yo students, of not being Indian enough, of being an apple, a wannabe, a pretender. I feel like I can't breathe.

With trembling hands I sit down and pen a letter in reply, and anger throws the words like blood over the page, black and red and endless. I am taking no prisoners because I am tired of my existence not being good enough, of my experiences being invalid, of the fucking reservation and the hateful people in it! When I'm done, I hand it to Rick. I watch his face metamorphose between wonder and horror. When he reaches the end, his head twists a bit. Then he looks at me and asks, "Who are you going to send this to?"

"The *Charkoosta*." I hand him the published letter to the editor and am thankful he doesn't argue about whether or not I should write a reply. Instead he looks at me and at my letter on the table in front of him and smiles. "How about if I help you write the response?" He adds wryly, "You don't want to piss everyone off up there."

I finally agree.

"Dear editor," I write, "I personally did not grow up in the white culture because of choice. I, like several people of my generation, judging from the letters searching for parents, was given up for adoption. I don't know whether the tribal members were given a choice to adopt me and my siblings, or not. Regardless, I grew up loved, white and very, very Indian (using your definition of the color of my skin). I never once was mistaken for Swedish. . . . I stand accused of being an 'apple Indian,' white on the inside, red on the out. I am, but not by choice. These are things that came to me. I've accepted it, why can't you? You talk of never having to undergo racial slurs? I get it every single day of my life living in white society, and I don't have the comfort of family to escape to on the reservation, where someone knows how I feel. . . . Regardless of what you like, I'm enrolled, I'm proud to be a member, and I will be very, very angry if you try to take my little bit of heritage away from me."

I signed it "Susan Devan Harness (Vicki Charmain Rowan) Fort Collins, CO."

Two weeks later, the blue phone on the wall rings three times before I can get to it. "Hello?"

"Is this Vicki Charmain?" There is a female voice on the other end. "Yes."

"This is your sister, Roberta. Ronni Marie, your other sister, is here with me. We've been looking for you since you turned eighteen."

I am in free fall.

They haven't forgotten me!

Fort Collins, Colorado, July 4, 1993.

Roberta had called in the middle of May because she'd seen the letter to the editor. In that call she'd invited my family and me to join a family get-together over the Fourth of July.

"Where do you want to meet?" she'd asked.

"A restaurant she likes," Rick mouthed. I repeated his suggestion.

"Do you like Chinese food?" Ronni asked.

"I love it!"

"Let's meet at the Mustard Seed."

Over the next few minutes we worked out the dates and the details, and as I hung up the phone I could feel my heart pounding with breath-stopping pressure. I turned to Rick and smiled, my eyes filling with tears.

Summer had been well into the nineties in Colorado, so we'd packed sleeveless shirts, T-shirts and shorts, having forgotten we've experienced snow on the Fourth of July in Montana. When we hit town, we made a quick stop to Walmart to purchase more appropriate clothing for the fifty-degree weather: heavy sweatshirts and jeans.

Rick and I had frequented the Mustard Seed many times, when they were located downtown. Now the restaurant is in the mall, and as we walked down the broad hallway I wondered what these siblings would look like. I remembered, years before, when the idea of reuniting with my family had been a long-tarnished dream. I had been watching an episode of Maury Povich. His guest had been a Blackfeet girl who'd been adopted into a white family as an infant. Maury had arranged a meeting between her birth family and her for the first time, onstage. I remember thinking her siblings looked absolutely nothing like her; where she was light, they were dark; where she sat almost regal, her siblings slouched and grinned at the camera, their long black hair twining around itself, uncontrolled. I could see by her looks that not only had her father been white; he'd been very white. Her dress, her mannerisms, and her makeup all endorsed the white, upper-class culture she'd grown up in. Over the hour-length program, conversation was awkward and disjointed; everyone on stage looked uncomfortable with her presence there, including her.

Would my meeting be as painful? I wondered as we located the doorway to the restaurant. We spotted the group immediately. I recognized them not for their similarity to me, but for the fact that they looked like they were waiting for someone. I'd expected them to look different; I expected them to look like me, mirrors to one another, like my husband to his brothers and sisters, whose genetics screamed, "same family." They shared physical characteristics among themselves: their hair black with smooth curls that cupped their face, framed their smiles, their eyes. The same set of dimples graced the gently round cheeks of Roberta and Ronni and Ronni's two daughters. I saw myself as different: taller and my short, dark hair lay straight and coarse and far away from undimpled cheeks.

But we were related, so we hugged, chatted, and caught up on one another's lives. *I was getting my questions answered*, I told myself, as I pinched pieces of beef and broccoli with my chopsticks and listened to their histories, sating my curiosity. I wanted to know what my family looked like, and now I knew. With a sense of disquiet I felt like I was in a quirky episode of *Sesame Street*'s "One of These Things Is Not Like the Other," its melody playing in the shadows of my consciousness:

Three of these things belong together
Three of these things are kind of the same
Can you guess which one of these doesn't belong here?
Now it's time to play our game.

That was yesterday. Now we are on the Flathead Indian Reservation, in Arlee, Montana. My two sisters (that still sounds so strange to hear myself even think of these labels) and our families are sitting on the hoods of our cars in a parking lot that looks across Highway 93 toward the powwow grounds. In front of us two opposing lines of cars cruise past us at a crawl. It is July 4, the morning of the Fourth of July Powwow; this is the town's version of a parade.

Some are hot rods; some are old; some are brand new. All are here to be seen and to be a part of something. The red Pontiac Firebird catches our attention, as does its driver, a late teen Native girl, tall and thin. I imagine the car was purchased with the per capita payments she received when she turned eighteen. The temp tags on the back indicate it had been purchased yesterday.

We watch as the girl drives slowly up the street, making a U-turn and coming back the other direction. A block away she cuts another U-turn and repeats the process. On the fourth cycle she decides to turn left, across traffic, onto Powwow Road. Except there's already someone almost there, a new Jeep Cherokee driven by an older couple, just passing through. Even though everyone was going relatively slowly, we watch in fascination as their Jeep slams into her brand-new Pontiac Firebird, the beautiful red metal on her passenger-side door crumpling and creasing from the impact, which results in a metallic *screech* and *thud*. We see her get out of her car, her tank top loose over a pair of tight-fitting jeans, and run to the passenger side to survey the damage. She's horrified.

She's angry. Because of the noise of the other motorists, I don't know exactly what she's saying, but I'm pretty sure it's a string of expletives.

Rick leans over to me and says in a quiet voice, for my ears only, "That's how rez cars are made."

The family gathering we have been invited to coincides with the pow-wow. Rick and the boys, and Ronni and I, walk the powwow grounds. I look through the wares in the vendors' stalls, some of which have canopies overhead to keep the sun—but more likely today the rain—at bay. There are star quilts and dance regalia. There are beadwork and quillwork in the form of earrings, necklaces, bracelets, chokers, and hatbands. The smell of frybread drifts over the grounds, and my mouth waters as I think of the golden, brown delicacy sprinkled with powdered sugar and drizzled with honey. One table has southwestern jewelry displayed on black velvet, distinctive styles that I identify as Hopi, Navajo, and Zuni. I am a fan of earrings, so I look at the choices carefully. Although I am drawn to the silver overlay of the Hopi jewelry, my eye is caught by a set of small Zuni-inlay Sun Face posts. I touch them, gently, admiring their work, the minuteness of the detail between the turquois, coral, onyx, and silverwork that melds all together. When I look behind me to talk with Ronni about them, I see she has fallen behind.

The boys, now ages six and three, want to go with Ronni, who agrees, leaving Rick and me to walk the powwow grounds together. On the far end three young men walk near us. One of them, in his early twenties, weaves and stumbles, three or four steps behind his friends. He recovers his footing, then turns and looks at me. He might have been handsome at one point, but today his dark-gold hair is greasy, and the alcohol has pulled his face into a lopsided grin. "Hi, Cousin!" He raises his hand in greeting.

"Hi." My answer is wary. I am wary, of his drunkenness, his famil-iarity, although we don't know each other. But mostly I'm wary of the look he throws Rick out of the corner of his eye.

"Who's your people?" he asks, jutting his chin toward my direction.

"Salish."

"I'm Pend d'Oreille." His smile becomes even broader. I miss the wicked line his mouth has developed as he continues talking to me while staring at Rick. "See? I told you we are cousins." He pauses and his eyes narrow; his smile becomes lazy. "That's something you don't see every day." He looks at his three friends. "A white man walking with an Indian girl." The grin turns malicious, and I can see Rick's hackles rise. It's not that uncommon, I think to myself, but I have to agree, the man-boy threw out the bait in front of Rick, and it was well placed. I put my hand on Rick's arm and say, quietly, just for his ears, "Just keep walking. Ignore him and keep walking."

Rick is angry. I see it in the way his jaw tenses, his blue eyes glinting dangerously. He has been singled out. But I can't get as angry as he is. Those slurs are not uncommon in the world I walk in. I want to say, "Don't like how it feels, do you?" but I don't. Instead I put an imaginary hand on my arm and tell myself to just keep walking.

A few moments later we meet up with Ronni, who hasn't wandered far from the vendor's area. I find the earrings again and sense Ronni standing behind me. My sense is confirmed when I hear her ask, "What are you looking at?"

I point to the earrings. "I love Zuni inlay. I think it is so beautiful." We move on to the next table, and the next, talking easily about the jewelry we've seen and the jewelry we have. I am so at ease with her, so calm. It's hard to believe that I've just met her this morning. I observe her daughters, ages ten and five, who look with open adoration at their mom and openly watch me with curiosity.

Ronni excuses herself, and when she returns she hands me the earrings I'd been looking at. "I can't," I say. I feel embarrassed that I'd so openly admired them. Plus, I don't accept gifts easily. I don't know how. Maybe I don't think I'm worthy. Or maybe I think I have to give her something of value, but I have nothing except that I'm here. Both of us, perhaps, are looking for adequate trades of acceptance.

"I want to introduce you to our uncle, Albert," Ronni says and pulls on the sleeve of my sweatshirt, leading me to the doorway of a metal building. She enters and I stop at the doorway and watch as she approaches a man, leans over, and talks quietly to him. He looks up and glances at me, then nods, says something in response, and returns to his game. When she gets back to me, she explains, "He'll be out here in a minute."

We step outside and stand in the little space of sunshine. This is where we are when he joins us. "Sue, I want you meet our uncle Albert and his wife, Delphine." I reach out to shake his hand, then hers. "This is Vicki Charmain," she says, turning toward the handsome, forty-something-year-old man. "Roberta and I talked with her a couple of months ago, and now she's here."

Delphine looked at me and smiled. "She looks just like Vic did, when she was younger." Delphine's voice is low and soft, and I barely overhear this statement that she says to Albert. She is slender, her long, dark-brown hair resting quietly on her shoulders, falling gently down her back. Within moments Delphine and Ronni have left, each to their own interests, and I am standing awkwardly near Albert, this stranger-relative. I watch him quietly for a few moments and note his upright stance, his arms crossed in front of his chest. There's power in the way he stands, a sureness of who he is, and I find myself thinking that I wished I'd known him forever.

"Ronni says you are Vic's youngest brother?"

He nods, throwing me a smile and a quick look. "I'm ten years younger than she is. I'm forty-seven."

I've been enamored with the appearance of Asian people for as long as I can remember, which is odd, considering we don't know anyone Asian. But looking at Albert, I realize why. Those characteristics, the almond-shaped eyes, are markers of our Cree heritage. Albert is handsome, with his smooth face and his kind eyes, whose gaze rarely meets mine. There is always a half smile that seems to rest, unbeckoned, above a strong chin.

"Did you live in Phoenix?" I ask, remembering Dad's description. *But he was a drunk, a no-good bum*; Dad's words enter my consciousness.

Albert shakes his head and then thinks for a while. "No, I never lived in Phoenix," he says.

"Did anyone in your family live in Phoenix?" I ask.

He considers my question, quietly looking into the distance. Finally, he looks at me, for just a moment, then looks away. "No," he answers, shaking his head again. "I don't know of anyone in the family who lived in Arizona. Why?"

"My dad said he thought a relative of mine lived in Phoenix. I just wondered who that might be."

Albert's laugh is soft and good-natured. "Well, I don't know why he'd say that. Unless he knows something I don't." His eyes sparkle, and at that moment I'm so happy that I've met this man, this uncle, and so angry with my dad and the picture he'd painted for me. I feel a sense of relief that none of it is true.

I look away, unsure how to have this conversation. What is it polite to ask about? What pushes the boundaries? What would seem rude? But if I don't ask, I won't know. "Can you tell me anything about my father?" He is hauntingly absent; other than a brief notation about nationality, there was nothing about Ronny Smith in the social worker's notes.

Albert looks at me then and smiles, a gentle smile. "Ronny had a beautiful singing voice," he said, then looks off to the distance, as if looking back in time. "I used to love going to the corral in the evening when he was taking care of the horses. I'd just sit there and listen to him sing."

I now know where I got my love of music and my ability to perform. My parents couldn't carry a tune in a bucket, as Mom liked to say. To have this talent and finally know that it came from one of my birth parents, someone related to me, well, I couldn't hide the smile that played on my lips.

Albert and I then talk about small things, light things, inconsequential things that really have everything riding on them: where I live, whom

I'm married to, the children I have, the life I've been given. And I wonder things, like where he had lived and if he had any memories of me. I wonder what he'd been like growing up. All those questions reminded me that I truly missed this man I didn't know. What would it have been like for me if I hadn't been adopted?

I don't realize I have voiced this question aloud.

"Don't ever ask that," Albert commands, his voice sober, his face serious. He's looking directly at me now as he continues. "You left, you escaped this place. Don't question whether or not it was right. Look around you. How many of these people are accomplishing things in their life? You escaped, and you be glad of it. I don't ever want to hear those words from you again."

It's as if he's slapped me. I wanted him to say he missed me, that he wished I hadn't left. But he didn't, and I'm embarrassed. The thing is, I don't feel like I've escaped. The world I'd been raised in has left me bruised and fearful, shaken of confidence. His words make me realize that this world isn't going to be a safe haven either. Albert has no idea how many times I've tried to return, because I haven't told him. He doesn't know that I've come up here while I was attending college in Missoula, just looking for familiar faces. Or that I've tried to find employment here, but jobs weren't open for me. Or that I'd come up here and spoken the Plant name as my family name, but no one I talked with seemed to know the Plants. He doesn't know the many ways people on this reservation have sought to keep me out; he doesn't know the heartache that made me stop trying nine years ago. But his tone tells me he doesn't want to hear these stories, so I smile, apologetically. And I don't tell him how much I've missed him, even though I don't remember anything about him.

I see him again later that afternoon, as the family members have gathered in an open, grassy area up the Jocko Valley. I stand near Rick; he is my rock. The boys run around as if they belong here. But of course— they have family, us. Therefore, they belong. We've eaten portions of a four-foot submarine sandwich and drunk soda, munched on chips and side dishes people have brought. And now we are standing in a clearing, between the dirt road and the Jocko River, which whispers secrets behind a screen of trees. Overhead the clouds hang heavy, and the air is darkened not just by the clouds but also by the pine trees standing guard around us, enclosing us.

The meeting is difficult to recall in anything more than snapshots. I am overwhelmed by the people here, what they look like, who they are, how they're related, what they know about me. There is too much information coming to my senses about who I am, where I'm from, who my relatives are. After a while the only cadence I'm aware of is my pulse that pounds in my ears and echoes throughout my body.

Aunts and uncles introduce themselves and begin filling in the blanks of why they are important in the family tree. Uncle Chuck has fair skin and obsidian eyes and a broad smile. "I remember you when you were this big," he says, stretching his hands about two feet apart. "I bought you a teddy bear the day you were born. Do you still have it?"

I shake my head but am thankful to have someone who remembers me as an infant.

"Yeah," Chuck says again, his gaze and his smile unwavering, "I remember the day you were born." Chuck is two years older than Vic.

There is Glenrose and Frank, their gift is a hot-pink dream catcher, which I cradle in my hands. Glenrose is Vic's senior by six years. There are others who become blurred almost as soon as I meet them, people who shake my hand, who say words of welcome, but these words never make it into my long-term memory. There is too much information, and my brain can only continue to take snapshots. Around me are groups: Vic's kids and Albert and Delphine. Rick stands behind me, our shoulders touching. Our sons run between us and the river. Aunts and uncles are off to one side, and across the green, on the other side of the fire, stands a group of cousins. I don't even know whose children they are.

We are ringed by tall trees whose tops sway in the afternoon breeze. Across the clearing, beneath one of these trees, sits a lone woman in the camp chair, her body hunched, her face turned away from me. I know who she is. People have pointed her out. She is Vic, my birth mom. When I see her, when my eyes focus on her small body, everything falls away, except for the sound of crows squawking their irritation at us standing between them and the crumbs we've dropped. I slowly become aware of people's gazes, shifting toward one another, toward me, then away. I'm nervous.

The sandwich I consumed a half hour ago sits somewhere above my stomach and beneath my throat. And as I watch this woman, look at her, think about how long I'd wanted to meet her, I realize I don't know if I can carry this meeting out. How do you begin to have a conversation with someone who birthed you but whom you never met? With someone who didn't fight to keep you, when that's what you'd do for your kids? With someone who was supposedly found at the bar down the street when they were given a court date they had to attend if they wanted to keep you? Vic steals a glance in my direction, and for a moment, a brief connection in time, our gazes meet. Then I look away, awkward at being caught with my curiosity around my ankles. I feel the pulse in my neck quicken.

Once I walk across that clearing, I think, *I will no longer be able to merely imagine her, to turn her into someone I could dream about, to give her whatever characteristics I want her to have, romanticized characteristics. She will become flesh and blood and all that goes with that.* And I don't know if I want to do that. If I *can* do that. My anxiety grows; it pounds at my temples. What if we don't share anything other than blood?

My breath is jagged, and my hands grow cold. I feel eyes watching me; I hear the whispers as they glide from one person to another. I look at Rick, who puts a hand on the small of my back and gives me the merest of pushes. I resist. I dig in my heels and refuse to move. Just for a moment. I close my eyes, take a deep breath, and inhale the aroma of the pines.

I take another deep breath, throw a small prayer to the wind, and begin the long walk across space, across time, across a generation, to the woman who sits in the chair on the far side of the clearing. I touch her shoulder and kneel down, placing my hand on her leg. Very quietly, almost whispering, like the trees around us, I say, "I'm Vicki Charmain. I've come home."

IO

Thicker Than Water,
Thinner Than Time

Flathead Indian Reservation, Jocko Valley, Montana, July 1993.

The stranger who sat on a chair at the edge of the clearing was Clara Victoria, my birth mother. She was surrounded by tall pines, whose tops swayed gently in the cool breeze, a breeze that never brushed the forest floor. The chair's fabric wove its own simple pattern, crafted against a natural world. Beneath her feet lay a carpet of short pine needles, long fallen and red, leftovers from countless seasons.

As I stared at her from my vantage point, my first thought was, *She looks so Indian*, just like one of those Edward S. Curtis photographs that capture the harshness of time laid on the softness of Native skin, burnishing it to dark copper, creating arroyos where none previously existed, a blurred prairie scene in the background. Prominent cheekbones broadened Vic's face, and like Albert, her eyes had an Asian appearance.

I shared her genetic material, same as Ronni, my blood sister, eighteen months my senior; same as James Allen, who is a little over a year younger than me. James Allen was not at the gathering. No one knew where he was, although people gestured vaguely to the west when talking about him. Perhaps he lived in Portland, perhaps in Spokane. He drifted in and out of their lives. Out of her eight surviving children, three of us had been removed from the home by social workers in 1960. I was the only one who had not returned. Until that day.

Every so often someone from the small gathering wandered over to talk with Vic, their quiet voices further absorbed by the fallen needles. And then, sometimes, her laughter erupted, rising low in her chest until it escaped, airy, through her throat.

"Baby! Go get me a beer," she demanded, then laughed as the small child, probably three or four years of age, ran toward the creek, where the beers were left in its frigid waters to cool. She ran, as fast as her chubby legs could carry her, returning with the familiar beige can of Coors in her tiny hands. Vic grabbed the flip top and pulled, opening the can with a *fzzzzz* and quaffing the drink with her head thrown back and her eyes closed. Obviously, this was the beverage of choice, judging by the eight or so cans that littered the space at her feet.

Vic pulled her thin coat closer to her chest as she hunched over, protecting herself against the cold that wasn't intimidated by the nearby fire. She held the beer in one hand and took a final sip, dropping the can alongside the others when she was finished. She then shoved a hand into her pocket and withdrew a pack of cigarettes, which she tapped against her palm, a gesture that I, as a nonsmoker, still don't understand. I just knew Mom also carried out this ritual each time she unwrapped a new pack. Extracting a slender white stick, Vic placed it between her lips and pulled a lit match to its edge, while she protected the feeble flame with a cupped hand. The end grew bright, as she inhaled, deep and slow, and her eyes squeezed shut against the smoke when she breathed out. It was evident she enjoyed this part of the ritual.

"Baby!"

While the toddler ran to the creek, Vic and I held each other's gaze across the clearing for an awkward moment before I looked away. Somehow the group had become aware of this exchange, and the already-muted voices quieted even further, allowing only for the whisper of the trees, the quiet rush of the creek, and the call of the crows to be picked up by my ears. A sense of expectation hung in the air, as low and confining as the ceiling of clouds. I scanned the group, my heart beating frantically against my ribcage, and butterflies took flight in my stomach. Once more I was a small child, fearful of strangers, fearful of her. But my curiosity mixed with fear and caused me to wonder what each of us inherited and what have we passed on. As always, I looked for familiarities.

My aunt, Delphine Plant, Albert's wife, leaned over to me. "You look just like Victoria." She'd made the same comment about our similarities to Albert earlier that day, when I first met them. But when she said it to me, I couldn't help but cringe as I looked intensely at the woman I "look just like." I didn't see the sameness Delphine described. Instead, I saw a face bloated with years of drinking and aged by difficult living. Her voice was harsh and guttural, and wrinkles carved deep into her skin. "I mean when she was younger," my aunt clarified. Had my reaction been so visible? Embarrassed, I turned away. "She was beautiful when she was younger, when she was your age."

Although she and I are both American Indian, our difference lay in the fact that while she lived among her own, sought solace among her family, and used them as home base from which she left and returned, I had been flung to the waiting arms of a world who found Indians repulsive, with our lazy, drunk, promiscuous ways. The wounds I was left with still bled under the right conditions. And my being in her presence put me in emotional limbo. I had longed for this moment, fantasized about it when I was six, dreamed about it when I was fifteen. But my soul filled with dread as the reality check of who I really am seeped into the cracks of my fragmented identity.

As I glanced around this small group of people, their brown eyes briefly met my own and they looked away, leaving me to my own decision. How could I have ever thought this was a good idea? How could I talk to this woman who'd given birth to me but allowed social workers to take me and ignored a court date to keep me?

"Baby!"

I watched Baby bring another can of beer and hand it over delicately, with love. Vic took it without any thought of the child. That beer can, like the previous ones, soon ended up at her feet. I took a deep breath; it was now or never. Leaving the safety of my husband, my family, and my aunt Delphine, I took my first tentative step toward her, and I felt the silence, palpable against my skin, my soul, as everyone in the group witnessed my journey, which lasted a lifetime but took only about fifty feet to complete.

"I'm Vicki Charmain," I told her quietly, as I knelt in front of her. "I've come home."

Vic refuses to look at me; her head is bent, so I am left to observe the haphazard part in her salt-and-pepper hair. My peripheral vision captures the shaking of her shoulders, and she bends even more forward, into herself, burying her face in her chest. Her voice is weak, supported only by the tears that I hear but cannot see.

"I dreaded this day," she finally says through soft sobs caught in her throat, strangling her words to bare whispers. "I thought you'd come up here and be mean. I thought you'd call me all kinds of bad names. I thought you'd be really angry and talk harsh." My own throat closes, and I can't speak. Her fear explains the number of beer cans that surround us, vestiges of distress. We are cloaked in silence, except for Mother Nature, who keeps talking, her breeze caressing the treetops, her water whisking over the glacial boulders that line the early lengths of the Jocko River as it flows from the Mission Mountains. After several long moments Vic looks at me, as if I am a spirit from a long ago past. I see fear in her eyes, tension on her face. Trails of tears follow the marked arroyos of age. There is silence, and I witness her face crumple with shame.

I push my own hurt aside, as I feel the familiar obligation to lessen hers. I place my hands on her arms, and even through her jacket I can feel their thinness. Soft as the pine needles beneath our feet, I say, "I

5. My first meeting with my family. *From left to right*: Ronni Marie, Vic, and Vern. Photo by Rick Harness. Courtesy of the author.

can't do that. I don't know the life you've led. My mom raised me not to pass judgment. I cannot judge you."

She cries openly then. I know we share the same pain, she and I. It's just called different names. Hers is a shame of relinquishment; mine is the hurt of abandonment. Both are two sides of the same adoption coin.

Flathead Indian Reservation, Ronan, Montana, August 1994.

I haven't seen Vic since last summer, and Ronni, not interested in visiting family, has dropped me off at the home of Vic and her husband, Ray, who live in tribal housing, in a small neighborhood tucked away off the main highway. Her home is like all the other tribally administered HUD homes in this development, a small one-storied structure cloaked in heavily weathered gray siding and surrounded by a fenceless lot, devoid of vegetation, save the hardy, slow-growing grass that erupts in the midst of the connected lawns. This grass could be mistaken for xeriscaping, but it's the result of people being too poor, or too disinterested, to plant, water, and maintain the lush lawns seen elsewhere in the United States.

The sidewalk from the street to the house is buckled, grouted with weeds that refuse to die. The door stands open, and I know I am supposed to just walk in without knocking (to knock is such a "white" thing to do), but I am uncomfortable with this cultural requirement. But if I'm to be really honest, there is nothing comfortable about this entire visit. I enter into the main living space and note that the linoleum is dirty and worn. Replacement is out of the question—too expensive. Beneath the picture window sits a brownish couch, whose springs have seen better days, evidenced by the sagging cushions that require anyone who sits there to defy gravity. Across from the couch are torn overstuffed chairs and an ottoman, and beside these stand a small table, where an ashtray spills over with cigarette butts that have been smoked all the way to the filter. Stale odors of cigarettes and bacon and eggs hang heavy in the air, and my stomach churns at this clash of sensory overload. Well, that and anxiety.

The walls are filmed by cigarette smoke; one wall holds a Catholic cross and clusters of photos in dime-store frames, where faces of smiling adults and happy children stare hopefully through the glass. There is one of a beautiful young woman surrounded by toddlers. There is a young man in military uniform, a proud, stoic warrior. I have no idea how he is related. There is the wedding photo of Vic and Ray, looking forward to a happy future. My eye, however, is caught by the photo of a young woman, whose long, dark hair, curved with gentle curls, is pulled back from her face, in a style of the 1940s. She is devastatingly beautiful. She is Vic at fourteen.

As I look from one photo to another, I try to find the resemblances between and among people. Some are clearly related, some are not. Who is the soldier? Who is the young woman surrounded by children? With an ache I am aware how visibly absent I am in these photos of family, and as a result I experience the familiar stab that comes from existing "outside." These captured moments commemorating achievements, events, and crazy-quilt pieces of everyday life sit in stark contrast to the heavy oppression within the room, this house, this development.

When I join Vic and Ray on the back patio, I am pointed toward an empty chair. Words are a hoarded commodity, made clear by the fact that no one is speaking any. Ray doesn't stand up or offer to shake hands; he just nods his head in my direction without looking at me. This is okay. I have no interest in meeting him—he isn't blood. And for me, right now, blood is all that matters.

I know from the family scuttlebutt that he'd refused to come to the gathering the previous summer, the one I'd attended, saying, "If she wants to meet me, she can damn well come to my home. I'm not going up there." I'm not exactly sure why he was so angry. Perhaps it was because I was the long-lost daughter that he and his family were forced to hear about, and I had returned. Or perhaps it was more visceral: I was the visible byproduct of a love that his wife had shared with some-one before him, a love she continued to revisit in stories and laments, especially after a long evening of drinking. A mythical love.

We sit on their back patio on white, molded plastic chairs and look out on a view that most Americans would pay a lot of money to see every single day of their lives: the bald-pated Mission Mountains rising majestically from the valley floor forming the eastern boundary of the reservation. In front of us, a gaggle of children, wearing dirty, ill-fitting clothes, play a raucous game of tag, screams of laughter escaping through white teeth, begging us to watch their every move. They are unfazed when we don't. These are Vic's grandchildren, the genetic remains of Robin, her second to the youngest daughter, killed a few years previous in a car accident, one of many, on Highway 93. A common motto that graces bumper stickers in the area is "Pray for me, I drive 93"—funny except that it's true. Vic is now raising Robin's kids.

I watch Vic as she watches her young charges. She looks different than she did the last time I saw her. Her face has slimmed down, and there is almost a regality in her posture. Gone is the hunching woman with beer cans at her feet. She turns toward me and measures my mettle with a steel gaze of her black eyes. We are definitely on her territory. She pulls the cigarette that is held delicately between her index and middle fingers to her lips and inhales deeply, her chin thrust forward, her eyes half-closed against the acrid blue smoke curling around her head in the breezeless air.

I remember sitting there for a long time that afternoon while the sun moved slowly overhead. What I don't remember are the conversations we try to have; I remember only that they are stilted and halting. I remember my stomach hurting and a headache playing around my temples. I remember thinking, *Blood might be thicker than water, but it's thinner than time.* How could we possibly bridge almost three decades, where I am but a fragmented memory, and she has been effectively erased, by my parents, by the system? I am painfully aware that for much of that afternoon she and I exist in minimal sentences and monosyllabic answers; her husband doesn't exist at all.

I try to find a gentle way to leave this physical discomfort when Vic's attention is pulled away by a child, perhaps a gesture, perhaps a scream. She growls orders, her voice raspy from too many cigarettes. The children stop their roughhousing for a few moments, and their black eyes jump between her and Ray, measuring her seriousness against his reaction. The moment passes with no action on anyone's part, and they return to their game, ignoring her continued brief rants. This, I can tell, is a long-practiced routine. I'm sure they'd pay attention if she'd come off the patio, but she doesn't. I doubt she comes off the patio for much of anything. She certainly hadn't come for me when I needed her, and that event was a lot bigger than a toddler asking for attention. I suspect she's not a patio-leaving kind of gal.

"You wanna beer?" Ray asks to no one in particular. Vic nods and he disappears, returning with two opened cans of Budweiser. He hands one to her and wraps the other in his fist and downs it in a few gulps. I glance at my watch; it's two in the afternoon.

After a few moments and a few sips, Vic asks, "You read much?" She'd lit another cigarette immediately after stubbing the previous one out.

"Yeah, I like reading."

"What kinds of books do you like?" Her gesture of the upthrust chin as she asks this is so Indian. I've seen it in fictional characters, those stereotypes of the American West, the Jim Chees, the Joe Leaphorns. But this is for real. This is also a loaded question. I know she didn't go beyond eighth grade; I know she doesn't work outside the home. I know the literacy rate on the reservation is abominable. I can't even begin to imagine what kind of books might be of interest to her. What kind of books would she have in common with me, a college graduate?

"I dunno," I say, playing it safe, vague. "I like murder mysteries, some romances."

I watch for signs of approval. She exhales and wrinkles her upper lip. "I could never get into those types of books. You like *Gone with the Wind*?"

"I loved *Gone with the Wind*!"

A few more questions later we realize we both like John Steinbeck,

James Michener, and the new one from Jean Auel. That afternoon I realize the love of reading is genetic, and I am humbly reminded that being uneducated is different from being stupid. This woman who resides in this impoverished, forgotten corner of the world known as the reservation is by no means stupid.

Flathead Indian Reservation, Ronan, Montana, August 2005.

I follow my sister Ronni, who this time has agreed to come with me to visit Vic, into the familiar gray house, the same one I'd visited years before. A bed occupies the far corner of the living room, where the dining table once stood, and on it lies a thin figure, curled, her shoulders convulsing while muffled sobs emanate from beneath the bedsheets.

"Vic, are you crying?" Ronni asks, as she steps forward. I'm shocked at the skeletal version of the woman I haven't seen in ten years.

"Oh, just feeling sorry for myself," Vic says with a rasping laugh, wiping tears from her face, which is even more carved with wrinkles from all her weight loss. She'd quit drinking two years before when she was hospitalized with a diabetic attack that threatened to move her into Catholic heaven sooner than she'd anticipated. It was during that hospitalization that she'd confided to Ronni, saying she wished she'd chosen her children over alcohol. That was as close to an apology as anyone was going to get.

"Who is behind you? Is that Vicki Charmain?"

I have to admit, hearing that name causes my throat to close, each and every time. When I was a kid, I used to think that Vicki Charmain was the baby that died, and I had somehow replaced it. I suppose in a way it's true, on some level: a child within a family is removed from view, which can be translated as dead, and is resurrected in someone else's family, well beyond the vision of the mother who'd given birth.

"Vicki Charmain! Come on over here."

I walk over and wrap my arms around her small, bony frame and look into her obsidian eyes. Their brightness says she is truly happy to see me. She is now seventy-one years old, still sporting harshly dyed jet-black hair spiked in the style of the eighties. This is her statement of unconventionality, the inability to color within the lines, which also explains my removal. Her unconventionality caused her and Ronny Smith, my father, to have me, a six-month-old, ride the rails with them to Minnesota. Her unconventionality led her to disappear for weeks, sometimes months at a time, leaving her children with various family members until she resurfaced, with no explanation of where she'd been or why she disappeared. Her unconventionality led her to shoot heroin in front of her five-year-old son, Vern.

But I recognize that she is the way she is and seventy-one years hasn't changed any of it. So I sit on the bed next to her, and both of us pretend ten years haven't gone by since I've seen her. We pretend her drinking hasn't caused the chasm in the family that is still an open wound, and we pretend that her kidneys aren't failing to the point that requires her to go to dialysis three times a week, as she wastes away before everyone's eyes. That's okay though—I'm really good at pretending; I've had a lot of practice. I've pretended for nearly four decades that I truly feel comfortable living in a country filled with people who often despise people like her and me, Indians. We are enemies of the state because we fought for our homeland, and we are constantly reminded how little we matter. According to various U.S. Census and CDC demographics, we are 2 percent of the population, our poverty rate is 26 percent, 83 percent of roads on the reservations are in unacceptable condition, we die at significantly higher rates than other Americans, our youth have higher suicide rates than other American youth, and we have an average of a 50 percent high school–dropout rate. Unfortunately, I think we have begun to believe we are as insignificant as our statistics portray.

"So how you been?" she asks.

Where do I start? Probably by explaining why it's been ten years since I've been back.

In 1995, two years after reuniting, Ronni and I became estranged, as did Roberta and I. But I don't know why. Really, the "why" is unimportant. What is important is there was nothing of substance to hold us together. We had no history, no shared memories, nothing other than a piece of paper that said we shared the same mother. And I didn't know anyone else in the family enough to feel comfortable just going to visit. I am not a person who pushes myself into a group and dares anyone to say I don't have a right to be there.

Therefore, ten years vanished. And how badly I want to say how much I miss her, how much I will miss the chance to discover our differences or, more disconcerting perhaps, our similarities. I want her to know that I need her in my life to prove that I am "real," a real daughter, a real sister, a real aunt, and a real niece. I'm not just a pencil marking on the genealogical tree that can be erased at whim when some family member determines I'm not real enough. I want to say these things, but don't. These words hurt, physically, as they sit bunched in my throat and, emotionally, as they sit bunched in my consciousness.

"Oh, you know, raising those two boys and making quilts."

Smoke encircles us with confining familiarity. "How's that oldest boy of yours? What's his name again?"

"Chris?"

"He the one that got me my beer from the river the first time you came up?"

I give a wry smile and nod. Chris became her minion of choice that summer at the gathering in the clearing. He replaced Baby, who sulked as she watched her grandmother create another "favorite," hard news for a three-year-old. Vic liked the brightness of Chris's eyes and the mischievousness of his smile.

She turns over on her side, facing us, her hand propping up her head, her face morphing into a familiar smile, the one that sits on my son's face most of the time. "That little shit. I couldn't believe it when I asked him to get me a beer from the river, and he'd run it back to me, shaking it the whole way! Each time I opened one, beer flew out of the flip top. I must have had three beers that he did that to." She laughs at the memory, her small shoulders shaking. She pauses and fixes me with a smile. "How old was he then?"

"Six."

"That little shit," she repeats, smiling. This term holds both endearment and high respect. She inhales, lays her head back on her pillow, and closes her eyes, the cigarette lying limp in her hands, the smoke drifting lazily from her mouth and nostrils toward the screen that covers the nearby window, its ripped fabric doing little to keep the flies out. They move easily through this nonboundary, being swatted by Vic only if she takes a mind to, which she rarely does.

"You see Robin's kids out there?" she asks, her voice suddenly tired. "I don't know who's going to take care of them kids when I'm gone." A tear slides from beneath a closed lid.

Out of nowhere Vic announces defiantly, "I hate black people." She stubs out another cigarette, adding it to the already overflowing pile in the ashtray and pulls another one from the pack. She watches my face, which I'm sure betrays a look of horror, and laughs at this reaction. "Don't think I don't hate white people too. I hate them probably more than black people. Coming up here, living on our land, telling us what we can and can't do. Making us feel bad about ourselves. That's what white people do." She pauses and looks out the window. "I don't much like Mexicans either."

I don't understand her issues about ethnicity. According to my adoption records, my biological father, long dead from a drowning accident, was white and one of Robin's partners had been from Mexico, a fact I'd learned on my last visit here. I don't know if that's how Vic really feels and she simply doesn't care who hears her opinions and states them proudly, or perhaps, as her youngest son claims, she's testing my reaction. All I know are these are the words she says. And while her chin is stubbornly set, and her eyes squint like flint against humanity, I cringe. These words are mirrors to the ones hurled at me as I was growing up, in anger, in laughter, in teasing, and in taunt: "I hate Indians." Although I can see where the unveiled anger comes from, and I can see where people get chips on their shoulder, I also see why I can't let myself go that direction: I have a white husband and two-eighth–blood boys that I would kill for, or die for, or just be for.

Flathead Indian Reservation, Arlee Cemetery, Montana, March 13, 2008.

A bitter cold wind blows across the wide valley, the kind that tugs at clothing, flapping loose corners like sheets on the clothesline. This kind of wind sandblasts our skin with pebbly-hard snow pellets, forcing our eyes to become slits against its onslaught. I watch the man in the Pendleton vest read from a Bible, his words flying away on a fickle gust, and I move closer to my sister, seeking shelter, if only for a few moments. I glance around the brown-faced group and note that there are about eighty of us huddled together in this rural cemetery, which holds the remains of ancestors buried over hundreds, if not thousands, of years. Unlike other tribes, we weren't moved here by the U.S. government; we ceded a large portion of our land and lived on the remaining 1,317,000 acres.

Ronni, James Allen, Aunt Delphine, and I face the empty hole. Two pine planks and a couple of iron bars keep the casket from falling in. It is a pine box with bare-bones decoration, the least expensive one the mortuary had to offer, the most expensive the tribal funeral fund could afford. We stand shoulder to shoulder, bent against the cold like bison. I know only five people, three of whom are standing beside me. I am the only one in a navy dress and heels. I am once more painfully aware of my outside status.

"When you go up to the funeral," another Native adoptee told me when I mentioned the passing of my birth mom, "it's customary for children to sit in the front row. You sit there, and don't let them tell you otherwise. You're as much her child as any of them."

I tried that out earlier this morning, at the wake. Ronni, James Allen, and I took our seats in the front row, next to Vern, Vic's youngest son, who'd sat at the wake for three days. The rest of the siblings, who had inhabited the front row moments ago, moved to the row behind us. This active shifting of place and location made it apparent we did not share the same status of "family." After a few awkward moments the three of us got up and returned to our seats back in the fifth row, next to Albert and Delphine, and watched the rest of the funeral from this sheltered vantage point.

Afterward funeral attendees filed around the chairs like the video game *Centipede*, shaking hands with each of the family members. An aunt approached me, shook my hand, and hugged me, pulling me close. She whispered in my ear, "You should be up in the front row with the rest of the kids."

I whispered back, "I know, it's just really uncomfortable." She stood back and appraised me with a sad smile, nodded, and moved on.

We were the orphans of highest magnitude.

But now, as I stand, huddled against the wind with a group of nearly perfect strangers, I wish I could say I had cried when I found out about Victoria's death, but I didn't. I couldn't summon up tears for this small woman who had given birth to me, allowed me to be handed off to the woman who raised me, and who wouldn't see me again until 1993, when I was thirty-four years old. My dry eyes focus on Delphine, who pulls gently on my sleeve and says quietly, "Let's go throw dirt on the casket."

I don't want to throw dirt on the casket. In fact, I really don't even want to be here.

But I am.

I I

In Memory

Fort Collins, Colorado, Spring 2002.

In 2002 my father died on March 27—my birthday—in Billings, Montana. Although the relationship he and I shared was, at best, contentious, the fact that he died on the day of my birth is a reminder it had not always been. People who think they're being supportive when I tell them this date say something like, "Geez, he couldn't even let you have your birthday in peace."

But I don't see it that way. I imagine he was trying to hang around long enough to wish me one final happy birthday. It was the one holiday he always celebrated through a card or a phone call, just a moment to let me know he was thinking of me.

It is March 24. When I went out to get the newspaper this morning, the air was chilled. Now, holding a cup of hot tea, I glance at the clock radio, which reads six o'clock. I have another hour until I have to be ready to head to the junior high where I student teach. I look outside and see that the day is already gray; large, white clouds dim the sun. I jump as the telephone jangles, then knit my brows in confusion; no one ever calls this early.

"Hi, Sue, I'm sorry to call you so early in the morning." It's Norma, Dad's wife, my stepmother. "The doctor says it's time to call and give you a chance to get here. Your dad's here at Deaconess Hospital. I had to bring him in about an hour ago; he was really struggling." I tell her I will be there by midafternoon. Rick helps me get ready by dragging out the suitcase and packing some clothes as I take a shower. He places a carton of Earl Grey tea in my purse and a supportive note, which I will find later. I am numb as I move through my everyday activities, the shower, a bowl of cereal, filling up the car with gas before I start down the road. These movements, rutted and defined, hold at bay the memories and emotions that swirl just beyond my consciousness—until I'm on the road. Then I try to separate them, like fighting children, so they don't overwhelm me, slamming my spirit all at once. I am fragile; I will break.

Forty miles north the temperature in Cheyenne has dropped to fifteen degrees. Snow flies horizontal to the highway, nearly obliterating the nearby landscape. I recall the stories I've heard from western cattle ranchers of their herds being caught in early spring snows, dying in pairs, mother and calf. I give a wry grin: here I am, American Indian thinking of cowboys. Sixty miles north of Cheyenne the storm ends, but the day remains gray.

Norma has taken care of Dad since they were married, in 1979. He was one of those guys who liked women to do things for him. This says everything about him: he loved Zero Mostel's performance of "Tradition" in *Fiddler on the Roof*. Dad saw his eastern European roots as very traditional, in the sense that the man ruled the family. I imagine he would have appreciated it if Mom and I saw it as traditional too, but we didn't. Evidently, his mom didn't see it that way either. She ran the house, and people did what she said without question, well, at least without audible questions. I think my dad didn't like his mom much. In fact, I don't think he much liked women, until he met Norma, who filled that compliant role and didn't complain. I've seen her get irritated at times, but she always waves it away like it was a mosquito and keeps on going. I, on the other hand, am not compliant, and that's where Dad and I often butted heads.

My parents adopted me when I was two years of age. That was the only story I knew, that I'd been adopted. There was no stork, no dark secrets—until years later. They made adoption sound wonderful, that I was chosen. When I was young I conceived adoption as people going through some kind of cafeteria line, where they got to a cash register, ordered a baby kept in the area behind the swinging stainless-steel doors, and paid for it when it arrived on the counter. I imagined my parents counting out their dollar bills as a nurse carried me out. As a young child, I had seen that this is the way someone acquires something; it was plausible.

But not everyone was so accepting of my adoption and becoming part of a new family. In fifth grade one of my friends asked why my parents looked so different from me. We had just gotten off the Bookmobile and stood beneath the plum tree that grew outside of our house. I told her that it was because I was adopted. Her look was worried, the same look I had associated only with adults. And like an adult, she said, "Oh, I'm so sorry."

As I drive up Twenty-Seventh Avenue, I am reminded of how little Billings has changed since I went to high school here in the 1970s. As a result, I am able to locate Deaconess Hospital easily, pulling into a relatively full parking lot. As I open the car door, my hands tremble, but I'm not sure whether this is from falling blood sugar or rising adrenaline. By the time I'm out of the car, my entire core is shaking.

The hospital doors open with a pneumatic *whoosh*, and I am immediately aware of the smell, the one that administrators try to mask, the smell of killed germs and dying cells. I approach the volunteer behind the desk. "I'm looking for the room of Jed Devan? I'm his daughter."

"Upstairs, third floor, the nursing station will tell you where he is."

Her answer is clipped but not abrupt, and she throws me a smile to take the edge off.

On the third floor a nurse points down a hall to where Dad's room is located. I stand outside his door for a moment and close my eyes and feel the knot in the pit of my stomach begin to tighten. My hands are still shaky, and now they're cold and damp. I wipe them on my jeans, take a deep breath, and push the door open.

My father is tangled in white cotton bed linens. His eyes are closed, and a clear, plastic oxygen mask covers his mouth and his nose. Beyond him a lone, bright-yellow daffodil sits in a cobalt-blue vase on the window-sill. He is dying of the lung cancer that surgery revealed five months ago.

Sensing my presence, he turns his head toward me and extends a skeletal arm, his hand motioning me inside. My throat closes, and I can't breathe. Tears threaten my composure, but I refuse to let them fall, to let him see me so naked in a grief I said I was never going to feel. I place a smile on my face and come forward, hugging him. He removes his mask and grins. His teeth are missing. "He had his last two pulled a couple of years ago," Norma says, at my unguarded reaction. My smile remains in place, hiding the shock at his thinness; he now weighs no more than seventy-five pounds.

When I was three he was the tallest man in the world. I would wait for him to come home from work, and when he did he'd lift me up and throw me into the air so high that I giggled at the weightlessness and anticipated the free fall into his arms. I never once doubted that he would catch me. One evening, however, when he came home he picked me up and wrinkled his nose, immediately handing me off to Mom. "She needs changing," he said, his tone accusatory. He had no idea how hard I'd tried, evidently unsuccessfully, to hold it just so I could see him and feel the joy of his happiness at seeing me.

I bite the inside of my cheek to ground myself in the here and now, as I turn my attention to Norma, who fills me in on all the details, assuring me that this isn't the first time he's been in the hospital. There'd been three other times where they'd patched him up and sent him home. "Who knows," she said, brightly. "It just might be the rest he needs before he can come home again." Denial never announces itself. Having not been privy to the intimate nature of caring for the dying, I believe her words, for the simple fact that I can't accept the alternative. And I try to be helpful. Being maudlin, I tell myself, isn't helpful. The inside of my cheek is now bleeding.

I walk to the window and look out at cars, lined up in unforgiving and regimented rows. The sun is now shining, casting sparks off the polished metal. These cars remind me of the cars parked outside the home of the family we knew in Missoula; they were longtime friends of my parents, and we visited them often. They lived in a bungalow near the campus, an old neighborhood where the maple trees were tall and yards well maintained. The younger kids and I often played tag. During one such game, when I was six, I ran out into the quiet street, in an abrupt, evasive maneuver. When I returned to the grass, my father, out of nowhere, caught my arm, his grip pinching its underside and leaving bruises. His face was angry, with the corners of his mouth pulled down, and his pupils black pinpricks in his widened brown eyes. I felt the slap of his left hand against my temple and I cringed. His hands grabbed my upper arms and he shook me, his face inches from mine. "You run around like a crazy person, never looking at where you're going. I don't know why you don't think about what you're doing. You get around these kids, and you just lose all your sense." He then illustrated my craziness by lolling his tongue out while waving his arms about his head and rolling his eyes.

My craziness must have followed me the whole time I was growing up, because the slaps just kept on coming. In my late twenties I remember reminiscing about something in his backyard. He sat, legs crossed, near his begonias; lit his pipe; and inhaled the smoke deep into his lungs. The familiar far-off stare visited his eyes, as he shook his head and looked, unseeing, into the distance. "You just never had good sense as a kid." My sense of self scattered, directionless, like dandelion seeds at his breeze of words. When I married, he praised my husband for taking over my care. "Maybe you can slap some good sense into her, because I sure couldn't," he said, laughing. My face burned; by then I knew I'd hated him for quite some time.

Behind me I hear his bedclothes rustling. I turn and study the shriveled person I almost don't recognize. In the brief moments since my arrival, my father has left this world and entered another; he now inhabits a morphine-laced dream where people, long-deceased or maybe just unseen, have stopped by to converse with him. He speaks in broken phrases, sometimes coherent, most times incomprehensible, while his arms, hands, and fingers are busy illustrating images visible only to him. Perhaps he's outlining a management plan; perhaps he's explaining population statistics. The doctor arrives and asks Norma if there's been any change. "Not really," she answers, "but he's only recently begun doing this." She gestures to my father's liquid movements and unintelligible speech. "That's normal," the doctor says and scribbles something on a form that hangs from the foot of my father's bed. He tucks his pen into his front pocket and says, with no eye contact, "Let me know if anything changes. I'll be doing rounds this evening." He leaves, his white lab coat flaring behind him, his feet marking time on the shiny, linoleum floor.

Since my father is occupied with his invisible guests, I tell Norma to take a break and grab something to eat down in the cafeteria. She hesitates and then, with a guilt-ridden look of relief, she walks out. I sit in the nearby chair and pull out a piece of embroidery I'm working on and glance at my father.

When I was in second grade, my father, for some reason, decided that we needed to take Fridays off—he from work, me from school— and go swimming at the hot springs up Lolo canyon. The first time we went the sky was a brilliant blue (cerulean—my father's favorite color), and the water literally danced, reflecting the sun's blazing rays in flashing shards of light. We each dived off the springboard and swam to the deepest edge. "Get on my back," he told me. I climbed aboard and wrapped my skinny legs around his chest, while my small hands grasped his shoulders, their muscles sinewy and hard. I held my breath and we dove. My eyes slit against the water, I watched in blurry fascination as the ripples undulated in bright patterns on the blue floor of the pool. I wondered if this was what it was like to ride a whale. We went the entire length of the pool before coming up for air. For the next two hours I loved being the center of his attention. We visited the hot springs six Fridays in row, and after that we never returned. Responsibilities of work had taken him away.

Norma has returned to the room, but my father hasn't. He is now somewhere else, slipping in and out of a restless sleep, talking to unseen people, spending less time with us. In the meantime Norma and I murmur in half tones late into the evening. At some point the nurse arrives, checks my father's vitals, and suggests we go home. My father is so medicated, she explains gently, that he won't be lucid until the morning. As we leave we both realize the doctor hadn't yet made his evening rounds; we should have seen him a couple of hours ago.

We return to Dad and Norma's house, where Norma begins her nighttime routine, and I escape to the guest room in the basement. It's been a long day. The last time I saw Dad was nine months ago, when he wasn't frail and dying. In fact, he'd looked healthy, and when he smiled he had a full set of teeth. I am shocked to realize they'd been dentures; no one had mentioned this fact. The drive and the unsettling experience of seeing him in this state leave me hyper and on edge. I walk over to where his small library collection stands at attention on shelves flanking the makeshift desk. I run the tips of my fingers over the spines of the paperback, hardback, and leather volumes of his most cherished books. There are scholarly books on the Bible, worn and tattered; and how-to books—one detailing how to build a log cabin, imprint 1916. There are academic botanical tomes and fiction and nonfiction texts that cover all aspects of American Indian history. With a wry smile I acknowledge my father's love-hate relationship with American Indian culture, with American Indians in general.

After he adopted me from my fractured reservation family, I think he believed if he could raise me just right, I wouldn't be Indian anymore. If I was white I would be free from prejudices, free from the hatred so entrenched in Montana culture. But in the American West, being Indian is what you are, not what you choose to be, especially if you look like one.

Norma and I return to the hospital early the following morning, and my father is less lucid than the previous night. "Has the doctor been here?" Norma asks the chaplain, who, judging by their familiarity, has been a frequent visitor. He shakes his head, "Not yet." Norma and I look at each other in confusion. Maybe he's in his office. Following the labyrinth of hallways, we take the elevated walkway that crosses over the street, connecting the doctor's building with the hospital. A few more halls and doorways later we locate him. He is sitting in his office at his desk, actively avoiding our presence. I know because he holds a manila folder in his hands, and he looks at it intensely, never touching a page. After several moments of awkward silence, Norma asks, "Did you go up to see Jed last night?"

He shakes his head.

"Were you planning on seeing him this morning?" Her tone requires an answer, and he looks at her with weary but unsympathetic eyes.

"There's no point," he says and returns his gaze to the opened file. I look at her face searching for a reaction, and I realize she's not going to argue with him, she's not going to contest his unprofessionalism. Instead, tears fill her eyes while she stands there mute. The awful truth of his words collides with the myth I've created, and the room spins and I stop breathing. My gaze catches sight of the yellow daffodil occupying a vase in the window of the doctor's office. And suddenly I hate that flower, and I hate the doctor; I hate this place, and I hate the fact that everyone else seems to know this is the end except me. Instead, I've decided to believe Norma in her goddamned delusion, and now I find out that she didn't really believe it herself. The tranquilizing numbness of grief engulfs my body and mind, and I follow Norma, like a calf, back to the other side of the hospital, because there's nothing else to do. The terrible reality of the situation has set in.

In the meantime my father has been moved to a room on a different floor, saved only for the immediately terminal patients. There are no daffodils in this room, and the colors of the wall are an unidentifiable tan. His bed is now surrounded by netting, the same kind that keeps babies from crawling out of their playpen. His gentle hand motions of the previous day have been replaced with the frantic clawing of someone trying to escape; however, whether it's out of death's grip or into his concept of heaven, I don't know. The netting forbids him from trying to get out of bed, which he attempts frequently. This is a good, because he's now hooked up to monitors and drip lines. And although the netting keeps him safe, I smile sadly at the irony—for him there is no more safety.

Each horrific coughing spasm produces copious amounts of blood, phlegm, and lung tissue. These are orally vacuumed by a nurse on a regular basis, and the contents are then stored, bright red, in a plastic jar by his bed. When the jar is filled, someone comes and empties it. It will not dawn on me until months later how many times someone has had to empty this half-gallon jar. At some point the chaplain arrives and talks with Norma in quiet tones. He asks how much chemo the doctors gave him, and he nods at her answer, replying, "Well, that's enough to make him think like he's doing something about the cancer, but not enough to make him really sick." Their betrayal leaves me ill and painfully aware of my naïveté; no one thought to let me in on the joke.

That evening, without warning, my father wakes up from a brief nap, his sudden clarity a stark contrast to the incoherence of an hour ago. His soft brown eyes are now clear, and they look at me with the adoration of that man who threw me into the air, of the father I went swimming with. With a large, unguarded smile, he says, "Happy birthday, Suz." His voice does not contain the rasp of disease, nor does it have the airiness of the dying.

"Are you hungry?" Norma asks, and he replies that he's starved. The nurse brings him dinner, and he carves the meatloaf with his knife and fork, asking about Rick, about our sons, about how my crazy mother is doing. He asks Norma about his garden, and if she'll remember to turn the canal water on for the plants in the next month. I am sure this is a miracle, although I don't believe in miracles. I have no other explanation. After dinner we sit on his bed, Norma one side of him, me on the other. I grasp his hand and am surprised its skin is not parchment. Instead, it is as soft as an infant's, and I contemplate how long it has been since I'd even touched my father.

Thankfully, my memories, the brutal reminders of my lived life, cease during my father's last hours. A heavy dose of morphine has placed him into a near coma, ending the incessant clawing that had begun again. Like the previous night, the nurse suggests we go home; she'll call us if there is any change. I return to my bedroom in their basement, where I can finally cry the heavy, wracking sobs that shred the depths of my soul, wave after painful wave until I fall asleep. The phone rings at four in the morning; it is the nurse telling Norma my father has passed away.

It is my birthday.

Norma and I begin the rituals that signify the end of a life, beginning at eight that morning. We go down to the funeral parlor, choose the urn, and choose his resting place—mausoleum or columbarium? After his cancer diagnosis my father couldn't make up his mind about how to deal with things afterward. "Being buried underground seems dark and claustrophobic, but I don't know that I want to be baked either." He decided at some later point that baking was a better way to go.

Awaiting the arrival of my family, I sit in the quiet of what is now Norma's house and look out on the garden he took so much pride in. When I was five, my father headed up a project that involved bringing back the trumpeter swan from the brink of extinction. I wasn't familiar with this part of his job because the birds were large and I was small, and he worried that I'd get hurt. But one late afternoon in early summer, he asked if I wanted to help him feed the swans. I immediately agreed. He drove the Jeep to the large aluminum grain bin, which stood near the edge of the lake, and I bounced along in the passenger seat, its ripped leather scraping the backs of my legs.

At the bin my father opened a small door at the bottom, and the golden grains of Montana wheat fell onto the ground. He shoveled grain from this small pile, filling the small rowboat that was tied up to the shore until the hull sat low in the water. He got in, tipping the boat slightly, and held out his hand to allow me to steady myself before we shoved off. The shore was covered with the new green of emerging grass, and I watched this grow distant as the lake grew seemingly larger. Gulls and other waterbirds wheeled overhead, calling, their sound carrying across the lake. Dad placed the oars in the iron swivels, which screeched in protest, and rowed steadily, *splash-pull*, *splash-pull*. Droplets from the raised oars made small rings that trailed behind us in the water. After a while he stopped rowing and set down the oars, and we drifted until the boat came to a stop of its own accord. As my father dumped shovelfuls of grain into the shallow depths, the swans swam toward us with surprising speed. With each stroke their massive size became more intimidating, and I felt better when my father rowed us away from their feeding place.

It was so quiet, except for the muted honking of the birds. The sun lay low on the western horizon, casting the air in a golden light, while the jagged summits of the Centennial Range drifted toward a shade of light violet against an evening sky of peach rimmed with red. Insects moved just above the water's surface. The only sound that broke the stillness was a splash that seemingly came out of nowhere. This splash was followed by a ringed circle that grew larger until it disappeared over the water's smooth surface.

"That's a fish rising," my father said, his voice soft, like we were in a sacred place. "It happens when a fish comes up, and its mouth breaks the surface. The fish is eating the insects that land on the water." His finger then pointed to a circle a little ways from our boat. "That's called 'rising,' when it comes to the surface. Like when the sun rises in the east." A smile formed as he scanned the surrounding landscape, and that smile reached all the way to his eyes. And suddenly, I'm not sure if I'm still in memory or in the present, because I hear his words and see his extended arm reach toward something unseen, his fingers moving rapidly to illustrate a point he was trying to make, what happens to fish when they eat and where they go when they're finished. Tears blur the world around me as I recognize these hand movements as the same ones at the hospital. I realize then that this is the place where he was talking to someone, perhaps me, about the one thing he loved best—the swans.

12

Too White to Be Indian, Too Indian to Be White

Fort Collins, Colorado, Spring 2004.

I am at Dr. Williams's office; she is the most recent in a line of therapists I've seen. Her space is comfortable: the furniture consists of one couch and two overstuffed chairs, upholstered in lush fabrics of browns and golds, as well as three heavily shaded lamps that throw subdued and delicate shadows on the softly hued, textured, saffron walls. New Age music floats in the background, and its tinkling bells, waterfalls, and birdsongs work to embed themselves into my subconscious, to the point that I am nearly unaware of their existence. I've chosen the brown chair instead of the couch, needing to be in control of my personal space— you know, the one that's about an arm's length away? I imagine that when the therapist arrives, she will come in, note where I sit, and then write that placement on her pad of paper, where it will become a clue, a guess, a sign, a definition. I inhale, filling my lungs; I exhale, pushing out my anxiety. I close my eyes and feel my pulse moving rhythmically, frantically, throughout my body. In curiosity I place my fingertips over the veins in my wrist. Yes, the rhythm matches the one in my ears.

This is the fifth therapist I've seen in twenty-four years. They don't last. Or rather, I don't. I never saw any of them for more than two or three sessions. They talk about things that don't fit or that I discount. Really? Exactly how does adoption fit with PTSD? Or they give me something, a word, a phrase, a diagnosis that grants me enough absolution to scuttle away believing that *now* I have the key for feeling better, for feeling cured. The last one I'd seen was Dr. Bernard, a marriage counselor who had helped Rick and me through one of our roughest patches, a barren area that had been scrubbed clean by the dysfunctional patterns each of us had grown up with. Suddenly, in the midst of his career taking off and me raising our two sons, our life's puzzle pieces became frayed and rough, no longer fitting neatly together. Perhaps they never had. Perhaps we had simply learned how to work around them. But we realized that working around them wasn't a good strategy when only a few connecting threads were left, two of which were our children. With each argument, each blowup, each collision, our marriage boat took on more water. That's when I got a recommendation for Dr. Bernard. It took us eight sessions and a lot of work, but we were able to climb out of the abyss in full survival mode.

Except I was still unhappy—not with us but with me. So I saw her one-on-one. By session three her frustration with my inability to reach down into the depths of my soul was explicit. "What is this?" she asked, her voice tired as she waved her hands around her eyes. I couldn't explain the tears that ran in an unstoppable stream for several minutes. I didn't know what they stood for or why they happened. I did know that her question and her tone left me angry and humiliated. I went home and canceled future appointments.

In the eleven years since our couples therapy, the sadness waxes and wanes, but it doesn't leave me. I am happy in marriage but unhappy in life. Something inside me is missing, which is why I'm sitting in the office of my fifth counselor, Dr. Williams, while my heart beats with anxiety. To pass time I look around this room, noting that the predominant theme is American Indian art.

Woven rugs and blankets hang on the walls, their patterns complex and abrupt. On an adjacent wall a bundle of sweet grass arcs near a cluster of arrows and a bow. A ledge runs along two adjoining walls, where the sheetrock has been cut in. On this shelf sits a variety of American Indian objects. Intricately painted geometric shapes march along the gently sloping shoulders of large clay ollas. Similar designs, drawn in reds, ochers, and browns, mark smaller Acoma-style pots. Basketry interrupts the spaces in between, their coils careful and deliberate, the fiber tight. An infusion of the indigenous permeates the room, and I wonder about its significance.

My attention turns to the forms in my lap, sheets of personal and impersonal questions seeking medical information. As I scan the words, I have no idea why she needs to know if I've had broken bones or allergies or my number of pregnancies and births. In spite of my questions I mark these appropriately. *Don't rock the boat*, the voice in my head says.

The next batch consists of several pages stapled together: a brief mental-health assessment. "Do you experience any of the following? (Mark all that apply.)" The list is extensive: anger, anxiety, sadness, depression, mania, apathy, isolation. "Do you drink three or more drinks a day? Do you take medication, or do you self-medicate? Do you have a plan?" I am a light drinker. I don't medicate, but I do have a suicide plan. However, it requires a season other than late spring. It requires snow and below-freezing temperatures. And I don't want the plan.

What I want is to have the pain of everyday living go away, the sadness, the anxiety, the depression, the anger, the isolation. But I don't have the confidence to address them, and no one knows they exist. It's surprisingly easy to keep these feelings carefully hidden from anyone's view. Rick, because of his travel schedule, is blissfully unaware. When he's home I put on the smile and do all those things that one does in a day-to-day existence: laundry, cooking, cleaning. I conduct all business over my phone, which means I don't leave the house unless I absolutely have to. I don't answer the phone but will pick it up soon after a call to see if anyone has left an important message. Friends who invite me to social functions are turned down easily with excuses of headaches, of head colds (an alibi that hides the fact that my nose is stuffed up from crying), of being tired, of having done too much this week and just needing to stay home, of having to take care of sick kids, of just wanting a lazy day. Across town Mom, who moved to Fort Collins from Billings in 1991, is battling her own issues, her own anxieties, her own depression, so it's easy not to have to check in. The phone calls and the visits fall off as people seek to support me in my aloneness, to give me space, to give me time.

But the kids are aware of the sadness that has blanketed me for years. Dan grows quieter; Chris becomes absent. When he was six Chris came into my bedroom in the middle of the afternoon. I tried to hide my tears in the pillow, the sobs in the handmade quilt. But I felt his presence. I knew he was there, and I was ashamed that I couldn't pull my act together enough even to soothe his worries. When I finally looked at him, he stood with his hands on his hips, indignant. "Are you crying again?" he asked, his voice loud and harsh. "I'm telling Dad!" Anger is fear made visible. How scared he must have been to observe my distress and be powerless to stop it. Perhaps he understood I was powerless to stop it as well.

So here I am, waiting for Dr. Williams, who I hope will be able to explain to me, point out to me, help me understand why I, a person who has a beautiful family, a wonderful home, truly amazing and supportive friends, and life experiences that become memories upon immediate completion, feel so apart from the rest of the world. It is as if I am moving through Jell-O, and I can only watch people live their lives through a Plexiglas window.

In 1999 I turned forty. I had never purchased anything in a liquor store. When Mom was forty she was buying a gallon of vodka every two days for Dad, who didn't want people to know he was an alcoholic. He evidently didn't mind people thinking Mom might have been. But me, as an Indian woman, I wasn't supposed to be in those places. That was the cadence of social training that drummed through my head and embedded itself into my brain when I walked through those doors: *Indians shouldn't be in these places. You know, they're all alcoholic good-for-nothings.* So, although I entered liquor stores, I never purchased.

To people who think I'm exaggerating I want to say, *C'mon, I've heard the whispers, the talk. I've seen the unconcealed contempt at the sight of their brown skin and the long black hair pulled back in a ponytail as they bought their booze off-reservation. And I've witnessed the hangdog posture of the person who is well aware of the eyes on him. Or her.* These remembered images are in stark contrast to my white mother, who could walk in almost anywhere unquestioned and buy the vodka with only a quick glance. If my dad had walked in, there wouldn't have been any question at all to his right to a drink.

So I stayed away from the counter, until I turned forty, and began to experience my first acts of rebellion. Educational rebellion: I, as an Indian woman, graduated with a master's degree in cultural anthropology. Social rebellion: I, as an Indian woman, became co-president of my children's elementary school's Parent-Teacher Organization board and worked, unsuccessfully, to get other minorities involved. Familial rebellion: I, as a daughter of a bipolar mother, refused to clean up after her most recent manic episode and listened, with such sadness, at her confusion as she wondered what the hell she'd done. Personal rebellion: I refused to be labeled as too old, too afraid. At thirty-five I began to study tae kwon do, receiving my black belt three years later. The following autumn I returned to school to obtain a teaching certification.

Although all these events began to form a redefinition of who I was, by forty years of age I could say I was definitely living on my terms now. Therefore, I discarded the identification that marked me solely as an Indian woman, and I entered a liquor store with the intent to purchase. But as I crossed over the threshold, I felt an overwhelming and immediate sense of vulnerability, embarrassment, and almost shame to be in this den of libationary iniquity.

Dr. Williams walks in, and I study her, the same way I study every person I come into contact with the first time. One of the first therapists I'd visited told me I carried out this kind of assessment because I grew up in an alcoholic family, and I had to watch people, my dad specifically, for any nonverbal cues as to what to expect: calmness or violence. I believe that is true.

I watch as she notices my choice of seat. That's when I feel my chest tighten with a constriction that chokes out my calm, as it buries the bells, the waterfalls, and the birdsongs beneath the pulse that drums in my ears. I feel myself readying for battle, as I seek to establish my own new personal world order. But I am well trained. In spite of my angst, my anxiety, my apprehension, I stand and extend my hand, keeping my smile tight but warm. Oh, the things we know how to do under pressure, as we hold our cards so close to our chest. *We're fine, everybody's fine; we're all fine here.*

Her handshake is firm, the kind of handshake career counselors suggest you learn before applying for jobs. But then she holds my extended hand in both of her palms, and I wince, not with pain but too much familiarity. I don't know if she notices that when she lets go, I wipe my hand on the side of my pants. She walks gently across the floor and takes a seat on the couch, smoothing the bottom of her skirt so it won't wrinkle. Her subtly ample figure is constrained in a dark-brown skirt-and-jacket suit. Blond hair, light brown at its roots, falls to her shoulders and rolls under itself. With a swipe at a wisp of her bangs, she reveals a pair of the darkest eyes I have ever seen. Her smile is broad and welcoming; mine is tight with uneasiness.

Moments later a heavy silence blankets the room, and Dr. Williams watches me, mute. I guess I'm supposed to start. I motion to the room around me. "I notice you have a lot of American Indian art." It's conversational—not a lot of pressure.

"I do," she says, wearing that brightening smile, while her dark eyes glint in pleasure. "I just found out I am a thirty-second Cherokee, and I am so proud of my heritage." She smiles more; my smile retracts.

"In fact," she continues, her Oklahoma accent thick like honey at the first frost, "I'm in the process of trying to get my name on the Cherokee tribal rolls. I've got my birth certificate and my mother's certificate and the certificates of all the women back to my great-great-grandmother, but I'm still trying to track down my great-great-great-grandmother's. Once I have that I can submit my petition to the tribal council and request my name to be added to the rolls."

The Dawes Rolls, created by the Dawes Commission and authorized by the U.S. Congress in 1893, were also known as the "Final Rolls of Citizens and Freedmen of the Five Civilized Tribes." The rolls are the bible of Native belonging and tribal membership in several tribes located in Oklahoma, ensuring their members are granted all the rights and benefits thereof. The designation "Five Civilized Tribes" was used by nineteenth-century white politicians to distinguish members of the Cherokees, Seminoles, Creeks, Choctaws, and Chickasaws from their "wild" counterparts, who still hunted for survival. Instead, members of these five tribes had adopted many Euro-American cultural attributes, including Christianity, literacy, a written constitution, farming practices, and market participation.

Rolls, or censuses, were a way to establish tribal membership to determine who had access to rights and goods as stated by the various treaties signed between tribal chiefs and the presidents of the United States. The earliest censuses were chaotic and unstandardized. Questions arose of who should be counted and who should not; how to deal with people who lived with the tribe but were not tribal members; how to deal with people who lived off the reservation but belonged to a tribal family unit; who was part of a family unit regardless of name; and so on. Although rules were established as to how to address inconsistencies, many times they weren't followed, making the rolls exceedingly imprecise.

Rolls became a central issue with the passage of the Dawes Act, also known as the General Allotment Act of 1887. The purpose of this act was to (1) support assimilation, (2) break up tribal units, (3) encourage individual initiatives, (4) further the progress of Native farmers, (5) reduce the cost of Native administration, and (6) implement a policy that could eliminate the federal-trust responsibilities over Indian lands within twenty-five years. Once all tribal members received their acreage, the excess lands were to be sold to white homesteaders for profit. Characteristics of allotment eligibility were determined officially as well as unofficially by the Dawes Commission. Officially, a person was required to be a member of a federally recognized tribe; unofficially, the Dawes Commission used a standard of blood quantum to help determine who should be counted. In the case of the Five Civilized Tribes, that quantum was one-quarter.

Membership determination regarding blood quanta, a double-edged sword, is left to the tribes to establish. It ensures recognition to receive what we are owed by right of treaty, but more insidiously, it is a way to ensure we breed ourselves out of existence. A "full-blood" American Indian woman is considered to have a 100 percent blood quantum. If she marries and produces a child with a non-Native man, her child would have a blood quantum of 50 percent; if that child produces a child with another non-Native, that grandchild would be 25 percent. By the fourth generation her great-great-grandchild will be ineligible for membership in many tribes, as many have adopted the "quarter-blood" quantum requirement. The Cherokees, however, do not require blood quanta to determine membership but rather rely on legal proof of matrilineal descent to women on the Dawes Rolls.

Under the Dawes Act, depending on age and family status, each tribal member would receive between 40 and 160 acres of reservation land that they could use, bequeath, or sell. The Dawes Act of 1887 didn't require the most assimilated tribes, including the Five Civilized Tribes, to participate; however, that changed with the passage of the Indian

Appropriations Act of 1893. At that point the Dawes Commission was established by Congress, whose purpose was to negotiate with the five tribes to get them to agree to participate in yet another land swap, this time exchanging reservation land for a piece of owned property. When the exchange was approved, the commission required a census, and the Dawes Rolls resulted from the final census. These are the rolls to which the Dr. Williams referred. But membership is never a given, especially when the Bureau of Indian Affairs is involved.

After I was born my birth mother enrolled me as a member of the Confederated Salish Kootenai Tribes. Within a few months of my adoption, Mom was contacted by a Bureau of Indian Affairs representative and asked if she wanted to sign away my Indian rights, meaning my tribal membership. The 1950s was an era of aggressive assimilation efforts: termination of reservation land and the rights of its people; relocation of Native people from rural to urban areas, where they competed for jobs and lived without the safety net of family or community; the continuation of the centuries-long program of Indian education, where administrators, both secular and nonsecular, commonly saw their American Indian students as, at worst, animalistic soulless beings and as, at best, not needing much more than a third-grade education because of their substandard intellect; and the placement of American Indian children into white families, far away from their tribes and their reservations.

Do you see the direction this is going? Do you see how legislators over the past several centuries have devised a myriad of ways we, as Native people, could lose our membership, our land, our culture, our children? Do you see the laws put in place to annihilate us; to dismantle our treaties signed in good faith with the Great White Fathers, as they liked to call themselves; to create avenues by which tribal land could be accessed and opened, our resources extracted without argument, without barriers?

In 1961 Mom understood the consequences of the representative's request. "Those aren't my rights to sign away," she stated. "Those are

187

my daughter's rights. And when she reaches the age of eighteen, if she wants to sign away her Indian rights, then she can do so. But I won't sign away what is not mine."

Bless her.

I've been Indian ever since.

"I'm Native," I tell Dr. Williams quietly, my smile still in place. Like a river's eddies in turbulent water, a dark anger begins to swirl, and it is directed at this person in front of me, who is so white. How could she possibly have any idea what it means to "be Indian," to know the price I've paid to "be Indian"?

"Really?" Her voice rises in interest, happy that we share this kinship, this blood bond of being. "What tribe are you?"

"I'm Salish. From the Confederated Salish Kootenai Tribes." *I'm not Cherokee*, I want to say.

She looks at me with a quizzical expression. "I've never heard of them. Where are they located?"

There's a certain sense of pride belonging to a tribe that no one's ever heard of. "Western Montana."

She nods while her dark-brown eyes attempt to pierce me. "Are you proud of your Indian heritage?" I hear it, her attempt to establish another kinship bond.

I level her with a steady gaze, and I feel the familiar lump in my throat. I have a half smile that I'm sure if I look in the mirror looks more frozen than warm. "Where I come from, you got beat up if you were proud of being Indian."

Her quizzical expression returns. "But you should be proud of what you are."

"I am who I am," I tell her. I explain, "I was adopted by a white couple, but I look Indian—so in the big scheme of things, I'm too Indian to be white, and I'm too white to be Indian. I am who I am."

By now my smile is gone. I realize I'm tired. I'm tired of justifying the paradox of my existence, why I talk so "white," or why I talk so "funny," without the reservation cadence to my sentences. I'm tired of explaining why I don't know how to speak "Indian" (there are 290 Native languages in North America alone), or why I don't know "my" culture. I'm tired of explaining why I'm not a "real" Indian, or how it is that I know so much "white" history, but no one asks me about "Indian" history. Perhaps because they are uncomfortable hearing that story.

But when she tells me, one last time, nearly pleading with me to understand, with a look of absolute confusion, "But you should be proud of your heritage," I want to scream. I want to get in her face and say, *You haven't walked in my shoes. You haven't had the hatred follow you through a place where people thought you didn't belong, like the Denny's in Missoula, where I met my uncle Albert and his wife, Delphine, in 1994.*

Albert's hair was short, cropped close to his scalp along the sides, a bit longer on top, a symbol left over from the 1950s, when Indians were pushed to "act like white people." But it didn't work—he was clothed in a Pendleton vest. Delphine was brown and slender, her long dark-brown hair draped loose about her shoulders. They'd seen me only one other time, so I was overjoyed to sit in the booth with them and visit—proud, even—except when I looked over through the wooden screen that separated us from the adjacent booth and saw the old couple, bent and bitter, their white hair reminding me of Q-tips. He was grumbling about his food; she was throwing us ugly looks, her brows drawn together like thin tubes of cotton, while her glacial blue eyes were filled with poison as she "tsk-tsked" and looked away, only to look back and do it all again.

Dan, who was four, began acting up. Not only was he tired of being in a grown-up world; he felt tension squeeze around us like the coils of an anaconda. I had to force my eyes away from the old woman, as Dan began whining and dropping things purposefully on the floor. When that didn't work, he swatted my face to get my attention, and when that failed he began screaming. His tantrum rose to such a level that I picked him up and took him to the bathroom. I swatted him on the behind, certainly nothing that could be felt through a pair of toddler underwear and thick corduroy overalls. It was a reminder that he needed to get a grip. And who walked out of one of the three stalls but the bitter old woman who, by now, was so angry with my obvious lack of parenting ability she sputtered her hatred of me and my kind, hissing that I had no business having children if I couldn't even take care of them properly. And by that time I was really tired, tired of having to defend who I was, where I was, and why I was. I was tired of my four-year-old's tantrums and of people barging into my life, uninvited, who feel they have a right to tear me down for no reason other than I was brown, a characteristic that somehow held deep meaning for them, which they were more than happy to share with me.

"Just mind your own business," I said to her, my voice nearly defeated but still audible. I picked up my son, who by that time was sobbing because he'd witnessed this hatred, and I pulled his head to my shoulder, turned his face to my neck, and rubbed the back of his head. As I walked out the door, I said with a quiet venom that matched hers, "Just mind your own fucking business."

"I am who I am," I repeat to Dr. Williams, and my smile is now entirely gone. "It's taken me forty years to be able to get to this point, and it is a place that I'm okay with, and that's the only way I can tell you who I am."

She tilts her head, and I watch her smile return. She says, almost playfully, "You stick with me; we'll get you proud of being Indian."

I've been emotionally slapped. *She doesn't get it!* I realize, stunned. But then again, how could she, with her blond hair and fair skin and advanced education and the ability to move unquestioned in this society because she looks just like them?

No, she would never know what it meant to be Indian in Montana.

Bottles stood in rows on the shelves, upright and elegant, the glass or the liquid within or both were tinted in ambers, browns, greens, reds, blues, and ecru. Long necks, short necks, wide shoulders, no shoulders—their forms varied; their bodies triangular, rectangular, circular. As I stared at the colors, the rows, the shelves, the labels, all whispered to me of the sins of my birth mother, the Indian woman who lost her kids to "the system" because she couldn't quit drinking. I winced, quelling the whispers, and reminded myself that I was in the decade of rebellion; I was not her.

Even so, I was self-conscious, heinously so. But I walked (strolled) to the wine aisle (wine seems to be more socially acceptable than beer, as least on the social-status ladder) as if I'd done this for years. I perused the labels, searching for the fine wine, the one that raised eyebrows in interest. I ran my fingers along the bottles of reds, whites, rosés, whose points of origin resided in South Africa, Argentina, Italy, and California. I read the labels beneath that described the flavors as "sparkling citrus" or with "hints of cherry and dark chocolate." The labels served two purposes, education and a way to hide my embarrassment by focusing on something as people walked by. *Good God*, I thought to myself, *I hadn't considered that someone would actually recognize me in this place! If I can't look at wine, I'm never going to be able to look at porn!* My face flamed as I pretended to be at ease in this place, even as I tried to push aside the fact that at forty years of age, I was still letting other people dictate my life and my actions through their judgments. But old habits die hard; I could quiet my trepidation, but I couldn't quiet my shame.

I breathed in resolve and settled on a $21.99 bottle of red (the price at least gives the appearance that it is better than the $7.99 bottle next to it), whose green bottle with the long, slender neck seemed more uptown, swanky. Balancing it in the palm of my hand, I looked at the label without really seeing it, averting my gaze from yet another newcomer to the aisle. It was heavy. I focused on the gilded label's French script, unable to ascertain even one word that looked familiar. *It must be good*, I thought with a wry smile. But really, I had no idea if the wine was good, bad, awful. That's when the panic set in. I was stuck. I couldn't put the bottle down, and I couldn't walk up to the counter and just pay for it.

I couldn't do those things because each of those actions would mean something, represent something that I wasn't prepared to acknowledge.

I concentrated on the label's red-line drawing, an estate of some sort, presumably where the grapes had been picked. The placard indicated the wine to be red, with a "rich" and "complex" taste of plums and black-berries. *Rich* and *complex*. I rolled those around on my tongue. Yes, those were words that I wanted to define me. So, despite my claustrophobic spirit, I forced a sense of rich complexity and approached the counter, behind two other people. I felt a thin line of perspiration trickle from beneath the fringe of my hair.

When I glanced at the checker I saw a college kid, but horror overtook me as I realized I knew him! He was six years older than my eldest son, and they were in Boy Scouts together! Good Lord, of all the people to witness my identity experiment! *He's a professional,* I reminded myself. *He rings up sales, asks customers if they want a receipt, puts bottles into bags or boxes, and he does this day after day after day.*

"How's your day?" he asked without more than a cursory glance, a practiced smile.

"Fine," I answered, my throat dry, my words miniscule.

"Great. $21.99 plus tax brings it to . . ."

I extracted my wallet and felt the palm of my hands grow damp. My fingers shook at I pulled the credit card from its pocket, and I was sick to my stomach, as I hoped the kid didn't think I stole this card and that's why I was shaking.

A lifetime. A lifetime of feeling that somehow I had done something wrong just because I was who I was. I breathed and pasted a smile on as I looked directly into his eyes. I waited then, for the judgmental look, the quiet sneer, the request for an ID or something else that would take a long time to find in my purse while those behind me waited, mut-tering their sanctimonious whispers with barely hidden irritation. The purpose of the exercise was discomfort, to make me so uncomfortable that I would leave and not return. I'd seen that game applied to Indian people in Montana too many times to think it wouldn't happen to me.

I waited.

"Do you want me to put it in a bag?"

My heart pounded with relief.

"Yes. Thank you."

"Have a good one," he said, his smile friendly as he looked at me, but only briefly. There was another customer right behind me.

I cradled the bagged bottle in the crook of my arm and walked out into the sunshine that bathed my face. I, at forty years of age and an Indian woman to boot, had purchased a bottle of liquor. Well, wine. And the world hadn't stopped spinning.

13

This Once Used to Be Ours

Flathead Indian Reservation, Arlee, Montana, August 2008.

I am flying home.

Home.

Until now the reservation has never been "home," and I wonder why it suddenly becomes home now. To me home has always been a place to return to, a place to belong, a place that provides a definition of self and connection with the land and its people. Therefore, with regard to me, the reservation does not meet the criteria for two simple reasons: I have no memory of living here, and my contact with my family over the past twenty years has been, at best, inconsistent.

Transiency has defined me, defined my family. Dad's federal government job transferred him every two to five years, and we'd always find ourselves the "new people in town." Consequently, these towns became places I *lived* instead of places I was *from*. I was born in Missoula and lived three years in Red Rock Lakes, near the infinitesimally small town of Monida, named for its location on the border of Montana and Idaho. I attended grade school in Stevensville and Naselle, Washington; junior high in Naselle, Great Falls, and Billings, Montana; and high school in

Billings. College was in Bozeman, before I was placed on academic leave, whereupon I moved to Gardner to gain a certain measure of maturity. I finished college in Missoula and grew mature enough to have a marriage and a family, moving with them in 1987 to Fort Collins, Colorado. Here we put down very deep and solid roots, on my recommendation.

Unlike me, Rick doesn't require a "home," a place to be from. He was a navy brat who lived on six bases, nationally and internationally, over a period of eighteen years, birth to college. He does not have the same yearning for home that I do. His home, he states, is wherever his family is.

But me, I yearn for a home, that place that marks my identity as being a "community member," and I don't have it. Therefore, it was important to me that our sons know home as a palpable, knowable place, distinct in memory: a sanctuary. By design we found a neighborhood where the school was at its center; they would graduate with kids they'd gone to kindergarten with. When it came time to sell our house and purchase another, we stayed within the same schools the boys had been enrolled in, moving only six blocks away. They were heavily embedded in the neighborhood as well as the community we actively built. In many cases the networks we cultivated replaced long-distant relatives. When everything was said and done, they knew who they were and where they were from, and they knew they were an inherent part of a well-established and carefully tended support network.

And this was my definition of home. But now that definition seems to fly in the face of my sudden redefinition. This newly defined home exists only in a relinquished memory of the family homestead on the Flathead.

Like much of the reservation land across the nation, the Plant family homestead was the consequence of the Dawes Act. It was designed to bring American Indians into a "civilized" society, becoming independent farmers, becoming entrepreneurs. For twenty-five years the titles to each allotment were held in trust by the federal government. At the end of that period the title transferred to the landowners, and the land allotment would be theirs to do with as they wished.

Problems were rife within this policy: the allotments were small, and therefore usually not economically viable, yet American Indians still owed taxes on the land. Not able to afford the taxes, they lost the land to white farmers or, worse, non-Indians who had buddied up to the Indian agents and were added to the Indian census rolls, qualifying them for Indian status and allotments. The kicker was the land that had been put into reserve for American Indian residence was being opened to non-Natives at phenomenal rates. Regarding my reservation, the 1855 Treaty of Hellgate stated, "Nor shall any white man, excepting those in the employment of the Indian Department, be permitted to reside upon the said reservation without permission of the confederated tribes, and the superintendent and agent."

The General Allotment Act of 1910 effectively opened the Flathead Reservation up to white settlement, stating that all Indians of the tribes who legally lived on the reservation would receive either 80 acres or 160 acres, and the remaining acreage would be open to white settlement. The Indians were never consulted, nor were they ever asked for permission.

My birth family does not know me as Susan Harness; they know me as Vicki Charmain, the name I was given when I was born. Some know me as Mainey. Vicki Charmain is the name I use now when I call Uncle Albert to ask him to take me to the family homestead. He considers the option for several moments. All of Albert's replies are slow, careful, methodical, an indication of why people come to him for his consideration on tribal matters; he is an acknowledged elder and as such puts a lot of thought into the issue prior to ever giving an answer.

"Well, there's not much to see," he responds after a few moments. "It burned down years ago."

Although I am disappointed, the feeling is fleeting. "But I just want to be there," I assure him, trying to keep the pleading tone to a minimum.

"I just want to walk there. I just want to see it." For whatever reason, the idea of the homestead and its specific location on the land has become nearly sacred in my mind. So sacred in fact that I need to make a pilgrimage, to examine its physicality, to feel the grass between my fingers, to get a sense of rootedness. And I need a guide to accomplish this. I want Albert to be that guide.

In his hesitation to answer, I sense a question: *why is this suddenly so important?* Perhaps I am trying to reconvene with my ancestors of long ago. Perhaps I want to reestablish my birthright, at least in my own mind. But a more shadowed possibility floats at the edges of my consciousness, whispering what I could not think aloud: *perhaps I am seeking to experience the last place I was before social services took me away.* I try to imagine what this might have looked like. I wonder who answered the door when the social worker arrived. Were members of my family surprised, or did they expect this person? Had someone made a call from this house? Or a concerned neighbor?

I push the questions away before they can begin to form into quicksand. These considerations map out dangerous territory, giving the ethereal "what-ifs" form and substance. What if social services hadn't come? What if Vic had come to the courtroom to claim us? Or even if she couldn't be a mother, what if we'd been kept in that community, raised by someone else? Or what if all contact with my birth family hadn't been severed?

These questions are dangerous; they illuminate the boundaries of who I am, where I belong. Mom would be devastated by their being placed onto the wind. She would ask, was she not a good-enough mother? Had she not devoted decades to my well-being, and why was that not enough? The questions are painful reminders to all involved, except for the child-placement professionals, that family ties are so fragile they can be broken and remanufactured and sold as the original. As long as the questions are never uttered and the answers are never found, they lose their destructive power. So I push them to the back of my mind and

6. Albert Plant. Photo by the author.

acknowledge that, for whatever reason, the thought of returning to this space has consumed me for years. But the "why" factor keeps coming up.

"Why is this so important to you to try to go back to people who aren't that interested in having anything to do with you?" Rick asks, more out of concern for my emotional well-being than anything else. "Why would you want to come back here?" asks my youngest brother, Vern, who has dreamed of leaving and having a different life elsewhere. "Why isn't being here with your friends and your family enough?" asks my friend Anne, confused by my compulsion.

Because.

I want to go because I believe it is in my blood, because perhaps I can get them to care about me as much as I care about them, at least in my mind. Perhaps I can fight the demons that chased me away with their racist tones and their judgmental eyes. Perhaps through claiming this space as my home, I can claim authenticity to my inheritance, genetic and otherwise. Perhaps, by being here, I'm staking a claim on my identity and will no longer accept ascriptions that aren't true.

These answers, however, remain unsaid. To my ears they sound romantic, laden with unrealistic sentiment, as if constructed in dreamscape. I can't imagine how they would sound to others. So my response is vague because it will shield the pain of being seen as illogical. "Because. I just do. I don't know why. I just want to go back."

Albert seems to hear my thoughts because he doesn't ask for an explanation. "Sure," he says, "I can take you there. How about Sunday, after church? Delphine and I can meet you at the North Valley Creek turnoff."

My vocal chords grow so tight I can barely squeeze the words "thank you" past them. When I hang up, I send a prayer of thanks to the Creator. I have scant knowledge of the homestead. I know several family members had lived on and off in the log cabin over the years, and that my birth father's only photo known to exist was up at the homestead. I'd heard it had been destroyed when the homestead burned. Ronni had mentioned at one time she'd had the photo, then lost it. Regardless, Ronny Smith's image remains a ghost in my imagination, having been bulldozed by the ethereal memories of others, abstract and elusive.

The following Sunday I'm sitting at the turnoff in my car. I glance at the clock on my car; it reads twelve-thirty. Albert and Delphine show up ten minutes later in their little blue truck. After a few pleasantries I put my Subaru wagon into gear and follow them across the sturdy wooden bridge that crosses the Jocko River. The dirt road hugs a low-lying bluff, then turns abruptly southward and continues across a checkerboard of grassland, where cattle graze contentedly in the August sun. This piece of land runs along the foothills that border the western edge of the Flathead Reservation. Few colors make up the palette of this place; however, the hues are stunning as the shades of gold and amber of the fields sit in contrast to the greens of the mountains and the cerulean blue of the sky. This feels like home.

Except that little voice in the back of my mind asks a question I'm not yet able to fully answer. *If this is home, why are you still looking? You've met your birth mother, you've met many of your siblings, you've met extended family, and yet obviously something is missing. Why else would you return again to this place?*

Psychologists say that memories typically begin at two years of age. That may well be true. I remember waking up from a nap in a room darkened by a pulled vinyl shade. I stood in my crib and stared across the seemingly vast empty space to the closed door, waiting. There was a sense of anticipation, excitement. I remember I didn't make a sound, but I was so surprised and so pleased to see the smiling face of the woman I would always know as Mom, as she gently pushed the door open to see if I was awake. Both of our smiles were filled with joy, and both of us were happy to see each other—we were mirrors of the same emotion. I can only believe this event had to have been days after my placement; why else would it stay branded in my memory as if cast in metal?

We pull into the property, and I get out of my car and experience a sudden sense of vertigo as I look back across the grassland to the highway that lies like a gray ribbon on the other side of the valley. I had driven on that road perhaps a hundred times with my adopted family, with my husband, or by myself, always on the way through the reservation to the Bison Range or Flathead Lake or Bigfork or Kalispell or Glacier National Park. Looking at that highway from this perspective I recall how each time I drove by I had looked across the valley to this very location and wondered what it would be like to live here, on the edge of these foothills. Sometimes I wondered if I could buy a plot of land and build a house and what that experience would be like. I am in two places at the same time, here and on that highway. I close my eyes, trying to capture a steadying breath at this tattered remnant of memory that has lain untouched, ready to come to life given the right circumstances, like a snowdrop blossom on the edge of springtime.

I am brought back to the present as a large shepherd mix walks stiff-legged toward me, sniffs my jeans, and wanders away. Another mongrel mix of some sort keeps its distance, barking, its head thrown back, its eyes as wary of me as I am of it. The third, a young lab, is so excited to have visitors that actually like him that he dances around us for quite some time. He turns out to be our key into this pack.

A stocky man with the straightest, coarsest hair I've seen on anyone besides myself opens the door, his Hawaiian shirt bright against the day. "Welcome!" he hails, his smile as infectious as his demeanor. This is Pete, the owner of the double-wide and the son of Albert's eldest brother, Peter, although he is the same age as Albert. He is my cousin, but later I will learn I'm related to many people up here, the vast majority of whom I have never met and probably never will. Pete's wife, Linda, fair with silver hair, stands slightly behind him and smiles, waving a welcome of her own.

There are introductions and handshakes, and then I step back, away, and take in my surroundings. Although the original homestead had been eighty acres, Pete's small piece of heaven that sits next to the homestead is probably five. Somewhere along the line the family had lost the land allotment, and the tribe, having first dibs on all property up for sale, purchased it to retain it in tribal lands. Pete was able to purchase the adjacent property, which allowed us access to the family's original allotment.

I turn back to my cousin and study him, looking for those shared similarities. For years I shared no characteristics with the people who surrounded me; now these faces are nearly as foreign but somehow more familiar. Perhaps it sits in our brownness, in our hair color, our eye color. Perhaps it's more intangible, visible only in our laughter. There's a quick sense of humor that weaves gently through this genetic family, one that I share with everyone I've met so far.

But for Pete and me the only similarity I see is the individuals we married. Not only are Linda and Rick non-Native, they are visibly so. Pete's dark skin, salt-and-pepper hair, and dark eyes contrast sharply with Linda's fair complexion, blond and silver hair, and blue eyes. In that moment I become aware of how much I take Rick's and my difference of appearance for granted; I experience a jolt of surprise to see it on someone else. I think of the line from Robert Burns, "Oh would some power the giftie give us, to see ourselves as others see us." And through this introduction I am finally handed the mirror.

"You sure you don't want to take the four-wheeler?" Pete asks, for the second time.

"No, that's okay. We'll walk," Albert replies.

"When you get done, come on back for some iced tea, and we'll go over the family photos."

Land is so closely associated with the people, the cultures, that sit on its soil. In 1984 Rick and I set out to see America. We began our trek from Missoula, Montana, driving through Wyoming and South Dakota, then dipping into Iowa, where the contrast of landscape shocked my system. We'd exchanged the arid high desert with a green lushness that I hadn't known existed, except in books or movies. Cornfields, staccato in their rows, flew by my window, mile after mile. Dotted between these fields were aspects of white: carefully tended whitewashed barns, large and sturdy; white houses with white Ford Fairlanes in their white detached garages surrounded by white picket fences. And tidy! There was not so much as a board out of place. In the West it was not uncommon to see junked vehicles of all kinds occupying land around the residences; here those scraps of rusted metal had long ago been disowned and hauled to salvage yards, leaving yards clean of debris. Of course, the majority of the settlers in this area were the Germans and the Swedes, known for their almost obsessive ability to keep things neat and orderly. Not only have they taken control of their lives; they've taken control of the land, their earliest ancestors forcing themselves in while forcing us out.

We Natives now live on the fringes, on reservations where many of the homes are not only unkempt but in some cases barely standing, while rusted metal sits in spaces once seen as yards, the representation of a middle-class life. Some may perceive this chaotic landscape as an active resistance to those ethnically white ordered spaces and ordered lives, while others might see this disordered environment as the product of an uncaring and lazy people. I think this is what happens to societies that have been battered by immigrating forces and made to endure their brutal governmental anti-Indian policies and practices. Each generation of people that remains on the margins loses a little bit more of their connection with one another, as well as their connection with themselves. This loss becomes visible on the land and in the system.

Delphine waits off to the side as Albert and I walk away from the double-wide. When we go about ten steps, Albert stops, put his fingers in the front pockets of his jeans, and gazes out over the long-grass prairie. When I look at Albert I feel such pride in our relationship, both blood and constructed. Standing nearly six feet tall with his broad chest and shoulders thrown back, he reveals someone committed to beliefs and values. It's clear why he's a beloved and respected elder. As I study him, I long for that sense of self that he so easily portrays. My gaze drifts to his face; although he is nearly sixty-four years old, his skin is smooth. The only wrinkles that ever become visible are when he smiles, and his cheeks become round and his eyes dance. That's when I feel the most joy. I go out of my way to say something funny just so I can watch him relish a moment of life.

But today he is serious as he looks out on the landscape. After a few moments he takes one hand out of his pocket and gestures as he speaks, his fingers following the terrain. "Our family," he says, the rez dialect clear, his voice quiet, "used to own everything from those trees up there, all the way down to the river." He pauses and looks at me, a sad smile playing on his lips. "At one time, we were rich. We used to have nearly a hundred horses that grazed this valley." But slowly, the smile disappears, as a shadow crosses his face and his brow furrows in distant thought. Then he shakes his head. "I'm not sure when we weren't rich anymore. But we lost almost all the horses. And now this land belongs to the tribe." This tract of land that he speaks so lovingly about is tinged in late summer gold, and his face betrays a sense of yearning, almost a pain. When the smile returns, grief crosses the air between us. His voice grows quiet, soft on an errant breeze. "But this once used to be ours."

He turns then and faces the opposite direction. "And there were three cabins here, the main one down here, then one about a quarter mile up the road—that was where guests went or people who just wanted to break away from the main house—and then another one a half mile or so beyond that, which was where our grandparents lived in the summer. We called that the summer house."

Albert walks slowly away, stopping about twenty feet from me. I follow but trip as the edge of my tennis shoe catches on something. When I look down I see a concrete foundation, the outline of the original house. It had been carefully poured, its edges sharp and defined. I walk along the top, trying to imagine the interior's layout, but my imagination remains blank. Finally, I look at Albert and ask, "What did it look like?" Then I wait, like a child for a story. And I am not disappointed.

"It was a two-story log cabin," Albert explains, his voice soft with remembrance, "with an addition added on at some point." He steps carefully over a piece of concrete, which, upon closer inspection, is actually a step to what would have been the threshold of the house. "This was where the front door used to be, and over here to the left was the living room. Back over here was the kitchen. Every day we had to get water from the creek, over there." He gestures to the embankment to the south, now heavily lined with willows. It seems a long ways to go, especially for a young child, the person, I imagine, who was most likely to fetch the water.

"The sink was here, and we had a wood stove here. And just over here there were the stairs that went up to the second story. That's where the bedrooms were."

As he speaks, time falls away and I see myself standing in a dark interior filled with people. Loud people.

"Oh, we had some really great times in this house and some really bad times," Albert says with a smile, interrupting my thoughts.

"When were the great times?"

"Oh, you know, when people came to visit. We'd sit around and play cards; we'd tell stories. And we'd laugh. We would laugh for hours." His eyes dance and his cheeks are round.

"And the bad times?"

"When Mom and Dad were drinking." He doesn't elaborate. Perhaps he doesn't need to. That's kind of how it worked in my family as well. Maybe drinking and its consequences are the same worldwide.

I look at this place and try to imagine myself here on that fateful day. Had Albert been here when I was removed? Had he witnessed the event? I had been eighteen months, which meant he was maybe sixteen, seventeen, perhaps. Had my eldest sisters been there? My grandparents? My mother, Vic? My father, Ronny? Who watched as we were taken from this space and put into the car and driven away? *Did anyone understand how that exactly had happened?*

When I became a parent, I was overwhelmed by the feelings of love and protectiveness that swelled my heart until I thought it couldn't swell anymore. Cradling each of my boys as infants in my arms, I would look into their faces, their eyes, Chris's green and Dan's blue, and marvel at their gaze back at me. I studied the shape of their noses, their mouths, wondering which parent they resembled most; I would laugh at their wide-mouthed, toothless grins. I ran my fingers through their hair, Chris's fine and light brown, Dan's coarse and golden brown, and held their tiny hands, feeling their fingers grasp mine and hold on.

When Chris was seven months old, I watched as he reached for the lip of the brick fireplace and lifted himself like a walrus, except gravity forced him to fall, his forehead hitting the fire-hardened bricks. He howled in pain, and it took a long time of rocking to calm him. I watched when Dan, at thirteen months, began walking quickly, if unsteadily, down the slightly sloped driveway. His body got too fast for his legs and he pitched forward, scraping his chin along the concrete. I winced with these and other attempts of theirs to get the world, and their bodies, under control. And most times there was nothing I could do to assist but stand by helplessly and watch.

But one of the most difficult times I experienced as a parent was when each of our children turned eighteen months old. As I watched their every move, their tests of nature, as my worry mixed with my joy, one question battered my psyche: *how could anyone give an eighteen-month-old child up, forever?* I couldn't imagine lacking the ability to adequately care for them, to the point of watching them being loaded into a car and driven away, with no plan on how I was going to get them back. *Would they be scared? Would someone hold them and assure them that everything was going to be all right?*

How did my mother let her decisions get to the place where my sister and brother and I needed to be removed from that home? This was the question rolling around in my head like marbles as I watched Chris and Dan play with their building blocks or their Tonka trucks, building a world that was safe under my gaze. *Under what circumstances could I allow them to be seized and driven out of my life?*

I stand in the house and imagine my place in it. "How many people lived here at one time?"

"Oh, let's see . . ." he counts off the names of parents and siblings, ticking each of his fingers and adding digits for husbands or wives, and children. He comes up with something like twenty people as an average number.

"Where did you all sleep?"

"Mostly upstairs. Mattresses covered every inch of the floor, and when that area was full, people slept downstairs. You just laid down wherever there was a spot." His laughter causes me to smile; it always does, offering the seemingly heartfelt invitation to join in. We turn and step back over the threshold, and when I turn to face the river it feels surreal, as if I am coming out of a dream. When I glance back into the foundation, I am surprised that the cabin isn't real, that it existed entirely in my mind. And then, as if welcoming me back, Delphine smiles and murmurs a greeting.

"Ready?" I ask, and the three of us begin the walk up the two-track toward the upper acreage of the land. The black lab also joins us, and I keep track of him by following the sounds of grass moving. He is well cloaked in the honey-gold slender stalks that stretch above my knees, except every so often that black wagging tail beats with violent interest as he tracks particular scents, betraying his tangential path. I've become so interested in the dog that when I look up I realize that Albert and Delphine are slightly ahead of me, their feet raising puffs of dust that dissipate quickly into the still air.

We pause on the gentle slope, and Albert points out two distinctly different sites. "These are the dumps," he explains. "That one over there is older; it's been filled over with dirt. And the one here? That one's newer; it's still open."

I can tell the sites are old. My parents found all kinds of antique bottles in places like these. I look at Albert and say, "There might be treasures in this dump!"

They both laugh, and Albert's eyes sparkle as he replies, "I don't know, but I doubt it's anything anyone wants to keep; otherwise they wouldn't have thrown it away to begin with!"

We turn and walk toward the upper acreage. We are silent. As I look around I drink in this landscape, pulling it deep into me like it is a cool glass of water. Montana in August is incomparable. This is when grasses wear their yellow and gold gently, brought to light by the angle of the late afternoon sun, which has softened the hues that blazed so vividly only a month before. When put against the dark green of the pines or the sapphire blue of the sky, these colors become truly stunning. And the aroma: I close my eyes and draw in the scents, a complex mix of pine, grass, dust, and . . . cow pies? Startled by the acrid whiff, I open my eyes and look around, but I don't see anything that hints at bovine feces. But what I do see is that Delphine and Albert have somehow gotten quite a ways in front of me again, and I have to walk quickly to catch up. Once more I've gotten lost in my daydreams, a lifelong tendency.

"I've never seen the creek this dry," Albert says, as we approach the site for the summer home, which sits a couple hundred feet away. The only evidence that water had run here recently are the willows that grow sturdy and plentiful along this shallow wash. And yes, dotted among the willows are numerous cow pies, evidence that this land is being used for grazing. As I scan the landscape, something catches my eye: a tall shrub with broad leaves that looks out of place in the midst of this community of willows. I touch Delphine's shoulder and point; she follows the direction of my index finger. "That's a lilac bush," I say, not being able to keep the excitement out of my voice. It is the vestige of human existence, a clue.

She squints to see it clearer. "No, I don't think so," she answers. She turns to Albert, her voice soft, fragile. "Albert, do you remember your folks having a lilac bush up here?"

"No," Albert says, shaking his head. "I don't remember any lilac bush." He pauses. "There used to be something growing by the front door, but I don't think it was a lilac bush."

While he talks Delphine walks slowly to the shrub in question and soon I hear a small exclamation of gentle surprise. "My goodness, will you look at that? Vicki Charmain's right. It *is* a lilac bush." Delphine studies its branches, its leaves, the seedpods left from the previous blooming cycle.

"Hmm," Albert mutters, bewilderment tingeing his voice. "I don't remember one being up here, but here it is. It must have been pretty small when the house was here."

The foundation of Albert's grandparents' house isn't as elaborate or cleanly set as the lower house, whose concrete lines clearly delineated the shape of the home. In fact, this foundation looks more like a collection of rocks loosely piled on top of one another, which indicates to me it is significantly older than the family house down the road.

Delphine gently pushes the toe of her tennis shoe against a large, half-buried boulder. "This is where the corner of the house sat," she explains quietly. "This is what it sat on, what held it up." With that clue I can make out the faint outline of where the original cabin had existed. It had been much smaller, big enough for two people and perhaps a child or two. What is surprising is how close it is to the creek that trickles by the boulder, practically on top of it. I furrow my brows. Surely the creek wasn't in this location fifty years ago or more; it must have wandered closer over time, the way creeks do. But where the creek's original path had flowed is not clear; the willows have encroached so heavily on the home site that it is difficult to tell what it must have looked like before.

As if reading my mind, Albert says, "It wasn't nearly this overgrown." He gazes at the landscape for a long time. "In fact, I don't remember there being any willows at all. They've come in here since the house has been gone."

Albert and Delphine then turn toward each other, their heads close together, a self-contained unit, and walk through their memories. Then the feeling overwhelms me, an overpowering appreciation of this gift they have given me, a chance to see this place through their eyes, a chance to get to know them. From the beginning, when I met them in 1993, they've embraced me, sheltered me. They've asked to meet my husband, to let him know he is a member of this family. They made way for Ronni, James Allen, and me to sit with them at a funeral where we felt unrelated among the relatives but safe within their being. They offer me a certain sense of solace when I seem to need it the most.

Like here.

"Did your mom practice traditional spirituality?" I ask Albert as we begin our walk back to the home site.

"Yeah," he nods. "She'd get up real early in the morning and go out and do those things that she always did. I don't know what they were," he clarifies quickly, "because she didn't include us in those things. She raised us Catholic, but she was traditional."

Like many conversations, ours ends abruptly, because there is nothing more to say. And although I want to dig deeper, I respect Albert's pragmatic nature; some things are better left unquestioned because questions require answers, and sometimes there aren't any. But regardless of how pragmatic my own nature is, the questions of my family, my adoption, the what-ifs, never abate and continue to swirl in the restless currents of doubt.

I stop and watch the black lab weave and bounce its way among the three of us and then veer off to the side, following a scent that draws his attention. My gaze drifts once more to the landscape, across the grasslands, along the ribbon of river, returning to the boundary of pine behind us, and suddenly I felt such a sense of longing rise within me. Here, I believe, I can view the world undetected and whole, where people would not question my reason for doing so. This was my homeland; this is my homeland. And I cradle this gift, given so freely by Albert and Delphine, with a ferocity that takes me by surprise.

Adoption. There is my experience, and there is how I should feel. My experience is that when I was removed from my blood family, then my birthrights, my membership in a family and a community, and the sense of who I was in the world were also removed from me. Therefore, while I was growing up, the positive and negative aspects of my adoption became both the most obscured and most visible. How I should feel, brought about by cultural pressure from the society in which I was raised, is typically stated in these ways: "Everything happens for a reason" or "There's always two sides to adoption; you can't just look at the negative."

The spiritual reason for my adoption escapes me. I don't know why I was taken from a chaotic family filled with alcoholism and dismembered relationships and placed in a family filled with alcoholism and dismembered relationships. And despite Mom's efforts to protect me, I heard the murmurs of total strangers, who described Indians as lazy, dirty people who lived off the government. It was devastating to be a child alone and isolated in a world that saw little if any value in me as a human being because of the color of my skin. But it may well have been just as devastating to live here in this family. I have no idea how to weigh, judge, or give value to the choices made on my behalf. So the questions keep circling, and the answers are elusive, and the currents continue to rotate in on themselves.

Has this line of our family always struggled? Or was this a particular struggle of the past two generations, with our permanent placement outside of the family the result? When did our family get placed in such jeopardy? When we lost the horses? Was that the beginning of the end?

Regardless of what Albert said that first day I met him, about my luckiness to "get out," I have difficulty agreeing with him. As I look out on the landscape, I consider the people I came home to, watching their traditional practices like a third-string player on a first-string team. No, I don't feel lucky. I feel cheated, and I can't explain or defend the sadness, the emptiness, that engulfs me when I'm here or the wistfulness I feel when I'm gone. So I don't try to explain, and that topic remains silent between us. I imagine it is a wall that makes its presence known only to me.

I am brought back to the present by Albert's hand on my shoulder. "The other house," he says, pointing to the flattened area to the north, not far from where we stand, "used to sit over here, in this area. It was a one story, smaller than the first, but larger than Mom and Dad's."

I nod. My head is filled with half-recreated images of half-recreated selves, and I've stopped asking questions. The silence sways between us, and Delphine, as if reading the tension, asks, "Ready to go back?" Her gentle voice beckons me to agree, and I do so with a nod filled with exhaustion. She smiles and walks with me, saying, "I think they said they were going to look at photos, and I don't want it to be too late before we get home."

The interior of the trailer is large and filled with the familiar trappings of a modern life. The living room holds a dining hutch, a grandfather clock, and comfortable couches that I can see from where I lean against the kitchen counter. This is where we stand and talk about our experiences off the reservation. Linda asks me about my research with other American Indian transracial adoptees, and I begin telling the small group how difficult it has been for us to come home and the reasons for it. It is easy to keep the academic tone out of my voice, because I am really talking about me.

However, in the midst of my telling, Pete launches into a story of when he left the reservation to go work elsewhere. "I think they called it 'relocation,'" he explained, adding that when he came back, no one here welcomed him home. "It was really hard to come home." Even now, forty years later, his voice holds a distinct hint of anger, of hurt. "Because we left, and lived in the larger world, when we came back we were different. These people didn't necessarily see us as being family anymore, let alone part of the tribe." His voice rises in frustration, and I don't interrupt; I don't want to turn this exchange into an argument of "who lost out more." Because here, in this no-man's-land of nonbelonging, there are no winners.

But I want to say, at least you were here. You were part of your family; people who knew you as part of the family, as one of the tribe, watched you grow up; they had memories of you in school; they knew who you married. You also had memories of your family, your friends, your community. You, my dispossessed cousin, at least had a chair and a place card at the table. You lived and breathed and came of age in this family's memory, this community's memory, this tribe's memory, not somewhere far away. You lived here all these years, and then you left. No one put you in a car and drove you away before your memories could even solidify, before your community's memory of you could solidify.

What I do instead is tell a story, my story. "I tried to come home on many occasions, but I had no idea who my family was. No one would tell me that information. Until I was given a file. Only then did I have a family name." I told them the earliest time I tried to make contact was the summer after graduating with my bachelor's in anthropology in 1983. I wanted experience doing archaeological fieldwork. I knew the reservation's lands were getting "loved to death," as more and more people hiked its mountain trails and fished its rivers. On a whim, I contacted the president of Salish Kootenai College and offered to map cultural sites, not the sacred sites, I clarified, but sites of everyday human habitation, so the tribes could have record of them before the old people who remembered these sites, had stories of these sites, had passed on. He and several other people thought this was a great idea, and I was encouraged to meet with this person, call that person, introduce myself to others. With each contact I mentioned that my family was the Plants, that my mother (I didn't mention she was my birth mother) was Clara Victoria Plant. Did they know any Plants? No one indicated they were familiar with the names, but I kept providing them, hoping word would somehow get back to anyone in the family that I was looking for them. I was depending on the Moccasin Telegraph to do its magic.

In the meantime my project made its way through the labyrinth of people and departments until I finally was able to present to the tribal council.

And then I waited for a response.

But none came—not about my family, not about the project. Not long after that the chatter of the archaeological proposal became silent. There were no phone calls, no emails, no correspondence of any kind. I had no idea why it failed. Finally, I got ahold of a woman who explained, apologetically, that the tribal medicine man had been consulted. The project had been scrapped when he stated, "There will never be an archaeologist on this reservation." And that was it, kaput. My last-ditch effort to come home had failed. I never tried again.

Delphine and Albert exchange quiet whispers. I stop talking, thinking they have something to add to the conversation. Delphine looks at me and smiles. "Albert has a story about that," she said, her voice soft.

"Really? Tell me." I lean forward anxious to hear anything he has to say to fill in the blanks.

Albert smiles and shakes his head. "No, I'll wait until we go home."

"C'mon," I chide gently, thinking he is just being shy.

"No," he says more emphatically. "I'll wait."

An uncomfortable silence stretches until Linda motions us to the kitchen table, and we gather around notebooks of photos. Gently opening the binding, I scan the sepia and black-and-white prints that document the lives and places of this family. I study the photos of the homestead, surprised at how different they are from the images I had created in my mind just hours before. These structures dated back to the turn of the twentieth century, if not before, and their rustic appearance reminds me that someone's sweat and labor built these cabins. A photo taken in the adjacent yard depicts a young Vic, beautiful and smiling for the camera. Ronni, probably seven months old, stands between Vic's legs, her hands overhead, clasping Vic's fingers in a tight grip.

As I flip through the pages I search these faces for familiar aspects of myself: the almond-shaped eyes, the smile, the round cheeks, the abruptly straight hair. There are faces that look back at me that mirror my sons' faces: their cheekbones, their jawline, their mouths. While my gaze and fingers follow the familiar contours of genetic connection, I become aware that this was a photographic story of a family, my family, and I am absent, even in time overlaps. It is as if destiny had already moved me toward something else.

These people who sit with me at the table are my guides on this journey of self and my relationship to others, who at one time were not others. But like any uncomfortable history, there are land mines. Unfortunately, the land mines are never apparent until stepped on, a badly chosen word, a perceived snub, too much pressure on a fragile relationship. After the blast the devastation left on the psyche is profound, and while one sits in a stupor questioning exactly what happened, the blood rains down on those who've witnessed the wreckage.

It is dark by the time we reach Albert and Delphine's house, and I feel antsy to get back to my sister's house—my night vision has deteriorated in recent years, and the highway, even on good days, is dangerous.

"What was the story you wanted to tell me?" I prod Albert after sitting for a few moments in one of the living-room chairs. To be honest, I'd thought of nothing else in the interim between leaving Pete and Linda's and coming to this home. My mind continues to return to his statement, turning the possibilities over like a worry stone.

He shifts uncomfortably in his chair, and when he faces me he looks sheepish. "I don't really want to say," he begins. The smile is there, but it is apologetic, guarded. His eyes watch me watch him. "I'm afraid that you won't think as highly of me afterward as you do now."

A jolt of adrenaline rushes along my chest, but I force what I hope is a genuine smile, an encouraging smile. "Albert, there is nothing that is ever going to change my opinion of you. What is it?"

He sighs and shifts again, clearing his throat, his voice somber. The sudden shift in mood scares me.

"Well, Johnny came to me one day. He told me about this archaeologist who wanted to record sites. We'd had so many bad experiences with people, with scientists taking knowledge and leaving us with nothing." He pauses and looks directly at me. "I was the one who said there would be no archaeologists on this reservation. I was the one who put a stop to that project. Of course," he adds, looking directly at me, with pain in his eyes, "I had no idea it was you."

My eyes cloud with unshed tears, and the familiar frustration stirs. How could he have known? Of all the times I'd been here, stating my name, who I was, who I had been, no one told him I'd been looking for the family. Just as in the summer of 1983, when I tried to offer the only thing I had to offer, my knowledge, no one in the family even knew I existed. My adoption had been closed, the records sealed, like every other adoption in the 1950s and 1960s. My amended birth certificate and my sealed records that could be opened only by a court order effectively erased my existence from this family, from this tribe. The fact that I had no access to my "before" life had forced a separation between him and me. I hate this iron wedge of policy!

My throat is tight with anger, with sadness, with bitter regret. But I smile at him across the space of the room, because none of it is his fault. I smile and shake my head and ask as gently as I can, "How could you have known it was me?"

14

Integration

Fort Collins, Colorado, Fall 2008.

In autumn of 2004 I entered graduate school, forty-five years old and classified as a nontraditional student seeking a master's degree in cultural anthropology. I'd visited Dr. Pickering, the department chair, the previous spring, hours after Dr. Williams had assured me that if I stick with her, "we'll get you proud of being Indian." I was finally exhausted of being "fixed" by therapists. I began to doubt that the problem lay with me, but I didn't really know with whom it lay.

"What is it you want to know about adoption?" Dr. Pickering asked. Was she interested? Confused? Just doing her due diligence, separating the wheat from the chaff in terms of assessing the seriousness of me as a master's candidate?

After providing an explanation, I summed it up, saying, "I want to know who feels they have a right to tell me what I am or what I am not, and why my statements of who I am are dismissed."

She smiled. "Sounds fascinating. Apply."

As I stood to say good-bye, Dr. Pickering lowered her voice and with a wink gave me an important piece of advice. "The key word you'll want to use is *identity*."

I had a place to start.

The problem is I wasn't expecting the swirl of confusion that the word produces within me, and I try various mechanisms to calm it down. Tonight I pour a glass of pinot grigio and reflect.

Two years ago I'd spent a week with my sister Ronni Marie, who'd been placed with a separate white family. We'd gone to the Oregon coast to reconnect. That's when I got the full story from her about the family she grew up in.

We'd built a campfire one evening, down on the beach, and roasted hot dogs. She popped a beer, and I drank my pinot grigio out of a plastic cup, and we talked, telling stories and sharing laughter: funny things, ridiculous things, like when she was young Ronni thought if you stood by a fire, your legs would get tan. Understandable, but wrong. In a moment of quiet, between, I leaned my head against a piece of driftwood and watched the stars shine against a dark, blue velvet night.

"When did you live in Great Falls?" I asked. "Were you there in 1973?"

Ronni nodded, taking a pull from her beer.

"That's when I was there," I continued. "I went to North Junior High. Which school did you go to?"

"I went to East."

The pinot danced along my tongue. "I almost went to East Junior High."

Ronni's eyes grew round, and a smile beamed across her face. "Really? My gosh, we could have met there!"

I laughed. "Maybe! Mom and Dad separated when we lived there." Well, that was the first time they'd separated. The second time, when I was a senior in high school, Dad left, packing up and moving to North Dakota. Mom filed for divorce soon afterward. But I didn't mention that

7. Susan and Ronni Marie. Photo by Rick Harness. Courtesy of the author.

to Ronni. Instead, I continued, "One day she just picked me up from school. I just had the clothes I wore plus a few things she'd grabbed for me. We stayed at a motel for a couple of nights, and I remember it snowed. My jacket was meant for breezy days, not snowy ones, and we weren't expecting snow in April. We went to Woolworths and bought me a couple of cheap outfits because she wasn't going back to the house. She drove me to school every day. She found us an apartment in a complex just a few blocks from East Junior High, but I didn't want to switch schools. But if we had stayed in that apartment I would have had to go. I doubt we would have met though. You would have been going to the high school at that point."

Ronni swigged a gulp of beer and stared into the fire. "That's wild. Why did she move you out?"

"Dad's drinking was putting us in jeopardy. It was looking like he was going to lose his job, and she didn't want to be around to watch the explosion when that happened. He was pretty unstable. I think she just wanted to ensure my safety, and she certainly didn't want to put hers on the line either." I lifted the glass and studied the stars through the filtered lens of wine. "What was your mom like?" I asked. In the three years prior to our estrangement, she'd never talked about the woman who raised her.

Ronni weighed my question as she looked at me, her eyes wide. She shook her head and finished her fourth beer and looked at me again. She chuckled, but it was devoid of amusement. "Not like that."

She reached for the fifth beer and popped the top. "Mom would do things. Mean things. Like when I was in grade school, I came home from school one day and changed out of my school clothes into my play clothes. I must have left my dress lying on the floor instead of picking it up and hanging it in my closet." She pulls the bottle to her lips and drinks. "Mom asked me a little bit later, 'Where's your dress from school?' And that's when I started getting nervous. I told her I'd get it, so I went downstairs, and I looked on the floor. It wasn't where I remembered it being. I looked all over the room, under my bed. I tore my bedclothes apart, thinking it got mixed up in the sheets or blankets. I didn't find it. I went to the laundry room and looked through the dirty clothes, even though I didn't remember putting it there. I went through all the clothes in my closet, thinking I must have hung it up, then I looked on the floor again thinking it must have fallen. That dress was nowhere, but I had to find it, because I knew if I didn't I would be sorry."

She paused and took another long gulp and stared into the white heat of the fire. "Mom told me then to go take a bath and get ready for bed. And just when I'm finally relaxing a little, she bursts into the bathroom and wraps her hand around my hair and pulls me out of the tub by my hair and marches me, naked, down the hall and down the stairs, all the time pulling me by my hair, and I'm crying because I don't know what I've done. And it hurts and I'm crying, and she takes me into the bedroom next to mine where the roll-away bed is, reaches in between the mattress folds and pulls out the dress. And I don't know how it got there. She yells at me, telling me that she thinks I'm retarded because I can't remember where I put things, and she throws it on the ground and tells me to put it away."

Ronni downed her fifth beer, and I watched a lone tear course down her cheek, which she wiped quickly away with the back of her hand.

"How did it get there?" I asked, totally perplexed.

Ronni opened her sixth beer, saying, "She put it there. To teach me a lesson."

"How old were you?"

"Seven."

And she drank.

I decide to call my brother, James Allen, the youngest of us three to be removed from the home. Leroy, his roommate, answers. Leroy and his partner, Toby, live with James Allen to help him with his disabilities. "Hi sweetie," Leroy says, his voice honey and sincere. "John's not here; he's over at Mom's house for now."

I am always a bit startled when Leroy or his partner, Toby, refers to James Allen as John. Like what happened with Ronni and me, his adoptive parents renamed him; James Allen had become John Roy. Names signify ownership, signify power. *Whoever has the power gets to name*, I recall from one of my anthropology classes. By replacing a child's original name, adoptive parents can pretend the child's past is erasable, if not absent altogether. That previous life can be forgotten and reframed; the child can be "theirs" instead of "someone else's."

A few months ago Ronni told me that when she'd been adopted, at age six, her adoptive mother had given her a choice of three names: Mary, Rita, or Christine. She chose Rita because she just liked the sound of it. "But I always thought it was a strange that of the three names that I was allowed to choose from, none of them was my birth name, Ronni Marie." She smiled, but it was a wistful smile filled with confusion.

Giving the adoptee a new name symbolizes not only a new beginning but a clean slate. But there's an assumption that somehow the child's previous life was "dirty." And this is where my confusion comes in. Why can't the child's life be just the experience of living instead of pretending it never happened at all?

"We're in the process of buying a house," Leroy explains, bringing me back to the present. "We want to make sure it fits John as well as my mom, who is sixty-three. But she's a very old sixty-three," he adds confidentially.

Leroy's mom battles intense schizophrenia; an episode can last three years. Five years ago he almost lost her because he was not able to get her to go in for psychiatric help. People, even family members, can no longer force others into mental-health facilities. "And God knows, they certainly are in no shape to make rational decisions!" he says with a flair for the dramatic. So he watched as she shrank to seventy-five pounds and hid herself away in fearful paranoia. I talk about my mom being bipolar; the similarities are striking.

The conversation turns to James Allen. "I remember James Allen when he was little," I tell Leroy. "A few years ago Mom told me that when they were thinking of adopting one of my siblings, they went to his house. She described a water pump being out front." Little by little that memory began to be filled in, so in a previous phone call I'd asked James Allen whether he'd lived in the country, in a brown two-story log house, with a hand-pumped water spigot in the front. "How did you know that?" he asked, confused. I told him that I remembered visiting him, but I didn't tell him why. "We'd held our hands under the stream of water, and Mom said that it was as if you and I had never been apart." The thing was I didn't just remember the scene, I remembered the *feeling*; I remembered that I liked him. We didn't adopt him; his foster family didn't want to give him up, so we went separate directions, and I forgot his existence.

"You know," Leroy says, "Since you've come into John's life, there's been a real difference. He sees you as the person who got out, as the person who has succeeded. And he wants to be a better person because of that."

I want to say thank you, that being that person is such an honor, but I feel pressure on my chest. What if people find out I didn't really "get out," that my success is a sham, that I'm as fragile as a laser-cut Easter egg?

Our conversation becomes quiet, and what I hope to be a healing exchange, isn't. We say our good-byes, and when I hang up I pour myself another half glass of wine, and I call James Allen at Leroy's mother's house.

In 2005, when I began my MA research in earnest, I had to find people to participate, specifically American Indian children who'd been transracially adopted by white families. But finding us is almost impossible: we inhabit every facet of this society and therefore blend in so well, culturally, not physically. I worked from the assumption that many of us had attempted to return to the Native community. I sent recruitment postings, attaching introductory letters, to the institutions I thought adoptees might contact: American Indian centers within universities, urban Indian centers, and tribal enrollment offices, among others. The task was challenging for very specific reasons: (1) although there are hundreds of thousands of us from the 1940s, 1950s, and 1960s, we are a very small percentage of the overall adoptee population; (2) I had to convince people they could trust me: I wouldn't have an agenda, I would let their voices speak, and I wouldn't use their experience in a negative way; (3) I didn't want to be the person to bring things up if they weren't ready; therefore, I urged them to assess how much they'd explored their adoption issues on their own; and (4) participants felt they had something to add to a silent conversation. After hearing these stipulations, a lot of adoptees said they weren't interested in participating. It was several months before I located my first participant and even longer before I was able to begin the conversation. The main reason it took so long was because, initially, I was hesitant to say I was an adoptee; I wanted to do the research as a scientific observer. But I wasn't just an observer. I was an adoptee, and because of that I could understand the challenges that could exist in this situation. So after many turndowns, I rewrote the introduction of the project, adding that the reason I was interested in the topic was because I was an American Indian transracial adoptee. From that point on, it became easier to recruit participants, as illustrated by one woman who responded, "Then you know what it's like!"

I knew what my experience was like; I wanted to understand theirs.

I constructed the research into three parts, each to build on the previous data. I was specifically interested in (1) how people classified themselves and others, ethnically; (2) adoptees' stories about their placement into the white culture; and (3) how many American Indian transracial adoptees had similar or different experiences. First, I gave a word-list exercise to forty-five people, divided into three groups: white, American Indians, and American Indian transracial adoptees. I asked each group what five words they would use to describe each of the two ethnic groups: white and American Indians. Taken together, these words framed and defined ethnic boundaries, revealing stereotypes of who "we" and "they" are. The next piece of information I was interested in was how adoptees described their lives. I conducted unstructured interviews with nine adoptees and asked them to tell me everything they felt was important for me to know about their experiences. Each interview lasted several hours, and data was collected over six months. The third, and final, aspect of the research consisted of a structured telephone survey to see how salient the information I'd collected was among twenty-five adoptees.

Data from the word list found that some of the words American Indians used to describe themselves were *proud, cultural, spiritual, family-oriented,* and *humorous,* while they described Euro-Americans as *materialistic, privileged, greedy,* and *ambitious.* The words whites used to describe themselves were *dominant, majority, privileged, greedy,* and

8. *From left to right*: Rick, James Allen, and Susan. Photo by Rick Harness. Courtesy of the author.

educated, while describing American Indians as *poor, proud, spiritual, oppressed*, and *struggling*. Although few had cultural ties to the American Indian community, Native adoptees tended to side with American Indians, who they described as *poor, beautiful, proud, spiritual*, and *humorous*, while describing Euro-Americans as *rude, selfish, fearful*, and *greedy*. That last description summed up our experiences in the white world.

I dial Leroy's mom's number and let it ring.

The second time I met James Allen was at Vic's funeral, in March. Ronni introduced us at the luggage carousel, where I went to retrieve my bags after landing. He was a tall, lanky man, with an angular face and jet-black hair that was gelled back. James Allen stood with his hands shoved deep in the pockets of his jeans, wearing a denim jacket with a sheepskin lining. His face had a half smile, which said meeting me wasn't a big deal. But when I hugged him I could feel his hands shaking through my coat, and I knew otherwise. For quite some time my aunt Delphine had been praying for this meeting of Ronni, James Allen, and me, asking her Catholic Christ to bring us back together. Now, with Vic gone, we were all we had left.

Of all the children in Vic's family, James Allen suffered the most. Though nothing was ever said, he'd been affected by Vic's drinking, showing telltale signs of fetal alcohol syndrome. His dyslexia didn't allow him to read, so I didn't write him letters, knowing someone else would have to read them. He escaped the abyss of full-blown AIDS a couple of decades ago by a doctor who gave him the cocktail drugs. He was one of the first one hundred people to be given the drugs. So now he's just HIV-positive—well, HIV-positive with a chronic smoker's cough and memory issues, thanks to the other cocktails of drugs he administered to himself in his party days.

At Vic's wake he tried to walk with Ronni as she mingled, following her from person to person, but her frustration at telling him the same information over and over got to her, and she brought him over to me; her command, unstated—it was my turn. So James Allen and I walked among the myriad of strangers, me looking for similarities, him looking for anyone familiar.

"Who is that?" he asked, pointing to one of our uncles. "That's Albert," I explained. "He's Vicki's youngest brother."

"Oh, I think I met Albert before," James Allen said as he searched what was left of his neurons, but to no avail; they failed him once more. "Who's that?" he asked more and more often, and each time I explained as if I'd known these people forever and not just for the funeral. Ten minutes later we'd begun our second lap around the room when he pointed to Albert and asked, "Who's that? Have I met him before?" And I started all over again.

When I've thought about James Allen, I take a tally and shake my head in wonder. *As if he doesn't have enough strikes against him from the perspective of middle-class America: being Indian, dyslexic, adopted, and HIV-positive, he's also gay.* But he's a fighter.

"Hello?"

His voice always makes me smile. James Allen and I talk on the phone about once a month, just daily stuff. Occasionally, he'll open up about the abuse he suffered at the hands of his foster parents, who didn't want to give him up. But mostly it's just stuff. Tonight, however, because of my dark mood, I find myself talking about death, how it can happen regardless of the things you put in place to hold it at bay. "My thoughts of death became different," I tell him, "when my husband's grandmother, a wonderful early seventyish person, sneaked out of the nursing home one morning with a gentleman friend to get some tea at a nearby coffee shop. She stepped off the curb, fell and broke her hip, and died three days after her operation. It's bizarre. All she wanted to do is have tea with a gentleman!"

But there is no insurance against it, no foreknowledge, no way to keep what's going to happen from happening. God love the old dame who thought escaping from the nursing home with her boyfriend would be a brief respite from the purgatory of aging.

I traveled a lot as I collected the nine adoptees' life experiences. I flew to meet them in their home states, and I met one at the Denver International Airport as she waited between flights. I talked with them over the phone, at powwows, on my vacation, or on their vacation—one happened to be passing through Colorado and stopped by our house. I talked with them whenever and however I could arrange it. And what a gift each of them gave me!

When I was coming of age in Montana, I'd met several adoptees. Only one, the friend and tentmate from Glacier National Park, ever let me in for a peek at her experience. The others didn't want to talk about their adoption, and now I could understand why. Our lives had been private for so long, and we were so busy trying to fit in that we didn't want anybody reminding us how much we didn't.

To be able to not only talk with other adoptees but to have them talk so intimately and with such willingness about their experiences was such a beautiful and valued gift. Stories, there were so many stories, of shame, of heartbreak, of pragmatism, of survival, and of resistance. Many of the stories pivoted around the issue of tribal enrollment. The ones who weren't enrolled told me they were placed before the birth parent could enroll them. They were a product of a secret affair, and the birth parent felt the child would fare better away from the reservation and could pass as white; or the Bureau of Indian Affairs was successfully able to get adoptive parents to sign away the child's American Indian birthrights, thus revoking the adoptee's tribal membership.

If they were seeking enrollment, they sought specific benefits, rights brought about by binding treaties with the U.S. government: access to tuition-free or tuition-reduced college programs, to health care, to an inexpensive residence through tribal housing. One woman wanted to adopt a Native child, giving him or her the same benefits she'd received through her own placement, and felt she had a good possibility through the Indian Child Welfare Act of 1978, or ICWA.

ICWA was enacted to stop the high number of Native children being adopted by non-Native families throughout the 1950s, 1960s, and early 1970s. The act supported and built on the argument that David Fanshel made in his book *Far from the Reservation*: the decision about Indian child welfare should ultimately rest with the Indian people. And Indian people didn't want their children lost to the colonizing society. Therefore, before allowing a child to be placed into a non-Native home, ICWA requires that serious attempts must be made to keep the child in a Native community, with a member of the child's family, a member of their tribe, or a member of a federally recognized tribe, respectively. If no one is able to take that child within these three placement attempts, only then can the child be adopted by a non-Native family.

In his 1974 address to the Subcommittee on Indian Affairs, William Byler, the executive director of the Association of Indian Affairs, estimated that by 1972 nearly a third of American Indian children had been placed with non-Native families. Such high removal rates have had a devastating impact on a group of people who have been marginalized so effectively, socially, culturally, and politically. Therefore, not only has ICWA been successful in preventing large numbers of American Indian children from disappearing into the dominant culture, but it has prevented American Indians and their culture from being entirely subsumed into a colonizing society.

But that's the larger picture. On a more individual level, as adoptees who grew up prior to that piece of legislation, we weren't effectively moored to any ethnic identity, and as a result, we experienced racism, both from whites and from American Indians. One woman told a story of running away from her adoptive family to her birth family. She became uncomfortably aware of her aunt's disgust when she knocked on her aunt's bedroom door before entering. "You can tell you're white, because Indians don't knock on doors!" And there was the flagrant laughter that followed that made her cringe even more. Another woman talked about the harassment she and her adopted American Indian sister received from other kids in her southern state. "They'd set fire to our hair, put gum in our hair, pull guns on us. They said we didn't deserve to be around white people, that we needed to go back to the reservation where we belonged." One man's adoptive mother used a nearby tribal community to teach him to be ashamed of his heritage. "She'd drive me out to the reservation, and back then it was dilapidated houses and fishnets and all that. She'd grab me and pull me out of the car by my hair, by the back of my neck, and she'd say, 'You want to go live in that house? After coming from my big beautiful house? Who wants to live there?' It was a punishment to her: 'Oh, look at the Indians.'"

Another adoptee described American Indians as a "nice little backdrop" to the Thanksgiving story. Another one felt like she was a tourist rather than a participant when she attended powwows. Yet another felt she was never chosen to be the angel in the Christmas Eve pageant because angels didn't look like we did, with our dark hair and brown skin. And the expectations, even among the people we married! One woman recalled, "When I was married to my non-Indian husband, everything was fine, as long as I didn't act Indian."

Painful anger seared the edges of adoptees' souls and was made visible in the stories they told me, the stories that were carefully hidden, guarded until someone asked. Until I asked. I asked not because I was curious but because I thought it was important that we talk about what it felt like to be American Indian in a white society. And it was important for child-placement policy makers who made, and will make, these arrangements to hear us.

I am still restless after my telephone call with James Allen, and the feeling of unease slides through my soul. I don't want to feel alone. Evelyn. I'll call Evelyn.

Evelyn Stevenson, a lawyer for the Confederated Salish Kootenai Tribes, was one of the first people to respond to my request for adoptee participants in relation to my study. "I think I can help you," she said. She not only helped but provided historical information as well; it turns out that she was among a handful of people who worked on the initial language of what would become ICWA. I called her a few weeks after our first conversation to ask her how adoption placement affected our tribes, specifically, how many children prior to 1978 had been placed into non-Native homes?

"Oh, we have no idea," she said.

"You mean you don't know?" I asked.

"We didn't think of what was happening until sometime in the early 1960s, when we realized children were pouring from the reservation. That's when we started counting." Evelyn didn't have the numbers off the top of her head, and I realized it probably wasn't important. What was important was that the number was significant enough for people to take notice.

"I was wondering when I was going to hear from you," she chides gently. In the intervening years Evelyn has become my friend and confidante, especially where adoption, namely mine, is concerned.

I put a smile in my voice and assure her that I've finally come up for air. I don't tell her why I've been in hiding. I don't tell her that there is a tremor in my soul caused by intensive self-reflection, leaving me feeling isolated, stranded, alone, and vulnerable. My little voice tells me the landslide won't be far behind. After a few moments, I think, *This is a bad idea.* I sense emotions, long dormant, stirring now, and I don't know why they've started, where they've come from. A look? A sentence? Thin air?

"Are you writing?" she asks.

"I am," I reply, my voice tight, cheerfulness pushed out by sheer force.

My writing has set this emotional landslide into motion. You see, I'm writing an essay (that will eventually become a chapter) about Evelyn and the surprise party her daughter and son gave her at Kwatuqnuk Lodge on Flathead Lake to honor her. I'd flown in just to let her know I cared and supported the role she played in so many lives. By the time festivities got under way, nearly three hundred people had joined. Her ex-husband got up and exchanged funny stories about her past experiences, their past experiences, leaving us with reflections of her tireless work to establish legal foundations for the tribe she loved and was part of. Her daughter relayed a story about Evelyn's health, telling all of us in attendance that several years ago Evelyn nearly died when a brush fire turned on her and she inhaled the flames, searing her lungs. From that point forward she was forced to have oxygen nearby, and as she grew older it was required 24-7 to live. One by one people stepped to the podium and shared their stories of the woman who helped so many, including a young mother of three. She'd turned to Evelyn for help when her money ran out, and she was in fear of being evicted from her apartment and losing her kids to social services in the process. Tearfully, she revealed how Evelyn gave her money and found the resources needed to ensure the young mother's children wouldn't be placed in foster care while she found a way to get back on her feet.

Then there was a pause. Everyone, it seemed, had told their stories. Except for me.

Heart pounding, I got up from the table in the back of the room and made my way forward. In the meantime her son began wrapping up the party, but upon seeing me smiled and stepped back, allowing me to speak. I stepped up to the podium and put my mouth near the microphone, wincing as I heard my voice broadcast through the large room. "First off, I am so thankful to have been invited to this gathering. Unlike all of you, I've known Evelyn for only six years. I know how hard she has worked in the area of child protection, having been one of the original voices in crafting the Indian Child Welfare Act. She has helped people who've been adopted find their families, their homes, themselves, in the process. I am one of those adoptees. My name is Susan Harness, and when I asked for information with regard to my research on adoptees, she gave it willingly. She's helped me find a way to open my records, through the signature of a tribal judge. She helped me establish who I am in this world of in-betweens. Evelyn, on behalf of adoptees like me, we thank you for the work that you have done. I am so honored to know you."

She gave me permission to be who I always thought I was. At that point I felt as if I was a salmon swimming upstream against a strong, strong current. She helped me to find a pool where the current disappeared. There I only had to worry about swimming.

The most difficult part of my research regarding the lived experiences of American Indian transracial adoptees was conducting the telephone interviews. Many of the questions I asked were painful and intrusive, inquiring about feelings of isolation, racial discrimination from within and outside of the adoptive family, and physical and sexual abuse. Knowing this, I was careful to warn people who were hesitantly considering participating.

"The survey will take about an hour," I explained. "We'll talk about your perceptions; we'll talk about race. We'll talk about your experiences growing up, and we'll talk about abuse. These questions will make you feel uncomfortable, especially if you haven't thought about these topics in depth or know how you stand on these issues. If you haven't intensely explored your feelings about being an American Indian transracial adoptee, you may want to reconsider participating." Several people withdrew at that moment.

I asked adoptees to choose from a list of positive and negative descriptions of American Indians, which they'd heard from people in the community in which they lived. Twenty-one adoptees heard *drunken*, sixteen heard *government-subsidized*, thirteen heard other terms (such as *slutty*, *good-for-nothing*, and *lazy*), thirteen heard *thieving*, and eleven heard *dirty* from the list of negative descriptions. Fewer adoptees heard positive descriptions and far less often. Of the twenty-five adoptees ten heard *proud*, six heard *quiet*, and six heard other terms (such as *craftsmen* and *artistic*). Sadly, only four adoptees said that *intelligent* was associated with American Indians.

This last piece of information churned my anger. We'd been placed into a society that prided itself on education and intelligence. We'd been "chosen" by our parents to be part of this society, yet *intelligence* wasn't a term used to describe the ethnic group we came from, wasn't a term used to describe us. I couldn't help but think back to the Economics Department adviser suggesting a better fit for me would have been vo-tech and not a university, all without looking at my transcript. Although all the adoptees in my study said they heard negative descriptions of American Indians from people in the communities in which they lived, several indicated they hadn't heard any positive descriptions.

We were marginalized to the furthest edges of society, pushed toward the Native boundary. But according to many of us, we were comfortable there. We were cloaked, almost invisible in our ability to finally blend in.

And as long as we didn't speak and let our white words sneak out, no one was the wiser. As one adoptee said, "Us Native American adoptees really long to belong, and if there was somebody to start something or do something, I would be all for that reconnection, not necessarily with family but with the culture—if the tribes were to say, 'Let us tell you our stories and our traditions,' so I can get the password to belonging. I don't think I've gotten it, whatever it is. I want to feel [like I] belong . . . because I don't know, when I go to powwows, I don't know that the umbilical cord should go in the turtle purse or the meaning of the fan. They think when they look at me, I should know that stuff, but I don't. And when I open my mouth, they're like, 'Oh, you're one of those!'" "One of those" is an American Indian trying to pass as white, thereby betraying our race.

The toughest questions had to do with abuse within the adoptive home. Before I began asking about abuse, I assured participants they could refuse at any time to answer any questions. I felt it was only fair, considering this would be digging around in the most painful part of their spirit. I also reminded them that their answers would inform policy makers, child-placement officials, and adoptive parents that these issues indeed exist, and we would take this conversation into the public arena. This was the area where trust was paramount.

Of the twenty-five adoptees who took part in the structured telephone survey, eleven experienced emotional abuse, nine experienced verbal abuse, eight experienced physical abuse, and seven experienced sexual abuse. I winced as I listened to those seven adoptees say yes to each item, their voices growing softer, until the last answer was given with just a whisper. One of the women on my committee, a Native lawyer who specialized in child sexual-abuse cases, was stunned at the prevalence of sexual abuse. "Why doesn't anyone know this?" she asked, staring at the screen.

We'd been so ashamed of who we were as people for so long, there was no way we were going to talk about being sexually abused. For our whole lives so many of us were made to believe that we were wrong to be angry, resentful, bitter at our placement in a world that despised us or within families who didn't do anything to protect us. We were made to feel apologetic when we attempted to claim our Indian heritage and were denied access, accused of being defectors and turncoats, as if we had any choice in the matter, as if the consequences of colonization didn't affect us but only our blood family.

Edwin Mellen Press published my research in 2009 under the title *Mixing Cultural Identities through Transracial Adoption: Outcomes of the Indian Adoption Project (1958–1967)*. So much of the previous research blamed the adoptee for their psychological paralysis. *They* were having an identity crisis. But that crisis, I argued, had to come from somewhere; it didn't just appear out of nowhere. I held both Native and white societies accountable for imposing identities on us that made us unable to integrate into either group. As a result, that "crisis" is really anger and confusion at our nonacceptance. But now? We were coming into our own and people were going to have to listen to us.

Evelyn's voice over the phone penetrates my thoughts, bringing me back to the present. "That was sure a nice speech," Evelyn says, her voice quiet, careful, like she's running a brush through my hair.

I swallow a couple of times, but I don't know where to go with the conversation. I want to cry. I want to lie down in the fetal position with my hands over my head and cry, because coming to grips with my history, our history, has taken its toll on my spirit. But I can't end this conversation now, where it is. There is more. "That was one of the hardest things I've ever done," I admit to my long-distance friend. "Telling three hundred people that I was one of the kids taken away."

"Really?" she asks, her voice gently confused. "Why is that?"

My throat closes again, and I fight for control. "I know my removal was out of my control, that it was something that happened *to* me, but I still feel a certain sense of shame."

"Why shame?" her voice sounds entirely perplexed.

"I don't know. Maybe it was the shame of being unlovable. Sometimes

I think if we'd been more lovable Vic would have tried hard to keep us. But she didn't. Or maybe she couldn't. I don't know." I tell her I have to go, and after I hang up I am entirely honest with myself. The shame comes because living in white America hurts. Being rejected by my tribal people hurts more. There is an anger that builds from the rejection, and that anger turns inward because where else can it go? I can't fight the masses; I'll lose even more.

I'm tired. I'm tired of carrying this burden of nonbelonging. It's not really mine to carry. It belongs to my birth family, who opted not to do what was required to keep us out of the system. It belongs to child-placement policy experts, who think removing children and erasing their past by erasing information about their birth family and then placing them in the midst of a society whose history promotes a barely veiled hatred toward indigenous people will produce healthy, happy, and stable children. It belongs to my adoptive father, who didn't question the racism that surrounded me and didn't protect me when it entered our home in his alcohol-driven tirades. It belongs to my tribe, who refused to offer "welcome home ceremonies" because, as one tribal member put it, we'll muddy the waters by bringing our white wives or white husbands to the reservation. It belongs to American Indians who see us as people seeking our birthright because we are trying to get something for nothing: the free health care, cheap housing, a tribal job. We are not interested in those things. We are interested in knowing who we are, where we come from, and who we are related to. We want to learn and know our culture. We want the legitimacy that these same Indian people have been given. But that burden should be heavily carried by white America, who can now pretend that, because we are being raised in a white, middle-class family, everything will be okay. For many white Americans, history and its consequences have no meaning. But right now I alone am carrying this burden and the emotional landslide has begun.

It sounds bad, but maybe I need things to fall entirely apart to rebuild a stronger me.

15

Custer's Ghost

Lodge Grass, Montana, October 2011.

There's no comparison to autumn in Montana. I've forgotten this until I look out across the lowland, where the Little Bighorn River flows between the bluffs, through the town of Lodge Grass, then stumbles over the rocks that scatter throughout its now-shallow bed. The previous May, flooding had severed the town from the rest of the world, as river water spilled across Interstate 90 as well as the two remaining highways in and out of town. Now thirsty cottonwoods crowd along the river's edge, their colors bursting in the midafternoon sun: yellows, oranges, golds, and rusts. On the opposite bluff sits some sort of fenced compound, and beyond that lies the vast emptiness that is the Crow Indian Reservation.

I'm parked on a makeshift pullout at the Lodge Grass exit. It is October 4 and, as much as I've looked forward to this trip, a feeling of uneasiness surrounds me. My plans have been liquid, changing shape from day to day, for no other reason than my inability to make a concrete decision. The only things I know are I want to get to Missoula, present at a writer's conference, and talk with my brother, Vernon. But our research center needs Montana schools to participate in a survey that examines youths' attitudes, beliefs, and behaviors about substance use. So here I am, on the edge of the asphalt, debating whether or not to make a cold-call appointment to the high school.

"I love cold calls," a professional salesman had told me the month before, when I explained my hesitation to him. "What do you have to lose? Nothing. I'll take a cold call any day. Those are easy."

I inhale a deep breath and close my eyes, thinking of what I would say. Then I dial the school's number.

The voice that answers is young, maybe a student. "Lodge Grass School."

"Hi," I say and introduce myself. "I'm here in Lodge Grass and would like to talk with someone in your counseling department about a national survey we're offering to schools with students in seventh through twelfth grade."

"I'll transfer you to our counselor, Mrs. Cummings."

Two clicks later the call is answered by a bright voice. "Counseling."

I explain the reason for my visit and ask if she has time for me. I could be at the school within a few minutes. "Sure, that would be fine. Do you know how to get here?"

The directions are abbreviated. So abbreviated, in fact, that at the railroad tracks I lose my imagined route, the one I had constructed in my head. That's also where I lose the route in real life. After crossing the railroad tracks I find myself at a T, facing Main Street, and I have no idea whether to turn right or left. The population of this town along the river is a little over five hundred people. How is it possible that I've gotten lost in Lodge Grass?

I turn right and within a few blocks find myself in a part of the town that had been ravaged by the flood. Trailers, bashed and battered, are scattered along the roadside; some still look inhabited. Broken cars litter empty spaces, accidental yards that hold rusting metal and disassembled parts, left where the ravaging waters dropped them. A group of young people, perhaps high schoolers, eye my little white Ford Focus with its Colorado plates with distrusting interest, glancing up from their conversations to stare. As usual, I am an outsider.

I pull a U-turn and drive up and down each street, looking for a name even similar to the road Mrs. Cummings told me. Nothing. I return to Main Street, where I turn the opposite direction and drive slowly past a park with a playground, wooden homes that sit back from a tree-lined street, the Indian Health Service building, and an early childhood learning center. But then the town ends, and I am suddenly out of its boundaries. Confused, I look around to situate myself and *whoosh!* two cars pass me on the left, far over the posted speed limit of fifty miles per hour. "Good God," I mutter, pulling over at the three-mile mark. "No wonder there's so many accidents!"

I sit for a few moments and gather my thoughts. This was too far out of town for a school. Kids walk to school. I think back and figure the compound I'd seen on the bluff must have been the school; I just needed to find the road that led up to it. I make another U-turn and within moments sirens whine and a police SUV screams past me, going in the opposite direction, its lights a migraine display. My stomach fills with dread.

I am uneasy, and the feeling fills my ribcage, even as I locate the road and wind my way up to the high school parking lot. After pulling into a space far away from dented student cars, I gather my materials and begin a leisurely walk up the concrete path. The space between my car and the school entrance is extensive and empty. A brown-skinned man wearing a blue T-shirt and jeans steps out from behind one of the opened doors, waving his hand toward his chest. I believe he is just indicating the entrance; however, his hand moves more quickly, its motion jagged. I cock my head, trying to interpret the gesture; then I hear him yell, "Come inside. Quickly! You must quickly come in here." I furrow my brow. "Hurry," he orders. "We are in an emergency—this school is on lockdown!"

In 1977, while the Irish Republican Army detonated anger in English trash cans, we had a bomb scare at our high school. As teachers and administrators escorted us out of the school, we talked excitedly among ourselves, guessing who was really responsible for calling it in. It was, perhaps, the most exciting thing that happened, because things like that never happened in Montana. But this? This is all too real, at a time when school violence is not that uncommon. The entranceway is cloaked in silence, as teachers and administrators peer out the narrow windows in metal doors, scanning for other stragglers who seek asylum, speaking to one another in muted tones. No one glances at me. A young woman to my right catches my gaze and smiles. "I was the one who took the call and transferred you," she says by way of introduction. A woman slightly behind her and to her right whispers, "I heard he shot maybe three people, an elderly person and at least one other person."

"Who was the elder?" someone asks.

The original speaker shrugs.

"Do they know where he is?" I ask.

The woman who shrugged turns to me and answers, "I heard he's on the southwest road out of town, but I haven't heard anything else."

Oh my God, I'd been on the southwest road! The people passing me, the police car, they were on the way to the scene. That would also explain the small groups of two to four people gathered along the streets, talking through car windows, across doors of pickup trucks, while they eyed my Ford Focus. I was an outsider. I didn't belong here.

"I think I've arrived at a really inopportune time," I say lamely to the young secretary. She smiles and nods her head. "Were the victims tribal members?" I ask.

She nods again.

"Was the person who shot them tribal?" I venture this question as gently as I can because it is none of my business. I'm not supposed to be here.

She shrugs. "I don't know. We haven't heard. I'll take you back to Mrs. Cummings."

The empty halls are wide, and our footsteps keep time along the newly polished linoleum, the clicks of our heels echoing eerily along the walls. The classroom doors, the same sky blue as the front doors, are closed, and I don't think to look inside to see if the children are seated at their seats or arranged in some other way. Instead, I take note that concrete blocks are the foundational structure of the school. *Sturdy*, I think. *Safe*.

The administrator's office sits squarely in the center of the building, its door closed. The secretary tries the knob, but it doesn't turn. She peers in the window and knocks softly. A male face, perhaps a custodian, peers back, first at me then at her. "Who are you looking for?" he asks, his voice muted by the safety glass.

"She's here to see Mrs. Cummings. She has an appointment," the secretary explains and then gives me a hesitant smile. "She'll be with you in a moment." Shortly after she leaves I hear the lock rattle, and the door opens. I'm led into an even more inner office.

Mrs. Cummings, a beautiful woman with dark shoulder-length hair and black eyes, smiles graciously. This small thing, this gracious smile, is successful at hiding whatever reactions she carries about the situation. "I began to wonder what had happened to you. No sooner had we hung up, the school went on lockdown. I'd asked them up front to keep an eye out for you. I'm glad you're here." The gracious smile turns to easy laughter as she shakes my hand in welcome. I am amazed then at how she slides into her seat and flips delicately through the folder of paper I've handed her, seemingly unfazed by our surroundings. That is a school counselor's job, I reason: to keep everyone calm and collected as they moved toward an unknown life.

"I'm sorry," I say, wincing with my words. "I came at a really bad time. But I think I'm the only person who has ever gotten lost in Lodge Grass." We both laugh, more to fill an awkward silence than anything else.

"Well, you certainly can't plan for these things." She gestures to the folder I'm carrying. "Tell me what you have."

I lay the materials in front of us and begin the explanation, all the while acutely aware that both of us are only half-engaged. Her glances shuttle between her cell phone and her monitor, while mine scans the room, checking for a hiding place. Her desk phone buzzes, and she looks at the caller ID. "I'm sorry, I have to take this. I'll be back."

As the door shuts solidly behind her, I can now consider the hiding places uninterrupted. There's a gap at the base of the desk, not a good place. File cabinets line the perimeter of the room; perhaps I can force a space between a couple and squeeze behind the row. I study every nook and cranny available for a plan B, a way out. I wonder all these things, but suddenly I realize with a certain amount of horror-filled guilt, I have not wondered about the children. How could I sit here and not think of the children? How many times have any of us imagined ourselves as the hero, what we'd do if something devastating happened? It's all so easy when devastation exists only in the imagination. It crept out of my imagination and became my reality, and I haven't, until now, thought about the children. *You don't know them*, a voice inside my head whispers, but my heart's response says, *That's not a good enough reason.*

Mrs. Cummings returns and reports that law enforcement still hadn't caught "the guy," a phrase that will come up again and again over the next few days in my interactions with other people. He isn't the shooter; he isn't a murderer; he's been relegated to some marginal space known as "the guy." Evidently, the guy is now headed toward Pryor. "Do you know where Pryor is?" she asks.

I nod, vaguely remembering one trip as a teenager with Mom and Dad in our sky-blue Chevy "pickum-up" truck. I have no idea if we ever *were* in Pryor, just that was where we were going. So, no, I really have no idea where it is, but I assume it is on the southeast road out of town, in the opposite direction of where I am.

As her attention shifts from her phone to her computer monitor to the door window, I become more aware that I am in the way. Perhaps I can leave, get out of this place where I am taking up the precious time of people who might need to move quickly. Here I am a stranger, an outsider, witnessing something I should not be privy to. It's like a horrible argument I've stumbled in on, one that the people involved don't want outsiders hearing.

"Mrs. Cummings," I broach, casting my gaze at the watch on my wrist, "I have an appointment in Hardin. In fact, I'm overdue. Do I need to stay here on lockdown, or do you think I could leave?"

Mrs. Cummings considers the options and makes a decision. "Since he's going the other way, I can't imagine you shouldn't be able to leave. I'll ask the vice-principal." She stands up and shakes my hand. "Thanks for stopping by. It was not a great time, but you'll have a story to tell," she assures me, laughing. I smile, but inside there is pain. This is a story I don't want to tell. Anybody.

The vice-principal meets me at the door, his voice confident, in charge in a gently caring way. "Since the shooter isn't in the immediate vicinity, I think it's all right. I'll walk you out. Where are you parked?" I point out my car from a nearby window. He nods. "We'll go down this hall," he says, leading the way. We make small talk about where I'm from and what I'm doing here. After a few moments he turns to me and says, "I hope one of the guys they say got shot isn't who I think it is. He is a really, really, nice guy."

My steps match his, and I don't know what to say in this quiet, empty space, where our cadenced steps are the only sounds in this long, long hallway. We stop at the door, and he peers outside. He pushes on the bar and the door swings open; a ray of sunshine hits my face. It should have been beautiful to feel sunshine, but instead I am on alert, on edge. We are ducks in a shooting carnival booth. I spy my car and note the vast expanse of space between us and it. There are no trees, no posts, no entrance signs, only grass trying to die in the October autumn.

As we cross the tract of deserted school grounds, I am conscious of the absence of sound: revving engines, screams of laughter, the thundering of children running for freedom from the nine-to-three school day. As I walk beside this stranger, I am uncomfortably aware of the danger he is putting himself in by the very act of being my escort. *It's one thing if I get shot, but to have him taken out because he's looking out for someone who isn't even supposed to be here? That's a whole other issue.* Uneasiness crowds around my guilt.

When I reach the car, I unlock the door and turn to wave good-bye. The vice-principal smiles and holds his closed fist in the power symbol. "The Cowboys will beat the Rams this year." He turns and walks back to the school. I start my car and find my way out of Lodge Grass in record time.

Hardin is forty minutes away, to the north, and my limbs are cold and my palms sweat as I drive the black ribbon of interstate. About halfway there I begin to search the bluff on the eastern side of the river for a familiar stand of pine trees that mark the headquarters of the Little Bighorn Battlefield National Monument. Until 1991 it used to be called the Custer Battlefield National Monument, but the name was changed as protesters asked, *Since when is a battlefield named after the losers?* Unfortunately, the battlefield still isn't named after the winners, the Cheyennes, Arapahos, and Sioux, who soundly defeated Custer's regiment, the U.S. Seventh Cavalry. The Seventh Cavalry swept in on June 25, 1876, hoping to surprise the tribes camping on the Greasy Grass, but the only ones surprised were the men of the cavalry. That war was only one of a thousand engagements the U.S. Army led against American Indians. I spot the familiar grove of pines, and like every other time I've driven by this site, a cold breeze runs through my soul.

Fifteen miles to the north, Hardin sits on the edge of the Crow Reservation. Its population is over 3,500 people, of which less than half are American Indians. In all the years I lived in Montana, I'd never been in the town of Hardin. According to the map, the town is laid out on a grid: numbered streets run east to west; named avenues run north to south. Five of the seven avenues are named after men in the U.S. Seventh Cavalry: Crook, for Gen. George Crook; Custer, for Lt. Col. George Armstrong Custer; Crawford, for Capt. Jack Crawford; Terry, for Brig. Gen. Alfred H. Terry; and Miles for Lt. Gen. Nelson A. Miles. Only two streets are named after tribes: Cheyenne Avenue and Crow Avenue. And there are no streets named for warriors: there is no Sitting Bull Avenue or Crazy Horse Avenue or Two Moons Avenue. In this town the Seventh Cavalry is history; the Indians are ghosts.

Hardin High School, whose Native population makes up 66 percent of the student body, resides on Terry Avenue. I park in the row nearest the school and walk toward the entrance. A Native boy, cell phone pressed to his ear, passes me as he looks across the parking lot. "I heard he's headed this way," he says to the phone. The pit in my stomach returns. *Surely*, I reason, *I'll be long gone before he gets to this town.*

Another young man sees me approach and holds the door open. I thank him and step into the chaotic hall. It is nearly the end of the school day, which explains the chaos, but it is a muted chaos. There is not much chatter, only movement. An efficient secretary shows me to the room, adding as an afterthought, "Oh, by the way, the counselor you had the appointment with is not here today." As I step forward to introduce myself to the only other adult in the room, she receives a phone call and quickly descends a staircase at the back of the room, holding the phone to her ear and whispering frantically until she disappears behind a closed door at the bottom of the steps. A tall, heavyset boy sits at the lone table, his eyes, behind black wire-rimmed glasses, are directed at the wall in front of him, while the surrounding world is kept at bay by earbuds firmly in place. A long, black braid hangs most of the way down his back. From his "don't give a shit" expression, I imagine he's in detention. Some looks are cross-cultural.

A male voice crackles over the loudspeaker, and my anxiety turns to fear. "Due to an emergency situation on the Crow Reservation, school-children are required to remain in their classrooms with their teachers while the school takes precautionary measures. The school is now on lockdown."

What were the chances? I run through the scenario: "the guy" is now a man with nothing to lose; he's killed three people, he is the focus of an extensive manhunt, and his next actions could well be to take hostages. And what better hostages than children? I look briefly around the room. There are no hiding places here.

Moments later the woman returns and asks for a brief rundown of why I am here, and again, like at Lodge Grass, both of us are only half-engaged in this conversation. This time it takes me five minutes. There are no questions, so I ask, "Do I need to remain here while you are on lockdown, or can I leave? I'm expected in Billings."

"You can leave," she assures me, her tone precise, her clipped words forcing themselves from between pursed lips. "I'll have someone escort you out."

"No. I don't want anyone to escort me out. I'll be fine." I will not jeopardize another human being, just because I am an outsider.

"Where are you parked?"

"In the front row."

"I'll keep you in visual until you get in your car."

In the fall of 1976, the start of my senior year, Steven and I had been on exactly one date. The one I asked him on. The only one I'd ever been on. The one where we sat in a movie theater and held hands. I don't remember the movie, but I do remember his hand was cool, and it shook slightly until I laid it, palm up, on my lap and intertwined my fingers with his. We both hunched down in our seats and thought our own thoughts while the movie flashed into the darkness.

A few weeks later Steven and I were as emotionally intertwined as our hands had been. I spent a lot of my time at his house. One day he and I sat in the kitchen while his mom, a gentle, quiet, petite person, went from cupboard to cupboard looking for something. At one point, while peering in one of the cupboards, she asked, without turning around, "Do you mind if I ask you a personal question?"

I froze. My mom was crazy, my dad was living in Minot, and I was just trying to keep my shit together while dating her son. Which personal question would it be?

"Sure," I answered hesitantly, throwing a puzzled look to Steven.

"What nationality are you?"

The world stopped spinning, but not in a good way. Nationality was code for "race." "I'm Indian." Immediately I felt the familiar heat of shame cross my face. I'd been told by so many people in so many ways, both overt and covert, that being Indian was a bad thing to be. Sometimes they told me because they forgot that I was Indian. Or maybe they figured I wasn't a real one. Either way the question made me nervous.

My nerves retracted only a little when she replied, "Oh," as she turned to face me, having discovered what she'd been looking for. "I was just curious."

My face still burned. People never seemed to be "just curious" about anyone else's ethnicity. Just mine.

That evening, when I reach my stepmother's house in Billings, I am grateful for its sanctuary. We sit in her backyard, the one Dad spent so much time landscaping with the half-dead trees he'd picked up at the garden center and nurtured back to life. We sip iced tea, protected by a fence, ensconced in a quilted tapestry of textured landscape. Nearby petunias droop, dying in the autumn days, while leaves of the neighboring buckthorn turn a fiery orange. Dogs bark in the distance, birds chatter quietly, and I am in hiding from a brutal world. I am well aware of my privilege of being provided this space.

My cell phone rings. It is a friend on the Northern Cheyenne Reservation whom I'd intended to visit but canceled at the last minute, my nerves having been shaken by "the guy."

"Did you hear about the shootings?" I ask, already knowing the answer. Of course she did; word spreads at the speed of light on the reservation.

"Yes! But I haven't heard any particulars."

I fill her in with what I know. "It's probably a good thing I didn't come see you," I joke. "He'd have followed me over there." We laugh and she wishes me a good trip. Five minutes later she calls back. "Law enforcement says he's on his way to Busby—the town I live in."

It is no longer funny.

Rick, working that week in Gillette, Wyoming, 230 miles southeast of Billings, calls me, saying, "They still haven't caught the guy. Even down here the schools let out early, and the police are encouraging people to stay in their homes. No one knows where he is."

Unpredictability puts everyone on edge.

The following morning, over breakfast, Norma hands me the *Billings Gazette*. "Suspect Sought after 3 Killed outside Lodge Grass" reads the black, bold headline. Below are two photos: one of Sheldon Bernard Chase, sought for questioning; the other of the log house, surrounded by cars and people, where the shooting had occurred. I shiver. That's where the people were headed when they'd passed me outside of Lodge Grass.

When I look up, Norma is watching me. "Evidently KULR sent a news crew down there to cover it. The guy couldn't even get close to the house. The Indians down there told the crew to stay away; if they got closer, they'd be shot! Gosh, he's just a young kid down there doing his job." She pauses, surprise etching her features. "There's always something going on down there on that reservation."

"Well, do you blame them?" I ask, leveling my gaze at her, as she holds her teacup in her hand. "The media always has a camera and microphone in people's faces, getting into their businesses, raking the families over, discussing and rediscussing their tragedies. The Indians don't want this splashed over the news. If this was a white guy, it would be three days of sensationalism, and it would be over. But the tribes? Well, they'll get blamed for the chaos for years to come. You know how the news will be spun—it's always that the Indians are so messed up. It's never about the history. So, no, I don't blame them for not wanting any white news people around."

She purses her lips, nods slightly, and changes the subject. Over the years, while my dad was still alive, both he and Norma consistently forgot which side of the blanket I was born on. Or maybe they didn't forget; they just refused to acknowledge my Indianness. But being Indian is what has defined me, especially in Montana.

I am on the road by eight, headed west on Interstate 90, grateful for a clear day, although the forecaster says rain is expected. I turn on the radio as soon as I get up to speed, trying to find one of the AM stations I used to listen to in the early 1970s, when the DJs were funny and the songs bubblegummy. But there aren't any; those waves have been taken up by right-wingers, left-wingers, sports chatter, and the Come-to-Jesus meetings of the audioreligious. So I cruise the FM stations, the ones that, in those same years, seemed to broadcast only National Public Radio, a staple of my dad's everyday existence. Now, however, I landed on FM Hot 101.9, with the "Big J show, playing today's hottest hits." Big J had the stereotypic voice of an FM DJ, loud, dramatic, attention seeking.

"And *he* had the audacity to call *me* a fat honky! Like you haven't seen any fat Indians around here! That's all there is! All you *see* are fat Indians! And this guy, with nothing better to do than send me an email, calling me a *fat honky*. I tell you, I don't understand it." My finger hovers over the power button, while Big J breaks to a couple of songs, and I debate whether or not to turn the radio off.

I should turn it off; it's garbage. But I can't turn it off because his anger, the ugliness of his words, slap me back to junior high and high school, when I lived in this town, and people felt free to voice their anti-Indian sentiment, sometimes to me directly, sometimes just within my earshot. Rarely did the people I know, or frequently come into contact with, view me as Native. Maybe it was because of my white mannerisms from the way I was raised. Maybe it was because I acted so white, spoke so white, and liked all the things white people liked, things that didn't include powwows or movies where Indians were the heroes. Either way they forgot because my actions indicated that I was *just like them*. Even if they'd questioned my feelings about Indians, I wouldn't have been honest. That was too scary to think how far outside of the boundaries of belonging, outside of the circle, I would be.

But this ranting over the airwaves? As bad as it might have been in the 1970s, it was never this overt. I let my hand drop away from the knob, waiting for Big J to return. The self-flagellation begins.

"You must have had guys falling over themselves to ask you out," Rick said one day a few years ago, as we talked about our high school glory days.

I shook my head.

"What do you mean, no?" He smiled, unbelieving. "You were adorable."

"I didn't have a date until the summer before my senior year," I said.

"You're kidding! Well, you must have been intimidating to them, you know, aloof in a way that made them shy."

"No," I clarified. "I was Indian."

"What does that mean? How do you know that?" The smile was gone, replaced by a tinge of defensiveness. Perhaps Rick didn't want to think of his wife being thought of as less-than. Or he might have been surprised that I was judging his ethnic group unfairly, that I had a chip on my shoulder. Whatever the reason, the defensiveness was there.

"That's just how it was. Mothers and fathers of great guys didn't want their sons dating Indians. They wanted them to end up with nice girls who are hardworking and God-fearing and would keep a good home. Indian girls don't do that. End of story."

"Well, that's ridiculous," he said.

I shrugged.

Rick changed his mind in 2008, the night President Barack Obama was elected. After attending a conference in Montana, he went to a bar filled with the conference attendees, mostly tradesmen, who became more and more agitated at the news stories that blanketed the broadcast stations. A few were shouting that a black man wasn't going to be *their* president, and after a few moments one announced he was going to get his shotgun and go shoot himself a nigger! And the whoops that followed chilled Rick to the bone. When race isn't an issue in your daily world, I think it's hard to believe it's an issue in anyone else's.

Big J is back. "You know, you try to do the right thing, and this is what you get in return. He says in his email, 'You fat honky,' and it's spelled like hockey with an *n*, so not only is he a fat Indian; he's a stupid Indian. Can't even spell. Just makes you not want to do the right thing." Again he goes to commercial, and I wonder how the advertisers are feeling about this conversation. Evidently, he wonders too, because when he returns, his voice is quiet. Calm. "You know, when I came in this morning the first thing I did was send out my prayers and condolences to the family of the victims and to the entire Crow Nation. And what I get in return is this Indian guy, shooting me off an email that says, 'We don't need your effing prayers and condolences, you fat honky.' But here's some more mail coming in now. Let's see what it says."

Suddenly, his voice changes to dulled interest, as if he's seen mail like this come through every day. "Okay, here we go. 'Big J, some people don't have a sense of humor. I think your sh— is funny, and I'm Crow from the rez. Keep up the great show. I listen all the time.' Here's another one from a young lady: 'I love your show, it makes me laugh. I'm Crow and they don't know what they're talking about.' Oh, and here's one . . ." His voice grows serious. "I am a member of the victim's family, and we would like to extend our thanks for your prayers and condolences at this time. It is truly appreciated by all the members in this family."

On Thursday, October 6, the *Billings Gazette* posted this story: "Investigators said Chase left his mother's home on North Dakota's Fort Berthold Reservation Monday. He took a Sitting Bull commemorative rifle, typically a Winchester Model 94 .30-30 caliber. . . . During the interview of one child, age 3 years, he disclosed Chase and [Jefferson] were fighting and Chase shot [Jefferson]. The child further stated Chase also shot [Cummings] and [Driftwood]. . . . Chase has a history of mental illness and had stopped taking his medication before the shooting. . . . He was arrested Wednesday afternoon without incident near the Spokane Valley Mall."

This is the thing, colonization has done a hack job on indigenous people. We've had our culture ripped out from under our legs, our traditions and knowledge replaced, our wealth of horses replaced by paper money that means only what someone in Washington says it means. We've had our land stolen, our children stolen, our pride stolen. Many of us have been given the worse land; our health care providers are paying off their student loans until they can land where the money is; many of our school administrators see their jobs as stepping stones and are out within three years if they can manage it. Our tribal money is used to pay lawyers to make sure we keep what we have, while our social services scrape to put programs together that are rudimentary, understaffed, and underfunded.

As a result, Indians have a 600 percent higher mortality rate from tuberculosis, 510 percent higher mortality rate from alcoholism, nearly a 230 percent higher mortality rate from car accidents, almost a 200 percent higher mortality rate from diabetes, and a 150 percent higher mortality rate from unintentional injuries. On top of that, we are killing ourselves and one another at appalling rates: homicide rates and suicide rates are 61 percent and 62 percent, respectively, higher than all other Americans. Is it any wonder that this kind of violence happens? That it doesn't happen more often?

I sigh as I add all these things together on the data sheet in my head. The bottom line is that Billings, Montana, and its vicinity is a powder keg. The dust of history sifts through the air, carried on a breeze of insinuation, anger, and memory. All it takes is a match and *poof!*

Custer whispers on the wind.

16

Vernon

Bitterroot Valley, Montana, October 2011.

We agreed on meeting at nine o'clock, but Vern, my brother, shows
up forty-five minutes early. I can't blame him, really; we haven't seen
each other in nearly two years. We hug, and his sturdy body is like a
cedar; he is like a bear, and I feel safe as his arms pull me in, encircle
me. When I stand back I immediately begin the search for similarity,
familiarity. His hair is black, cropped close to his scalp, with only his
temples shimmering in silver, as opposed to my hair, which is also short
and black, but iced with wide swaths of pure white. His eyes are darker
than mine, almost black, and his smile . . . I think we have the same
smile, but perhaps mine's a little less guarded. And our noses are almost
the same. At ten years his senior, I imagine I've changed a lot, but he
doesn't look any different than when I first met him eighteen years ago,
at a family gathering on the Jocko, when I first met Vic. When I first
met all my family.

I have a photograph of him, cut out from the tribal newspaper and
placed in our family album. Vern is standing with a group of police
officers, dressed in the sharply creased, dark-blue uniform of Tribal

9. Susan and Vern. Photo by Rick Harness. Courtesy of the author.

Law and Order. It was taken when he graduated from the academy. I've never told him how proud I was to hear of his becoming an officer or that I'm still so proud of him.

Three days ago I had called him at the spur of the moment to ask him for a favor. I was nervous. I hadn't called him in years. After punching in his number, I held my breath and waited for an answer. Maybe he wouldn't know me. Or worse, maybe he would and deny my request because I was going to ask too much, of him, of us. My heart stopped when he picked up on the third ring.

"Hey," he said, his smooth voice taking me by surprise. "I haven't heard from you in a long time."

He had answered so quickly I didn't have a chance to tell him who I was, to remind him of our relationship. I was afraid that without those reminders, he wouldn't know me. The thing is, I feel the need to do this each and every time I talk with one of my relatives: explain to them our connection, my place in the lineage. I see myself as forgotten, but his greeting tells me I'm not. I smile.

"Where you been?" he asks. His voice is like a spring rain.

Our relationship, the one between my birth family and me, is, at best, unsettled. Since our reunion in 1993 my visits are sporadic, their response to them, guarded. I drop out of their lives for years at a time, and they never beckon me back. There are no invitations, no phone calls, no emails, no letters. There is no exchange of news of any kind. Communication is one way: me to them. I know the rules and I accept them. From this description *reunion* is misleading—perhaps *remeeting* or *reconnecting* is better. There has been no reunification of our family, and maybe there never will be, although I continue the efforts.

But I still feel uneasy around this reconstructed family. The edge I walk, being one of them and not being one of them, is fine and razor sharp. I never know if I'll be welcomed, let alone accepted. We are separated by too many years, too much tragedy, too many tears, and too much difference. Plus, I tell myself, they all have one another; I am a satellite that has been knocked into a different orbit. In my mind they gather together like lambs in a huddle against the wolves. It takes work to insert myself into that huddle every time I return. They observe with practiced distrust my white mannerisms, my white speech, gathered from living for so long in the white boundaries. I could, they may presume, be a wolf in disguise. When I do return, however, they move apart, far enough to let me in. And when I leave, the circle closes tight behind me.

So when I called Vern three days ago, I was asking to be let in. "I have a favor to ask." And that's when my adrenaline started pumping; my fingertips felt on fire with the energy. I'm preparing myself for his rejection. That's not a new reaction; people have said no to me a lot. Sometimes that no means "no admittance," like the time I was sixteen and the saleswoman didn't want to sell me a pair of jeans. Like the time, thirty years later, at an upscale store in Fort Collins, when a saleswoman followed me from room to room as I browsed the merchandise, always within six feet of me, always folding, fluffing, moving items from one space to another. Always there. She met my gaze only once but dogged me until I left. I never returned to that store.

It's taken me over forty years to realize that I have been taught to believe I don't carry enough value as a human being for someone to say yes. So I hold my breath and hope Vern sees beyond that nonvalue and says yes. That little voice, the one I hate, whispers, *Why would he? We have nothing, no foundation.* This relationship that I'm trying to build with Vern is far from solid. It is the thinnest layer of ice that hides vacuous depths below, shattering under too much weight.

But it didn't shatter. Vern replied, interest tingeing his voice, "What do you need?"

I pulled air deep into my lungs and began my sales spiel. "The last time we spoke, a couple of years ago, you'd mentioned that your family lived in a campground for five years." I paused. "That conversation has been playing in my mind ever since. I want to see where you lived. Will you take me there?" Again I held my breath, but not for long.

"Sure, I'll do that."

What if he bails? What if my request carries too much pressure? Too many memories? "Promise?"

"Yeah, I promise." I heard the barely restrained smile.

"You won't back out?"

"No, I won't back out."

"I'll call you when I get into town."

"Ready to go to Hamilton?" I ask, pulling on my raincoat.

"Let's go." His words are clipped, sounding more like he is from Minnesota than having been born and raised in the Rocky Mountain West. We walk toward my rented Ford Focus, and I scan the parking lot for the new truck he'd told me he purchased.

"I didn't bring it," he answers, reading my thoughts. "I don't even know why I bought it. It's a ridiculous size. It's immense," he says with a wry smile. "I don't know what I was thinking." He points to the car he did bring—his son's. "It's a mess; it's better if we take yours." I grimace and wonder how he defines "mess," as he gathers up the loose papers I've thrown across my passenger seat and tosses them to the back.

We pull out onto Reserve Street, and although the street has changed, my memories of Missoula haven't. We drive by areas that had once been open fields, now filled in with big-box stores. We drive by Third Avenue; Rick had worked in an engineering office, where the street intersected with Higgins. We drive by Rosauers, the grocery store located just two blocks away from where we rented our first home together. We pass the golf course, where I remember walking with Rick on a beautiful June day when he said he wanted to be a millionaire by the time he was thirty. Don't we all?

We turn right on Highway 93, where if we'd gone straight we would have eventually, through some twists and turns, landed near the home we first bought, on the hill. So many memories. I am soothed by the town's familiarity. The rain pounds against my windshield, bringing yet another memory: why we left Missoula in 1987. In winter it was not uncommon to go six weeks without seeing the sun, except from our house on the hill, where we lived for three glorious years, or by driving out of the valley in any direction. Fort Collins, in contrast, experiences over three hundred sunny days a year. The rain feels oppressive.

As the windshield wipers slap the rain away, we talk about his job as a tribal cop. It's clear he loves his job. I think he loves the adrenaline. I tell him about the legal case I found online, from 1999, where it says that he, Vern Fisher, "testified he was afraid Brown was going to shoot him." Back then, he was just afraid.

Three years ago, Vern *was* shot. "Were you afraid then?" I ask.

He shakes his head. "No, not really. I was on a case, though, where my boss was shot. Twice, in the chest. I laughed because I thought he was goofing around, that he'd stumbled. Then I saw him go backward and knew what had happened. Kept him down, called an ambulance. He was wearing a piece of sheet metal outside of his armored vest. That's the only thing that saved him."

Regardless of our relationship, I am intensely aware I have a cop in the car, so when a traffic light on the highway turns yellow, I slam on the brakes from sixty miles per hour, trying to come to a stop. Both of us brace ourselves against the sudden stop. But I realize with horror I can't stop in time. I have to make a decision. I pause.

"I'd have gone," he says easily.

"Really?"

"Yeah."

I hit the gas and slide through just as the light turns red. "I'm sorry if my driving makes you nervous," I apologize.

He shrugs. "No, not really."

We sit in silence for a few moments, and I recall a conversation I had with Uncle Albert recently and what I was supposed to tell Vern. "Uncle Albert says he hasn't seen you in a while. He wonders why you haven't been down to his house, since you live right up the hill." Vern smiles but doesn't reply. "He's your uncle," I remind him, as if my reminder carries any weight at all. *I am an outsider.* "You know, he and Delphine are not going to live forever. They're your elders; go see them," I chide.

He cups his chin as he looks out the window. "Yeah," he says to the fogging glass, "We're not a very close family."

Colors of the autumn trees bleed outside the car windows, their hues heightened by the moisture. "What's the hardest thing about being a cop?" I ask.

"Probably when the kids die." As an afterthought, Vern adds, after looking at me, "Did I tell you I'm also the tribal coroner?" I shake my head. Vern is the first tribal coroner to be on the reservation. Those duties have typically been handled by the county.

"That must be tough."

Vern shakes his head. "It's not much different than being a cop," he says in that matter-of-fact way I'm beginning to get used to. "People are usually dead when you see them, regardless."

Dull gray clouds lay heavy on the Bitterroots, their edges brushing the knees of the mountains. As I watch the lace of golden-leaved cottonwoods race by my window, I'm aware that Ravalli National Wildlife Refuge—now called Lee Metcalf National Wildlife Refuge—lies just on the other side of the Bitterroot River. That refuge was my family's turning point, when Dad went from being a biologist to a refuge manager, from a casual drinker to an alcoholic. He liked working with animals, not people and budgets and bureaucracy. That's what he told me when he finally went to Alcoholics Anonymous when I was sixteen. But we'd moved to the refuge when I was five and then moved to Washington when I was ten. But I don't share the personal information; I don't want to open our dysfunction for review.

Vern forces my attention from the refuge by pointing out my driver's side window to a semicircular stand of cottonwoods. "That's one of the campgrounds we stayed in," he says. I look in the rearview mirror, and I debate whether I should stop and turn around. I want to stand in that space, to think about what it must have been like to be the child, Vern, even for a few minutes. His life is difficult to fathom. The very same year he lived in a campground, I was living the middle-class life in Billings, Montana.

"You know," he says, breaking into my thoughts, "We didn't stay in just one campground. We stayed in a lot of them. There's no way we could visit all of them in one day."

"Why did you stay in the campgrounds?" Are my questions painful? Intrusive? Evidently not, because Vern just keeps answering.

"That's just what we did," he says with a shrug. "I think Dad liked it; he liked camping. He didn't like living in a home, a structure with walls. And as a kid? It was great. We could do whatever we wanted; go wherever we wanted to go. There were no boundaries, whatsoever." He laughs. He then points across the car, to my left. I follow his finger to see the small, cabin-style bar. "I used to wait in front of that bar a lot. That one too." He points to the one across the road, a little farther ahead.

I smile. "What, waiting for someone to buy you beer?"

"No. Waiting for my folks."

I frown in vague understanding. "You were the designated driver?"

"Sometimes. Mostly I was just waiting for them to go home."

"How old were you?" My mind races to conceptualize what this means.

"Grade school."

I'd heard stories of kids driving their drunk parents somewhere. I didn't actually know anyone who had done that. I look at Vern and consider the life he must have led. Vern shifts in his seat. "I got a ton of stories. Funny stories, but none of them don't include alcohol."

Our car jolts as the pavement ends, and we muddle through puddles that dot a construction zone lasting several miles. "This stretch of road here? One time Dad was driving, and Mom and all of us were in the car, and they were arguing really bad. Then, all of a sudden, Dad kinda slowed down, opened up the driver's side door, and just bailed. Just left us going down the road without a driver. And we're sailing along, and you know? Then Mom just slid over the bench seat, behind the wheel, and just kept driving." His laugh is deep in his chest, and it rumbles like faraway thunder. "That happened more than once. Sometimes she'd turn around and pick him up. Sometimes she didn't."

He indicates for me to turn left down a narrow road. "And here? I walked this road a ton of times. Always in the dark. It was a long way home." He pauses and looks out the window again, his voice quieter. "A long way."

I've always been scared of the dark, my imagination conjuring fearful and violent images, both natural and supernatural. "Weren't you ever scared?"

"Naw. Animals never scared me. People do. But everything just left me alone." He points again. "Turn here. I'll take you by where I lived."

"It's surprising you stayed such a good kid," I say.

"Well, not always. I was pretty wild when I got into my teen years. One time I backed up to a bar and unloaded everything I could from it: beer, kegs, bottles, you name it. Everything went in the back of my pickup truck."

"What did you do with all that stuff?"

"Sold it." A wry smile crosses his features, and he looks at me for a reaction.

I imagine he's a great cop; he's been on the other side of the law.

Suddenly he smiles, his black eyes full of mischief. "You know how you want to write that book of what it was like to be adopted? I think I'm going to write a book about it was like *not* to be adopted."

We laugh and the laugher fills that tiny car with warmth.

But Vern's statement raises an interesting question that our society assumes about adoption—that to be rescued from a chaotic family and adopted is always better than not being rescued. And to hear his stories, it's hard to argue with that. But I have my own stories to tell, but for now I hold them inside my mouth and remind myself that this journey we're on, the one right now, is not about me. It's about needing to hear what happened to my brother when I wasn't part of his life.

So I follow the asphalt that winds along the outskirts of Hamilton as the road turns to a narrow two-lane. Houses, small and cottage-like, dot the landscape, their yards growing progressively larger until after a mile or so, when these yards slowly turn into small acreages. Willows grow everywhere; their rust-colored leaves hang limp in the rain.

"I used to walk down this road too, but it sure seemed a lot farther than it does now," he laughs at his confusion while he watches the land slip by and the years catch up. "Okay, that's one of the schools I attended."

A small, one-story brick building comes into view. I'm sure when he was here in the 1970s, that building looked old. It now looks ancient.

"Here, turn left at this road. And slow down, we're coming on it." There's a hint of excitement in his voice. "Turn left in here."

I slow down and eye the painted Quonset hut and adjacent white clapboard house. I feel uncomfortable being here uninvited. But then I feel uninvited in a lot of places. It's the hazards of being Indian. "You sure it's okay?" I wince with my question; I am such a rule follower.

"Yeah, it's a business."

We park and get out of the car, standing in silence for a few moments while he scans the countryside, getting his bearings. Pretty soon he paints the scene with his fingers, pointing at the various sites. "When we lived here all of this was open. The guy who lived here, in that house, had a potato farm, and my dad was basically a laborer. He did work for the farmer, got the fields ready, planted, weeded, harvested. He fixed machinery and did a lot of welding. Originally, he was a welder. We lived over here," he says, gesturing toward a grassy meadow straight ahead of us, "in a military tent, and we swam back in that canal." He points toward a screen of willows. "You can't see it now, but that's where we swam." He's quiet as he looks past the grass, the trees, into another dimension. "I don't mean to make it sound like growing up this way was all bad. It was great. Here, as a kid, I got to drive the tractor. A lot of times I'd work side by side with my dad. I enjoyed that." He turns to me, a half smile on his face. "But that's where we lived."

"Did kids make fun of you in your schools?" I could only imagine the brutal taunting any of my classmates would have received if they lived this lifestyle.

"No, no one said anything. I had a lot of friends, did well in school. Best thing was probably the fact I had no TV, so I read all the time. But we were usually the only Indian kids in school. But a lot of times Mom would just up and leave, for weeks, months at a time."

"Where did she go?"

He shrugs, "A lot of times she'd just go up and live with my grandparents, her folks. Other times no one knew where she was."

"Who took care of you then?"

"Dad," he answers simply.

"I don't know how she kept you guys," I say, shaking my head in complete confusion. "I have no idea how she didn't lose you to the system. I heard she did heroin once."

"She did. I watched. Rosa, our sister, said it was the one and only time Mom did it because I was crying so hard. But who knows?" Vern looks at me, studying my face, again with that unblinking gaze. I knit my brows and shake my head, trying to fit the puzzle pieces together.

"How did she not lose you to the system?" I ask again.

Vern returns his gaze to the field and settles his feet until they're shoulder-width apart, sliding his hands into his fleece-vest pockets. He is silent for a long time, and when he answers it is with a quiet voice. "We moved a lot. I went to a lot of different schools. By the time I was in eighth grade, I'd changed schools thirty-five times. I'm sure any time someone started sniffing around, we up and moved camp."

My smile is lopsided, but my voice holds no humor as I echo the logic. "She'd already lost three kids to social workers. She didn't want to lose the rest of you, but she didn't want to change either. She just tried to outrun it." I shake my head, but I'm careful to be honest with myself. As much as I would like to judge her actions with sanctimonious anger, I can't. I myself have gotten into a car and driven for hours, leaving my husband behind. I didn't leave in anger, but just as a way of racing the claustrophobia of reality that seemed to chase me once in a while, settling around me, trapping me until I want to scream in protest. Yes, I admit I have done that pretty often. And those drives, when they happen, on dusty roads or endless asphalt, clear my head. I scan the horizon, watch fields of grain fly by my window, feel the endlessness of the high-prairie landscape in which I live. While the white line disappears hypnotically beneath my car, the chaos is calmed, focus restored.

My eldest son, in the midst of his teenage angst, gave me so much grief I thought ceaselessly about getting into the car and watching Fort Collins disappear in the rearview mirror, becoming a green dot on the high-plains landscape. Years later, when I confessed this to my husband, he looked at me and said, "You think I haven't thought of that?"

It is on these drives that I churn events and conversations like butter, replaying them, reviewing them, revamping them. But sometimes I just drive. Sometimes I seek a sense of adventure that begins deep in my genes, to take a journey, to discover something. This usually happened every spring and fall, when the road trips were the longest, when I was the happiest, when I could do the hundreds of miles required to get whatever this was out of my system. I've been to Oregon (three times), Montana (numerous), Durango, Colorado (several), Missouri (three times), and the desert Southwest (often). Sometimes these forays occurred with the family, sometimes just with Rick, many times by myself.

The familiar requirement for self-assessment is apparent on this journey I am currently on: it is autumn and I am a thousand miles from my home. I could have flown but chose not to. I needed to think, reflect, to dream, to comb through the rubble of adoption and see, with new eyes, who I am in relation to my families and honestly assess how it has affected me throughout my life. I'm now finding out how this also affected my brother. Although I can draw a similarity between Vic and me in our escapes, there is an important difference: I never left my family when they needed me.

"Another thing Mom liked to do was ride the rail," Vern says, bringing me back to this time, this space.

I smile. "Yeah, that's what I heard. I heard Vic and Ronny went back to Minnesota once. They took me with them." I look at his face. "Evidently, it didn't go so well. I heard his family disinherited him because he was living with an Indian." I don't wait to see his reaction because anger still colors mine.

I start up the car and drive the back road to Corvallis, a tiny town tucked between Hamilton and Stevensville. "I think I went to that school," Vern says, indicating a somewhat more modern structure than the last school, but his eyebrows are furrowed in thought and he tilts his head.

"But it doesn't look right. It's like that one, but not that one. I think it was on the other side of the road. Yeah, there it is." This school is as old as the first, but it is not abandoned; children are playing inside the chain-link fence, while above them, over the door, the letters of the school name are rusted and askew.

The road is narrow and curved; the drive is slow, calming. "So have you ever wanted to look up anything about your dad?" Vern asks, after a few moments' pause. I'm uncomfortable with the turn of the conversation. I hadn't planned on talking about my birth dad. I hadn't planned on talking about me at all. But that's not fair, I tell myself. He doesn't know me as much as I don't know him.

"No."

"Are you curious?"

No, I think silently, I'm not.

Ronni, James Allen, and I are in the middle of the pack of nine children. We are full siblings to one another; we are half siblings to everyone else. The three of us share our father, Ronny Smith, a person of unknown Euro-American heritage who somehow made his way from western Minnesota to Montana, settling eventually with Vic on the Flathead Indian Reservation. It is no secret among all the kids that Ronny was Vic's true and only love. For decades she spoke of him constantly, many times in booze-filled conversations with one of her daughters as they drove her around the countryside. But I wasn't privy to those stories, those yearnings, those sonnets of longing. For me there are only scraps, bits and pieces of stories carefully wrapped around his memory like so many layers of papier-mâché. Uncle Albert was the only one who'd offered a memory, the beauty of Ronny's voice when he sang. When he'd told me that, I remember feeling elated, like finding a long-lost puzzle piece under the couch. I'd always wondered where I got my love of music.

Neither of my adoptive parents sang or played any instruments. But they purchased a piano for me when I was six. I assured them I would practice every day if I took lessons. As I moved through school, I took up the violin and eventually taught myself the guitar in college. I sang in choirs since I was six, played in orchestras, and found bit parts in school musicals. I never tried out for the leads or even speaking parts. I knew myself well enough to know that my nerves would cause me to self-destruct.

As an adult, I took classical guitar lessons but quit because I began growing irritated when my kids, ages five and seven, interrupted me during my three- to four-hour practice sessions. I'd become compulsive, so I stopped, not just guitar but everything—singing, playing, learning. It was no longer fun. But at least now I know where the love of music began.

The only other hard evidence I have of him is his death certificate that says he drowned in Moses Lake, Washington. He was fishing, and I was five. I never knew him. And then this is where the rumors, the hearsay begins. Evidently, I've been told, Ronny hadn't planned on having five kids at the age of twenty-five, so he gave Vic a choice: the kids or him. He'd left for Washington to give her time to think about it. Or according to another source, his ultimatum was either the booze goes or he does. When Vic didn't immediately choose Ronny, he left to go to Washington, hoping to force her to stop drinking and join him, counting on her love for him to make that happen. It was, as one sibling said, an effort to pull our fractured little family together. I have no idea how it all played out. But he was missed, not only by Vic but by her youngest sister, Darlene. The family knows her as Doll. "I really liked him," Aunt Doll once told me. "He was a really, really nice guy."

What's real; what's not? I know nothing beyond what I've been told, that he loved to sing, he rode the rails, and his family disinherited him because they didn't like the ethnicity of the woman with whom he'd had three children. And that last one, the racist ideology of his family, is to me the most threatening of all. So, no, I don't want to know anything about them. I don't want to meet them. I've known enough people like them to last me a lifetime; I don't need to know any more. I tell myself the "not knowing" is fine, but it's not. He disappeared, leaving no trace by which to know him, and the scraps I've been offered, the maybes of who he was, aren't filling. I want, I need, so much more, but that will never happen. So what am I left with? Unrequited love? Unrequited anger? I don't know.

"Why don't you want to know more about your dad?" Vern asks, quietly.

My answer is a shield, a self-protective device that gives me permission to not know anything, to not be hurt by people who would cut a son out of their life, who would, perhaps, pass that hatred on to their children and their grandchildren. What I say is unfair, untrue, and terrible, but it stops the anger that rages in me about the entire situation. "As far as I'm concerned, he was nothing but a sperm donor."

By now the rain is coming down in sheets. I pull into a parking lot adjacent to the Corvallis High School's football field, which is enclosed within the running track. It just feels like it's time to sit, that we are moving into serious conversations that pull at us like an eddy on the river. For a while we say nothing, as we stare at the dark-blue Bitterroot Mountains through the rain that runs in rivulets down the windshield.

"So when did you first know you were Flathead?" Vern asks, breaking the silence. It's interesting that he refers to the reservation when asking about my tribe. *Our* tribe, I silently correct myself. I glance at him, but he maintains his forward gaze, and I feel like I'm in a confessional booth without a dividing panel.

"I've always known I was adopted. And I've known I was Salish since we lived in Stevensville. But Dad wouldn't tell me anything else. He never wanted me to get in touch with you guys."

"Why not?" Vern's gaze shifts to me, then, but only for a moment. He's back to looking out the window.

Suddenly, conversation becomes difficult, pocked with the promise of hurt feelings. "Because he said you guys would come and camp on my doorstep and ask me for money. That's what he told me years later when I asked why he never gave me information. You know how Indians are," I say, mimicking his words. I have to avoid his gaze; otherwise, he'll see the stain of shame that sits on my cheeks.

"You're kidding," he says and stares at me, chuckling. I know he stares because I can feel his scrutiny like sandpaper on my skin.

"I'm not." I exhale. I'm on the witness stand, and I hate it. I feel like I will be held accountable for my dad's actions. I look down into my lap as I continue. "He told me all kinds of things about Indians that made me stay away. How you were all drunks, how you were into drugs, but more importantly how you would take advantage of me if I were to contact you."

I steal a glance. Vern is shaking his head as he looks away, the humor gone from his voice. "Your dad sounds like a piece of work." He gazes out the window. "What you've told me about your dad? I don't think I would have liked him."

"No," I say softly, "I can't imagine you would." I turn away so he can't see the tears that threaten to spill down my cheeks. Instead, I take a deep breath and change the subject. "You'd mentioned that you wished I had come back from wherever I was and take you away from all of this?"

"Yeah," he smiles. His brown eyes are kind, captivating, but always studying my reaction. "That was a big fantasy of mine when I was a kid."

I nod, silent. After a few moments, I clear my throat. "I tried to come back, Vern. I really did . . ." I stop and catch my breath, catch myself from falling entirely apart in front of this brother-stranger. I don't want him to see my vulnerability. I want him to see me as strong, as in control.

My throat closes, and I stop speaking. Instead, I stare out the window and see how much it's fogged up from our conversation, while the rain continues to fall. Clouds along the front edge of the Bitterroots part enough for me to see a fresh layer of snow. Silence fills the space between us. And suddenly this car is too small, too crowded. And words rush out, trying to find a safe exit, but there is none.

"I really tried," I continue, forcing the words across my vocal chords that try to dam them, limiting their release. "I went to the state social services offices. I talked with two separate social workers, who never once told me there was anything I could sign, or check with, to help me get in contact with you guys. I had no idea you had signed the information-release forms when I turned eighteen. The social workers never mentioned anything! And I tried to get jobs up on the reservation. I spread the Plant name around everywhere I went, thinking somehow it would get back to you that I was looking, but nothing ever came back, even though I asked. I even wrote a letter to one of the tribal elders . . ." I stop then, because I can feel a sob rise up within me, and I choke it back down. But the tears that now threaten are tears of anger, not sadness, tears of bitterness, of loss. That elder, of all people, should have helped me come home. That was, a friend assured me, his role as an elder.

I told him of the letters I'd written all those years ago, the one to Vic and the one to Mr. Snipe.

"What did you say in your letter to Mom?" Vern asks, his voice quiet.

"I told her I was fine. Not to worry about me. That I'd had a good life."

"You lied." This is said without judgment.

"Kind of. But I didn't want her thinking badly about herself. That wasn't going to do anybody any good. But after I sent the letters, I waited. I waited for weeks, months, years. And nothing came back." I pause. "Ever." I shake my head and bite my lip in frustration, anger still edging my words. "That's when I realized the elders, even if their job is to help, don't have to do anything they don't want to."

When Roberta, Vern's full sister, called me in 1993, I had asked her if Vic had ever received a letter from me. Roberta couldn't recall Vic ever saying anything about hearing from me at all. When I met Vic the second time in 1994, I had asked her if she'd ever received the letter. "No," she answered definitively. "I never received any letter from you."

I have no idea what happened to those letters. Perhaps the elder had never opened them. Perhaps they ended up in his circular file. Perhaps, like so many other people, he didn't want to get involved in a sticky family situation. Perhaps, I think tiredly, things would have been different so many years ago, if he had made a different decision.

"But everyone knows the Plants," Vern reasons, his voice filled with confusion.

"I figured they were a pretty big family. I figured the reservation was small enough that if I threw their name around, someone would tell one of them that I was there. I don't know what else I could have done." How do you deal with someone who isn't supposed to exist? A ghost in a memory? A marker of a lost self? A reminder of failure? I am all those things; I am nearly invisible.

"So many barriers didn't allow me to come home," I explain, fatigued. I sigh and continue. "I spoke to a social worker from here, from the Flathead, who asked why I wanted to meet my family. At the time, I was twenty-three years old. I told her, because I want to find the people who look like me. 'That's not a good enough reason,' she said. Then basically she told me not to come back. 'How do you think they'll react when you walk back into their lives?' she asked. 'You've been dead to them for over twenty years. You'll do nothing but remind them of the scars that are now starting to heal. How do you think that would make them feel?'"

I level Vern with a stare. "No one, not one person, ever asked if I was ever made to feel uncomfortable with my adoption, but I was not supposed to make anyone else feel uncomfortable with my presence? My questions?" Again that lump in my throat rose. "So I stopped. I stopped trying to find you guys. I stopped trying to be one of the tribe. I figured I didn't want to hurt anyone because of my actions. I didn't want to be hurt anymore. So I just stopped."

Anger and frustration wrap around each other until they form a tight ball that lodges in my stomach. I am angry that so much has been kept from me: my family, knowledge of my birth father, knowledge of who I was in relation to this group that I somehow belonged to. And I am frustrated at the people who could have done something about it, who could have helped me return home all those years ago but chose not to. Too much time has allowed pain and resentment to grow, to fester.

"And the other social worker?" Vern prods.

"She left records for me to find," I explain, and told him what the files had contained. "They said that Vic was given a court date. If she wanted to keep her children, she needed to come to the courthouse on such and such a date." I look at Vern.

"She never showed up," he finishes.

I shake my head. "A note said she was found in a bar down the street."

"That true?"

I shrug. "But when I told Rosa about those files, she flipped out. 'They're lying,' she yelled. 'I remember when they came and took you from the house. We were all crying. They're fucking lying!'" I stare out the window again. "Maybe the truth is somewhere in the middle. I don't know. But that's what the records stated." I am numb. I am beyond crying, as I recount the dismemberment of our family, its carcass thrown aside. I am testifying.

"When did you find out about us?"

"When Roberta and Ronni called."

"They didn't mention us kids in the records?"

I frown, rummaging through my memory for what the yellow legal-length paper read, the one I'd scribbled my cryptic notations on. I threw it away once I met everyone, thinking I didn't need it anymore. Bad call. Now I'm a hoarder when it comes to keeping records. "I think it was just Vic's name, Gloria and Rosa, and us three kids. I know it listed a lot of her last names, but I can't remember if you guys were mentioned or not."

"But when Roberta called, that was the first you knew of us." The cop, pressing for information.

I nod.

"Hm."

Perhaps he's wondering if they were as forgotten in the legal system as I was. We sit for what seems like a long time. What more can be said?

"Ready?" I ask.

"Sure, where are we going?"

"Stevensville." I start the car and pull out once more on the two-lane back road into our pasts, this valley our connective tissue.

Stevensville is a small western Montana town in the heart of the Bitterroot Valley. When I lived there, between 1964 and 1969, it was a quiet collection of shops and businesses: an IGA, with a filling station next door; a bakery; and a clothing store, where even I could tell the mannequins were severely out-of-date. There was the bank, the realtor's office, a law office, and other buildings, all connected to one another in the way buildings in small towns are. Beyond the town limits were the farm co-op and veterinarians and farther out small farms turned into larger ranches in the sagebrush-covered hills of the valley.

I gained my first steps in education in Stevensville. I went to kindergarten and grade school, then joined Brownies and Girl Scouts. I pulled musty books from dark-oak shelves in the immense library on the second floor of the grade school. I adored the first principal and was in awe of the second, Mr. Barlow, a Blackfeet man who went on to change Indian education policy in Washington DC.

There used to be a huge oil painting that hung over the main doors of the elementary school. It was a collage of people and events that defined the valley: a dark-haired man, a covered wagon, and the little cabin-styled Catholic church a few streets over, among other things I don't recall. One day, as a first grader, I asked the silver-haired, blue-eyed principal who the man in the painting was.

"That's Governor Isaac Stevens," he'd answered. "That's who this town is named after."

Pride made him smile broadly and push his chest out. Wow, to live in a town that was named after someone with so much power!

Decades later I understood the irony. Governor Stevens, in 1855, negotiated the Treaty of Hellgate with the Salish, Pend d'Oreilles, and Kootenais. According to the treaty, the tribes ceded more than twenty million acres to the U.S. government, while retaining only one million three hundred acres, an area that would become the Flathead Indian Reservation. Important items in the treaty were that (1) the land was to be occupied by these three tribes, as well as "friendly" tribes that could be placed there at the will of the president of the United States; (2) no white man could reside on the reservation without permission of the tribes, as well as of the superintendent and the agent; (3) any roads could be placed on the reservation at will; (4) the tribes would retain their hunting and fishing rights; and (5) the tribes would be paid for the land at a sum of $126,000 over a twenty-six-year period. An Indian boarding school would be provided, which taught agriculture, industry, and the trades of blacksmithing, tinsmithing, carpentry, and wagon-wheel making. The government would also construct a sawmill, a flour mill, and a hospital. White employees would be kept in service for twenty years. Every tribal member would earn a salary of $500 each year for twenty years. The Dawes Act required that the reservation land could be surveyed and divided into lots at the discretion of the president of the United States.

To keep peace, tribal members would be required to "acknowledge their dependence upon the government of the United States, and promise to be friendly with all citizens thereof, and pledge themselves to commit no depredations upon the property of such citizens," or consequences would follow. They would also agree that the use of "ardent spirits" would be excluded from their reservation, and they were to prevent their people from drinking the same.

This treaty brought the downfall of many Native people; the Dawes Act brought homesteaders by the wagonload. By 1904, when allotment was initiated, these same homesteaders, or their offspring, found themselves the owners of tracts that totaled nearly a half-million acres. Tribal members, not seeing the value of ownership, either sold their allotment or lost it because they couldn't meet the federal land taxes. The purpose of boarding schools were not to teach leadership but to teach trade labor, thereby creating an economy constructed and maintained by outside interests. Although the government stressed independence, its treaties and ensuing policies actually forced dependence, which further served to break and dehumanize the human spirit, while at the same time bringing about the cultural and social destruction of a once self-sufficient and proud people. And those "ardent spirits" that were banned? They became the substance of choice to numb the pain from the loss of their culture, from the loss of themselves. Those ardent spirits also created the dysfunctional space within my family that allowed me to be removed.

But Vern and I don't talk about these things; we've said all there is to say, for now. We are quiet on the ride back to town; as we eat our lunch at Double Front Chicken, near the old train depot; as we drive up and down the roads looking for the Snow Bowl ski area, only to find ourselves at dead ends in beautiful housing subdivisions. Perhaps we are quiet because we've run out of things to say. Or maybe we've said too much, opened up too much, required too much, wagered too much. And we're tired, and we hurt.

I will continue to hurt because today wounds have been opened and scars have bled. But maybe the bloodletting is required. In the process I've learned I haven't been forgotten. I've told someone else they're important to my life, and I've become important in his. Perhaps this is where the true healing begins, when old stuff is dragged out of the closet and aired.

17

Will You Be Here Tomorrow?

Fort Collins, Colorado, March 2012.

Mom is lying on her bed. This is what she does most days since arriving at the nursing home nearly a year ago. In this position she looks small, her dark hair wild amid the white scrambling of bedclothes. She weighs all of eighty-two pounds. Her dark-brown, widened eyes are the color of the rich, dark loam in Ohio, that state where she was born. They contrast sharply with her pale Scottish skin, which settles like parchment on her frail bones. Her eyebrows rise in recognition, and she smiles; it is a look of pure happiness. That same smile has greeted me more times than not over the past fifty-plus years. I return her smile, but with a pinprick of pain, as I am once more forced to acknowledge her aging.

Her single twin bed is in the middle of the room, clad in the Laura Ashley quilt Rick and I purchased twenty-five years before for our bed, just before expecting our first son. Once it was decided she would live here, she made it clear I was not to waste money on another quilt. "It's still perfectly good," she said, scolding my interest in material things. She was raised during the Great Depression, and her family was extremely poor, but they ate well, having two acres on which to grow their food.

10. Adoptive mom, Eleanor; and Susan, age four. Photo by Jed Devan. Courtesy of the author.

Her mother would begin food preservation as soon as anything came to fruition. As a result, Mom was not fond of blind consumerism.

Sometimes when I visit I lie down beside her and we watch the large-screen television on the wall, commenting on Jerry Springer or Dr. Oz or golf or football. Today, however, I sit on the edge of the bed and begin once more to survey Mom's limited collection of personal belongings, starting with the simplistic collage of photos in the inexpensive gilded frame. They are photos of me, at various times of my life. Some are school photos; many are not.

The most prominent is my baby picture provided by Montana Department of Social and Rehabilitation Services to accompany the announcement of their adoption of me. In the photo I am eighteen months old, clad in a pink dress, reaching for something out of the camera's eye while a small smile played hesitantly on my face. When I was in my twenties, Mom explained that photo to me: "You know, when we found out you were up for adoption, we came to see you. 'She is the most adoptable baby we have,' the social worker said. And when we came into the room, you sat on a chair and looked at me with your dark eyes and that Indian stare—you know the one, the one that measures people to see if they pass the test before making any kind of judgment? That's the stare you gave me, and I knew, right then and there, I was going to have to earn your trust, that I was being measured as well."

In the adjacent photo I am three, standing in a meadow filled with gray-green prairie sage, with pines, aspens, and mountains providing the background. I are surrounded by black-eyed Susans. The original photo had been black and white because color film was cost prohibitive for a young biologist with a new family, so Dad had added color dyes. As a result, the yellows of the flower, the reds of my overalls, and the blues of the sky are soft, almost pliant. In the meadow my small, pudgy hand is clutched around a green stem, and I look at the camera, smiling.

Next to that one is a photo of me, taken in 1966. I am standing on the lowland near the Bitterroot River, where the soil is rarely moistened by the gently moving water. I am seven and wearing shorts and a sleeveless shirt. My hair, flighty and fine, is pulled back into a dark-brown ponytail.

"Here," my adoptive father says, as he moves me from place to place, his hands on my shoulders, guiding me, forcing me, while my feet stumble on the rocks that are too big and rounded to rest smoothly against one another. "Sit here." "Stand over there." Always, the Bitterroot Mountains laced by cottonwoods are my backdrop.

My father takes the shovel that he has brought with him and places the blade into the rocky earth, near a soft-pink flower. With his foot

11. Susan, age three. Photo by Jed Devan. Courtesy of the author.

he forces the blade in, uprooting the plant with its papery petals, lifting it from its home. He is careful to keep as much of the soil around its branched roots as he can, but little by little the soil falls away as he transfers the plant into my small hands.

"Hold this. It's a bitterroot," he says, stepping back as he looks into the square box at the top of the camera whose two perpendicular eyes stare at me from the front. He checks the small, brown light sensor in his right hand. "Smile." He snaps. He frowns and looks at me through the box again. "Smile," he says, his voice now edged with irritation. "This flower is the bitterroot," he adds by way of explanation. "For the Salish, the tribe you belong to, it is sacred. It has important meaning. Now kneel down on one knee and smile." I do, but the rocks dig into my skin that barely covers the bone, and the smile I produce is fake. "Do it again, but this time hold the plant away." "Hold the plant here." "Hold the plant down and in front of you." "Stand up." He is always looking into the box, always checking the light meter. The only time he looks at me is to show his irritation of my inability to follow his simple directions. By the time we're done, that plant doesn't feel very sacred. I watch him place it back into the hole from which it was extracted, but the soil is now broken, scarred by its removal.

I've since learned the plant is sacred for its medicinal properties and high nutrition value, but its most impressive characteristic is the fact that it can withstand drought for several years, during which time it doesn't bloom. But when the rains come, these delicate, long, pink petals shoot up and out, producing the floral display that resides in my heart. Oh, so many metaphors. I breathe deep and look away. I ask Mom how she's feeling.

"I'm doing pretty good.

This is her standard response.

Mom is eighty-four years old, an age neither one of us thought she'd ever see after sixty-some years of smoking, four full-blown manic episodes, two marriages, and a lot of loneliness in the most rural locations of the American West. I'm thrilled she's still with me, and I tell her so. I don't tell her I can't imagine a time she will not be.

She gives me a cryptic look, one full of confusion. "I don't know why I'm still here," she says, her voice wavering and unsteady, more from nonuse than emotion. "Nearly all my family is gone." Her brows now knit together in consternation. "Who do I have left?" She shrugs and raises her hands palms up.

In that small gesture and that short question, she's raised a delicate subject that dangles awkwardly between us, one that we have never addressed. What are we, really, to each other? To me, she has always been my mother, because any memory of my birth mother has long been wiped away, cleansed, erased physically, legally, and psychologically. But I haven't always been her daughter. On a certain level there is an awareness of a "before" time, when other people constructed my family, when she was childless.

That question defines this razor's edge of being.

In the early to mid-1970s I began to explore, through poetry, what it meant to "be Indian," but also what it meant to be me: being Indian and living white. Even in those early years I perceived that a decision was involved; a requirement to be one or the other. I couldn't be both; I couldn't borrow; I couldn't pretend. Perhaps I was trying to order my world. Or perhaps the world was trying to order me. Regardless, the pressure was palpable. "With what will they bury me, flower or song?" I asked at the end of one such poem, referring to the white lilies that graced the funerary sanctuaries or the drums and the harsh ululations of grief I'd heard in the movies, read about in stories. Shadow memories.

A year later I switched mediums, trying to fit those two identities together in a fairy-tale happy-ever-after type of way. This time I sought something three-dimensional. I purchased beading string and beads in white, turquoise, rust, and bright red, as well as a three-inch-long narrow, stainless-steel needle. In my fifteen-year-old mind's representation, white beads represented white people; rust beads represented American Indians; turquoise represented the world in which we lived; the red represented the blood spilled for us to survive in that world. I skewered several rust-colored beads at a time and watched them run down the length of string, until the line ran several inches. I then strung a few turquoise beads to indicate a break, followed by a few white beads. The white beads really weren't white, but pearl, possessing a luminescence that caused me to fall under their spell. As I worked, my fingers stopped shaking, having become comfortable with the machinations of working on a very small scale. Inch by inch the single line of beads grew, rust, turquoise, and white. Then I changed the pattern. I alternated ten rust beads with ten red beads, interrupted by a brief turquoise section. Then I interspersed the rust with white, intermingling them, breaking up their cohesiveness. I tied the ends, and it became a necklace, which hung midchest in a single strand that looked to outsiders like chaos, but to me like a new world order.

Mom smiled when I showed it to her, narrowing her eyes in intent study. "That's quite creative, Susie," she said, moving that study to my face. "Tell me what it means."

"It shows the world before, when just Indians were here, then it shows the white people arriving, then it shows the wars, and then it shows how we live in the same space." Her study returned to the necklace, and she nodded, a look I didn't fully understand crossing her features. I can place it now. She was surprised at my awareness of assimilation, though neither one of us at the time knew what to call it.

How uncomfortable is that subject for an adopting parent?

"Who is that?" Mom asks, pointing to a framed photo on her dresser, the one where a woman is wearing a colorful paper conical birthday hat, its elastic string pulled taut beneath her chin. Dan, who turned two, sits quietly on her lap. In front of them sits a large piece of birthday cake. The woman's smile is large; Dan's is shy.

"That's you," I explain, slightly taken aback that she can't see herself in the photo. "It's Dan's second birthday, and you were celebrating with us." Mom peers at it for a long time as if she is trying to bring her two selves into focus. A decade ago she'd mentioned sometimes when she walked by a mirror and caught her reflection, she was shocked at the face staring back at her, wrinkled and old. "I still feel like I'm twenty years old; imagine my horror at being seventy-five!"

She doesn't laugh when she says this.

Mom arrived in Fort Collins in 1991, just six months before the birthday photo. She and I had talked of her moving to be closer to me, and as I waited for that to happen I imagined her life once she was here. In my mind I moved her into the small, yellow townhome near our house, the one surrounded by a border of black earth in which she could garden, her hobby for the past sixty years or so. I saw us around a glass table eating dinner on her patio or sipping tea and laughing as we watched my children, her grandchildren, playing in the small yard. In that house, I believed, she would watch them grow into young men.

But that dream was shattered when she flew into Denver's Stapleton Airport one late morning. She'd left behind her second husband (a retired investment banker), her membership at the Billings Country Club, and her friends in the life she'd carved out in the seventeen years of living in Billings. As I bundled her and one overnight bag into my car and drove north on Interstate 25, I began to realize, with a sick feeling, that she was in the midst of her second manic episode, sputtering words and ideas at once true and fantastical. Her husband, she whispered that night after dinner, had been a drug addict; she'd seen the needle tracks on the inside of his elbow. Warning bells went off. He was seventy-five and an alcoholic. Neither Rick nor I had ever seen any needle marks.

That first week in our house she slept very little, perhaps fifteen minutes a day. For the next week or so she was animated, filled with guile, extroverted and creative, composing small intricate drawings, symbolic and deep, whose meanings were known only to her. Within days of these drawings the paralyzing paranoia crept in, and her drawings then became dark scrawls, scattered and jagged. She was suspicious of anyone who looked at her for more than a few moments. But the odder her behavior became, the longer people stared.

In early May I found a psychiatrist whose office was located in the hospital. He was able to see her the same morning I'd contacted him. I had reached my limits of not sleeping and watching her antics with my children become more bizarre as time went on. The psychiatrist diagnosed her as manic-depressive, and she walked out in a fit of rage. The doctor called 911 and asked them to contact him if a woman matching her description was called in. A half an hour later the doctor received a response. Evidently, Mom had begun knocking on doors and asking people to let her in. The woman who allowed her admittance then placed the call and assured the dispatcher that Mom was "harmless." "I just think something's not quite right," she said.

By the time they got there, Mom was gone.

In the meantime I'd returned home. This is where they reached me when she'd been spotted at a school. Could I meet them there? Yes, give me twenty minutes, I answered. The thing that didn't make sense was that the school they said was located all the way across town.

"No," the secretary said, warily, when I'd entered the building and introduced myself and my reason for being there. "We didn't call about your mom. The woman you describe never came here."

I wanted to vomit. Where the hell was she?

The phone rang and the secretary reached over and picked it up on the second ring. "Yes? Yes? Why yes, her daughter's here. Sure. I'll tell her to go over to the other school. No, no. That's all right." When she put the phone down, she informed me that dispatch had given the name of the wrong school. I was to go to the one near the hospital. She laughed. "Well, they start with the same letter of the alphabet! Good luck!"

Jitters coursed through my body as I pulled up behind the police cruiser, by which two officers towered over my five-foot-three mother.

They wore dark-blue uniforms and dark-gray sunglasses. Mom grinned and waved. I could tell she thought she was important, having these strong men so interested in her life that they'd come to find her! I cringed.

Then Mom looked at me, and a sly smile creased her face. She glanced at each officer, then announced she knew karate and took a stance, raising her hands into straight-edged sharpness. Oh, God. They didn't laugh. They didn't find it even mildly humorous. Instead, one officer touched his fingers to the butt of his pistol, while the other wrapped my mom's hands behind her back and placed her in handcuffs. Putting his hand on her head, he manipulated her into the police car, ignoring the angry sputters that escaped her pursed lips.

"We'll take her to the mental-health facility," he said to me, without preamble. "You can follow us there." I drove through the neighborhood, which melted in my tears, but whether I cried from witnessing the scene of her madness or from witnessing the scene of her enforced control, I am not sure.

That afternoon dark clouds gathered above us, breaking into a storm whose rage swirled violently in green anger, while bolts of lightning called forth sheets of rain that fell on the thirsty land. Its brutality mirrored my emotions. The life I envisioned for her was disintegrating into soul-shattering shards. The dream died entirely when I learned a year later that she hadn't gardened in years; arthritis in her knees caused her too much pain.

Within six months Mom moved into low-income housing, a far cry from the country club lifestyle she'd shared with her second husband. When he died the following year, she didn't receive anything from his estate. Evidently, she'd signed a prenup that allowed an inheritance only as long as she lived at their residence. Like many women in her generation, Mom was too trusting. They had sat at his lawyer's office, after having had a few drinks, when she signed the document willingly. She believed that her husband-to-be had her best interests in mind when he called it a formality. His lawyer hadn't suggested she get her own legal representation. Gone was the money for ten years of "service," as she liked to call her marriage, her country club lifestyle, and her status. She'd grown up in severe poverty. It had once more become her identity.

My thoughts are interrupted by Mom's quiet voice, and I slowly return to her small room in the nursing home. I ask her to repeat her question.

"Did you have trouble finding me?"

"No," I assure her, with a smile. "I always know where you are."

"You're so full of bullshit," she says, laughter shaking her small frame and her brown eyes shining with mischief. But I can tell she's waiting for an answer. I ignore the question; there's no appropriate answer I can give.

She is here because her lungs are compromised to the point that she gets winded after walking only twenty feet or so. Plus she's no longer able to take care of herself in the traditional sense. For one thing there are too many medications for her to keep track of. Many of the pills and inhalers treat her chronic obstructive pulmonary disease. Other pills and capsules treat her bipolar disorder. Unfortunately, the medications have a tendency to manufacture new side effects, for which she requires additional medication. Each day is a tightrope walk of being agitated or sleepy, engaged or confused, independent or helpless, happy or sad.

I've begun to hate the television advertisements that romanticize aging while denying the reality of the life she's living, all with large grins of the unconcerned. In one commercial a woman smiles as she pushes her grandson on the swing, both of them laughing with wild abandon in the face of pulmonary disease. In another a man smiles through his depression when the sun comes out of hiding behind a cloud. In daily programming there is a succession of people who, with the right medications, beam their joy as they move through their various diseases and malfunctions. They grin despite what their bodies and minds are telling them: the end is near. But watching these commercials is a bit like watching the last movies that the dying people see in the film *Soylent Green*. The end is not awful. It is green fields and flowers and blue skies.

A small table sits beneath her window, holding items that are reminders of her previous abilities, most of them books. She hasn't read any of these in a decade and probably wouldn't be able to concentrate long enough to enjoy them now. There are four Time-Life books of literature, the biographies of Albert Einstein and John Adams, and two volumes of poetry by Robert Frost, as well as a well-worn copy of a green, cloth-bound Audubon bird book.

"What have you been up to?" I ask, drawing my attention back to the small woman beside me, the one whose fingers hold the afghan I once crocheted.

"I played BINGO, today," she says brightly.

"Did you win?"

"I did. When you get a BINGO, you win a quarter." She beams, then her eyes grow dark and her brows knit together, as if she is trying to reason through a puzzle. "I wonder what you get when you get a black out. That's when you black out all the numbers on the card," she explains, quietly and carefully. She focuses on me with the wide-eyed awe of a child. "That has to be worth a lot."

I smile and nod in agreement, knowing that in her mind, she is once more a child, when a quarter meant so much more.

But then, just like that, her smile, her awe, her wonder, disappears, and her face takes on a tension that was absent only moments before. Like clouds moving quickly over the eastern Colorado high desert, confusion, embarrassment, and sadness cross her face. I am suddenly aware that she is no longer "pretty good."

Her expression has gone blank as she surveys the room in which she's lived for the past year. Uncertainty shadows her face as her gaze wanders over the photos that document our lives, my mother and me, my husband and me, the kids and me, all of us together. It deepens when it settles uneasily on the lightweight wheelchair that sits near the foot of her bed, an oxygen canister hanging from its handles. After several moments of intense study, she points a shaky index finger (a neurological condition she's always had) toward the chair and says, politely, "Someday, when you have a bit more time, I'd like you to show me how that works."

I don't tell her I have time now because it doesn't matter. Her confusion will increase with compounded interest if I attempt an explanation. So, instead, I say in a soothing voice, "Sure, Mom, I can do that." My throat grows tight, and tears blur my vision. I am once more aware of the inversion of our roles: me as caretaker, her as the one taken care of.

Her gaze continues around the room, and she points to the bathroom and the armoire, respectively, and her voice becomes steadier. "That's where I take a shower, and that's where my clothes are."

My soul shatters just a bit. She is not explaining her room to me; she's explaining the room to herself, reminding herself that she still knows that the world has order. And then she falls silent, because suddenly it's all gone, her memories as well as her ability to converse about them.

Mom is tired. Her eyes are rimmed in red, and the scattered remains of her thoughts ricochet off of invisible ideas. As her memories slow down, mine pick up. She viewed her role as a mother with paramount importance. It was visible in everything she did, with care and patience. She improved my fine motor skills by having me place raisins on gingerbread men. She taught me how to read recipes and decipher ingredients, explaining what a "dash" or a "pinch" or a "scant teaspoon" meant. Unfortunately, even with this instruction I didn't become interested in cooking until my midtwenties, not because she didn't try to teach me but because I just wasn't interested in learning. She made a myriad of Barbie doll dresses from the odds and ends of fabrics left over from her upholstering projects and other sewing projects. She created grand ball gowns from pink floral ticking and scraps of golden jacquard. She knit chic sleeveless dresses with the smallest of needles, their stitches fine and precise. She sewed a woolen skirt and jacket set, trimming the neck with faux leopard fur, a fashion requirement of the 1960s. Eventually, she taught me to sew my own dresses. She spent hours driving me to and from my piano lessons, violin lessons, singing lessons, and orchestra, choir, and theater rehearsals. She taught me to read, listening to my stuttered beginnings of Dick and Jane and soon graduating to Dr. Seuss, *Grimms' Fairy Tales*, and Winnie-the-Pooh. She taught me to embrace creativity through writing, painting, pretending, acting, and music. But most important, there was always time to talk, in front of a fire, sipping a cup of tea, about the gossip, the boys, the teachers, the future. And then she sent me out into the world with all the tools she provided.

Sometimes I failed. And sometimes I cried. With the exception of her first manic episode, she was always there to help pick up the pieces as I was coming of age. That's the way I remember her.

"Will you be here tomorrow?" I hear the fear in Mom's voice, and I cringe because she's never been a fearful woman.

"I will," I assure her.

"Will you know how to find me? You know, sometimes they put me in different rooms."

"No, I didn't know that. But you know what, Mom? Anytime you look up and see that picture that Aunt Ann painted, if it's in the room, that's the room you're supposed to be in. They will always have that in your room."

She leans back and thinks about what I've said and nods, as if to convince herself the statement is true.

I can't imagine the fear of not knowing where you're going to be the next night. Evidently, I went through it when social services removed me from my home and placed me first with a caseworker, then with my parents.

Mom has erased much of that for me.

I am trying my best to do the same for her now.

18

Gifts

Flathead Indian Reservation, Montana, October 2012.

It's been a year since that early Thursday morning, when Vern and I drove down the Bitterroot Valley and I heard the stories of his life, when I watched the mountains slide gently by our car windows and met his version of Vic, our mom. He showed me the places he'd lived as a boy, and I stood on the land he'd walked. I thought of his life in the campgrounds, migrating from one place to another so many times that the chaos caught up to him. He left school to shoulder the responsibilities of adulthood and babies of his own by the time he was sixteen.

That Thursday, a year ago, I was introduced to another reality of what it meant to have the life I lived. And I drove away with a new awareness for the price I paid, that we all paid, for the choices that were made for me. There is a significant difference between my arrival last year and my arrival this year. This year's visit is a homecoming.

My schedule is busy: on Wednesday I'm giving a radio interview at two o'clock and then a lecture at five at the University of Montana; on Thursday I'm attending a meeting with the tribal council at eleven thirty; and on Friday I'm giving the opening lecture at the Presidential Lecture Series at Salish Kootenai College on the Flathead Reservation at noon. These discussions will revolve around the research I did regarding American Indian transracial adoption. The weight of adoptees' stories is heavy, reminding me of the responsibility I have to share them, with names changed, identities protected. What I am hoping is that my sharing them will change adoption policies and protocol. As I lie in bed, I feel a raw energy, an electricity that never leaves my body. My mind swirls, and the question *what exactly am I trying to do here?* comes around and around again, the eddy of emotion not letting it go. *Am I lecturing? Am I helping? Am I asking for something in return that won't, perhaps can't, be granted?*

I toss and I turn as I unknot the threads of *why*. Why am I so agitated with these upcoming lectures when I haven't felt this way anywhere else? I sigh. Although I may not want to admit it, I know why. Unlike other lectures and presentations, where I present information to an interested audience, I am now in my homeland, where it all began. I could make a lot of people in these circles very uncomfortable with my experiences laid out, boned and filleted for all to see. *This is what happens*, the wind whispers, as if agreeing with me, *when you let your children go.* Soon the rain begins and the lightning throws shafts of light across the room, and I finally fall asleep, heavy with uneasiness.

The interview and the lecture go well. Healing words are spoken. Gifts are given in the spirit of a homecoming: a Pendleton blanket, an intricate traditionally beaded clamshell purse, a shawl, a beaded necklace, all given to symbolize a welcome home. All make me cry tears of gratitude and joy. However, as beautiful and as symbolic as they are, they do not assuage the ghosts that walk in the valley of my soul. And I don't know if anything will.

Roads, some paved, most gravel, mark the Jocko Valley in one-mile grids. The Jocko is located on the southern end of the Flathead Reservation. It is nine in the morning, and heavy clouds lie close to the ground, pregnant with the threat of rain. Again. Once in a while the sun breaks through, but most of the time those golden rays of early morning light beam elsewhere, far away from me.

I am searching for the cemetery that sits next to a white wooden church located somewhere in this valley. It's been three and a half years since I'd been there, so my memory of its location is vague, at best. But the valley is not so large that I won't be able to spot it from a distance. Therefore, I drive slowly along the still-green fields punctuated by cliques of blazing yellow cottonwoods. The houses that lie scattered on the valley floor are a mixture. Some sit grandly on acreages that could be small farms, but aren't used in that way, while others are hunched, their roofs buckled and tired. And then there are a lot of in-betweens.

My gaze is drawn across the valley, captured by a slash of white against the autumn palette. It is the church, the steeple a dead giveaway. I zigzag across the lowland, eventually turning left onto Agency Road, which then veers to the right, by a fence that marks a boundary more than it acts as a barrier, into the churchyard. The church itself doesn't appear to be used anymore. There is no statement of denomination, even on the sign that once held removable letters announcing service times. I assume it's Catholic; Vic was Catholic. I imagine she'd be buried in a Catholic cemetery. I pull alongside the church and cut the engine.

It is silent. A mid-October breeze seeps into my car and then into my bones, and I shiver from the chill. Although I am here to visit Vic's grave, I'm not entirely sure why I've come. I tell myself it is a result of a detour I've taken as I drive from Missoula to Pablo, an interest, a curiosity, perhaps even a requirement. But all those reasons ring hollow.

I close my eyes and wrap my fingers around the door latch and breathe deep to alleviate the familiar jolt of adrenaline; I don't want to do what I'll do next. I pull the latch and get out of the car. Shutting the door creates a cacophony, and I scan the landscape, soon spotting the source: a flock of thirty chukar partridges, frantically beating their wings against the wood of wild shrubs as they seek a new haven. I smile wryly at my jumpiness. After a few moments, the silence resumes. I begin to walk, as gravel whispers beneath the soles of my shoes.

This cemetery is different from those I'm most familiar with, the ones that exist within the urban landscape of middle-class America. It is not filled with manicured lawns and engineered spaces that stretch out in rows of military exactness. Here, families, rather than individuals, are buried in clusters. Few graves are marked by traditional slabs of granite, concrete, or marble, on which names are delicately carved into the polished surfaces. There are no angels, no praying hands, no Celtic crosses, no historical photographs in oval frames. Instead, many of the markers are thin wooden crosses that, unlike stone, will melt into the soil in a decade or two. Its overall appearance is overgrown and cluttered, as runaway shrubs and graceful strands of long grass, now golden brown in their dormancy, fill the spaces in between. There is a tension here, between love and pain; therefore, much of this space is left untended. Some might misinterpret this as forgotten.

Vic's grave is easy to spot because of the mound of black dirt that lies nearby, covering her grandson, Nathan, who was buried only a couple of weeks prior to my arrival. Nathan lies at the foot of his mother, Vic's daughter, who is interred next to Vic's niece, who rests next to Vic's husband, who is buried next to Vic and is the only one who has a granite headstone, a gift from the Veterans Administration for his military service. The wooden crosses above lean delicately to one side or another, names painted black on their white enameled surfaces. These are my relatives. I can't say as I ever really looked at them from this perspective before. I shiver and cross my arms in front of my chest in hopes that it will afford me some protection from the seeping chill, but it doesn't. Instead, the cold mingles with a surge of loneliness, overwhelming my senses, allowing memories to escape.

March 2008: I remember James Allen, Ronni, and I walked along this road with a hundred other mourners to bury Vic. Ronni wore black pants; I, a navy-blue dress and heels; James Allen a suit. Vern, Vic's youngest son, was dressed in a suit as well and moved easily in this space and among these people. His bearing was protective, of Vic, of his family, of the traditions required of this rite of passage. He'd arranged it all: the obituary, the vigil, the memorial, the burial. He'd given her the best service her tribal burial monies could buy, including the beautiful pine box that sat to the side of the freshly dug hole that would soon be her home.

I remember speaking to him briefly at the vigil, lending some words of comfort and knowing they offered little, if any, solace. What right did I have to comfort? Me, who hadn't known Vic at all? I remember the guilt when the tears didn't come. I remember Aunt Delphine touching my arm as she led me to the edge of the grave, where each of us, among the rest, threw a handful of dirt on Vic's casket as we filed past. I didn't know what to say, but felt words of some sort were required. I whispered, "Good journey," through a very tight throat and only loud enough for Vic to hear.

Afterward I remember the way Vern sauntered over to me, hands in his pockets, and asked how I was. The information we exchanged was superficial, required. And then there was silence, the awkward silence of not knowing. Anything. About anyone. Ever. Vern broke the silence by pointing to a group of young people who stood across the circle from us. "See those kids over there? Those are my kids."

"Which ones?" I asked.

He laughed, his brown eyes sparkling. "All of 'em."

To Vern, family is everything.

So much lost. So little known.

Where do I fit in all this?

I stare at the grave, at the long grass surrounding it, at the irises that grace Vic's feet, and I wonder what color they are. Suddenly I am wondering all kinds of things: her favorite color, the things that made her laugh, her hopes and her dreams. When she drove away, did she like to drive fast? Like me? After a couple of beers? Did she experience pain that never left her soul? Did she, like me in college, dull it with mind-numbing substances or mistake the closeness of another human being with love?

Did she ever wonder what happened to me?

Suddenly, I'm startled by this simple question. I had wondered for much of my life what happened to her, but had it been returned? My throat closes, and it hurts to swallow, and that's when the tears finally come, at first gentle, but then full, blurring the world around me as they roll down my cheeks and disappear into the soil at my feet. And I can't stop them. I begin to hurt inside, a deep wrenching pain that begins in my gut and surges upward and shakes my shoulders with huge wracking sobs, a heaving eruption of longing and the repression of longing. I gulp deep breaths of air, but the tears continue, a deluge in the drought of feeling, and I just let them come. I don't have a choice. But I don't just grieve for Vic, I grieve for the destruction of me, for the destruction of all of us.

I glance at my watch when I enter Pablo—11:15. I'm scheduled to meet with the tribal council at 11:30. During the drive my thoughts swirled like a snowstorm: how things were, how things are, how they might have been, even how they should have been. By the time I arrive my emotions have settled, and I can concentrate on the next thing I need to do: find a parking spot and see if my eyes are puffy. They are, but only a little. I press my cold fingers over my lids and hold them there, unsure of how much good I'm actually doing.

Two weeks ago I'd requested to be added to the council's agenda, because I wanted the council to pass a resolution to hold a cultural event that acknowledged and welcomed home people separated from the tribes because of adoption or long-term foster placement. Now that I'm here, my stomach does a series of gymnastics, and I can't seem to pull enough air into my lungs to calm my nerves. Vern has come, as has Ronni, with her granddaughter in tow. They are there for moral support. Evelyn, my source of support throughout my journey home, has once more been there for me by acting as my liaison, introducing me to the council. She arrives, dressed professionally, wearing creased slacks and a matching jacket. She sits down and places a gift into my hand, wrapping my fingers around it. It is a necklace, which I clasp tightly. She smiles and nods, and we wait to begin.

Soon the clerk takes me aside and tells me that council is running late; there were a lot of walk-ins. We'll have to wait and see if the schedule can be rearranged. She adds that we have been allotted a half an hour. Soon we are instructed to go in, and we seat ourselves in the front row. Vern, seeking anonymity, sits in the back. I surreptitiously study the seven council members, who sit on the curved raised dais in front of me, and wonder how they'll react to my statement. I prepare for the worst. The words I will say address my own personal experience of living with racism on the outside, as well as the racism experienced when I attempted to return home. *Don't leave us hanging in a brutal world*, I want them to know. *We want to come home. We need to come home. And there's a whole new generation of foster kids being outplaced that will be where I was thirty years ago. Unlike mine, I want their homecoming to be successful.* The barriers to acceptance need to come down; they affect all of us.

The council moves through the business requests quickly. The tribal police chief, who is ahead of us, wraps up, then returns to the back row and sits next to Vern instead of exiting through the main doors. "He wanted to stay and listen to you," Vern will tell me later. "He was interested in what you had to say." I appreciate the show of support from this person I do not know.

Evelyn and I slowly make our way to the table in front of the council. I avoid looking directly at the members before we start because I'm trying to find the balance for my asking and feeling guilty because of my asking. After Evelyn introduces me, telling the council why she believes this is an important request, I begin to speak. A council member interrupts me briefly, explaining how to operate the microphone. I turn it on, bend the mic toward me, and smile. Then I begin.

"My name is Susan Harness. My birth name is Vicki Charmain Rowan. I was removed by Montana State Social Services from my home in 1960." I tell them about the ethnic slurs, the verbal and physical abuse. I tell them about the racism on the outside and the racism when I returned to the reservation. I talk about adoptees' deeply embedded pain of nonbelonging and tell them that by passing such a resolution, they will begin to heal the destruction caused by assimilation policies that have assaulted us as Native people. I speak for ten minutes and feel the tension simmering in the room. I look up from my statement and see the council members leaning forward in their chairs as they listen to my words.

When I finish, there is silence.

The silence makes me nervous. *What right do I, as an outsider, have to ask this of anyone or for anyone?* Soon I hear murmurs of appreciation, and I immediately hear each of the seven members, in this very public forum, add their own private story, of being ostracized within the institution of a predominantly white school, of coming back to the reservation after being away for a period of time and experiencing a similar type of ostracism, of extended family being outplaced, of people returning home. I am humbled by their stories, fragile gifts of a shared past.

I hope they seriously consider my request.

The previous afternoon, at the invitation of Dr. Gyda Swaney, the director of the Indians into Psychology program at my alma mater, the University of Montana, I presented a lecture about my research and my findings. Prior to the lecture Dr. Swaney had arranged for me to tour the new American Indian Student Services building. No longer housed on the edge of campus, this architecturally symbolic building stood at its center, on the edge of the oval, just a few buildings away from the administration building.

The number twelve is a central theme to the building's design, spaces that represent the twelve tribes living within Montana's borders: Assiniboines, Blackfeet, Chippewas, Crees, Crows, Gros Ventres, Kootenais,

Little Shells, Northern Cheyennes, Pend d'Oreilles, Salish, and Sioux. Inside, along the wall separating the interior circle from the hallway, are twelve doorways, each having the name of the tribe inscribed overhead and their traditional parfleche design inlayed in the flooring below. I saw the richness of the woods' hues as symbolizing the richness of each tribe's culture. How far removed this place is, both locationally and culturally, from the tiny turn-of-the-century house that used to be home to Native American Student Services. I am swelled with pride.

At a quarter to five I crossed the oval, locating the building where I was scheduled to lecture. Entering its hallways, I was slammed back to 1982, when I'd taken my first creative-writing course. The instructor was a well-known writer; he'd entered the classroom, clearly marked with a "No Smoking" sign, and after a few moments proceeded to grind his cigarette butt into the linoleum. Definitely a statement.

The room was located in the basement, and I was pleased to see Dr. Swaney as she approached me, wearing a beautiful smile that reached her dark eyes. After a quick hug, she said, "Before you begin, Joe Pablo, a Salish elder, will say a few words. I've asked him to talk because he will add important knowledge to the information you'll present. Ready?"

I nodded and took a seat in the second row, on the end. Behind me sat an older American Indian man, an oxygen cord draped below his nose and over his ears, connecting him to a tank on a wheeled holder. Nearly black braids, thin plaits with wisps of silver, hung to his lap. He glanced at me briefly, nodding a greeting as he spoke to the woman beside him. Moments later, following Dr. Swaney's introduction, he stood and walked to the podium. This was Joe Pablo, and his message was clear: American Indians in today's America experienced not only a dilution of our culture but a dilution of ourselves, because of the historical policies that framed us while stealing our very strong cultural foundation of family. The result was this destitute place where fractured families were defined by dysfunction, through no fault of our own.

"People mistake tradition with culture," Mr. Pablo stated, his voice soft but carrying great strength. "Tradition is what we do. Culture is who we are. Even though Ms. Harness wasn't raised around us, she is very much a member of our culture, because we are a culture that has experienced assimilation with such negative consequences. So," he said, turning toward me, acknowledging me with his smile, his nod, "you may not know our traditions, but you are most definitely of our Salish and Kootenai culture."

My own presentation was an illustration of his words. All the assimilation policies that were put into place—removal, Indian education, relocation, termination, and child placement—created a space for us to argue among ourselves who is real and who is a "wannabe," even though status had been granted by the Bureau of Indian Affairs. These policies meant to fracture us, turn us on ourselves and one another. Those of us at the margins were the vein of soft mineral that ran through rotten granite, crumbling us even further.

Several of us, including Joe, went out to dinner after the talk. At one point he turned toward me, with tears in his eyes. "Never stop telling people what has happened to us, what's been done to us. They need to know. Please promise you won't stop telling this story."

I promised. Joe passed away a few months later. I lost yet another person who could have provided guidance had we known each other all those years ago.

It is now afternoon, as Vern and I drive the lower road of the Bison Range, which skirts about a third of the mountain. The upper road, the one I most like to travel, had closed a few weeks earlier due to snow. Both of us are disappointed. Vern likes the view from there. I like the feeling of being part of the reservation community in an invisible kind of way. As we drive the lower road I feel more visible but not necessarily more grounded.

"So what did you do this morning after breakfast?" Vern asks, as the brown rolling hills, dotted in rusts and golds, slip by our windows. I drive slowly because this one-lane gravel road is gently scooped with potholes. I look forward to this time with him, when our conversations are easier, my words less guarded. By knowing him, I'm coming to know me.

"Not much," I reply. "Just drove up here from Missoula." Then I pause. I don't weigh my next words, but I know as soon as they are out of my mouth I have just landed in quicksand. "I stopped by Vic's grave this morning." I stare at the road in front of me as if I'm driving dangerously fast, not twenty miles an hour. Only then do I steal a look in Vern's direction.

He steals it back. "Why?" Those brown eyes are unblinking. Piercing.

"Why, what?" My heart speeds up, and the evasive maneuvers begin.

"Why'd you do that?"

"I don't know." I shrug my shoulders and look straight ahead. "I just did."

Vern, the cop, pushes. "I think you know. Why did you stop?"

"I just wanted to."

"But why?"

And this goes on.

"I just felt like it."

"What made you stop?"

"I just did."

"What were you looking for?"

"I don't know." Panic sets in because I'm being backed into a corner. I've just opened myself up to examination. *C'mon, you can do better than that.* Okay. I was establishing a territory: Vic was my mother too, not just Vern's, and I sought to defend my right to her. However, the doubts, the continuing doubts of whether or not I even have a right to this territory are assaults in and of their own. But I have to defend it, because if I don't and I lose it, I will have nothing left. Suddenly, I am playing a very foreign and dangerous game, with someone I can't afford to lose. "Why doesn't she have a headstone?" I ask, venturing in another direction. "Why is it just a simple white cross?"

"Why are you changing the subject?" He chuckles.

"I'm just wondering why she doesn't have a headstone. Something more permanent."

The chuckle is gone. Vern looks out the window. "Because I know that if I want anything done, it will fall on my shoulders. Headstones are expensive." He looks at me. "Why do you think she needs a headstone?"

There are only two of us here in this space, and somehow I feel like I'm being flanked.

"I just do."

"But why?"

"Because she should be remembered."

"Why are you so bothered by it?"

"I just think it's important."

Silence descends, as I've run out of room. My back is to the wall. "I'll go in halves with you," I counter. I'm buying time.

"Really? Why? I mean, what do you care? She's not there."

My throat tightens. *Because she is there. She will always be there. Because I don't know where else I will put her. I don't know where she fits. I don't know where I fit.* Silence fills the space between us, and I'm feeling vulnerable, exposed. I cross my right arm over my chest and massage my upper left shoulder. Tears threaten to spill, but I bite my lip and stare straight ahead and clench my jaw so the words don't escape. I swallow them down. Once. Again. And then I shake my head; the rhythmic rubbing continues.

"You know," Vern says after a few moments, his voice quiet, "it's okay."

But it's not okay. This collision of worlds is not okay. I can't say where Vic is or where she is not. I can't say why it's important that she have something more long-lasting. I can't say why I care anything about the woman who let me go, who has lain in that space in the ground for three and a half years.

But I do care. I care so much it hurts. And having this conversation hurts. I feel as if I'm defending my ideas, beliefs, and attitudes of kinship that may not be defensible. But they're mine. They're all I have.

"Because she should be remembered. Regardless of her choices." My words are quiet, shaky, but they're out. Massaging my shoulder is now a compulsive act; it takes attention away from the pain. The pain of existing in between: sister and not sister, daughter and not daughter, self and not self. This space of between, of being nothing and both, has created a dilemma in my consciousness. *Whose rights win?*

How much of a daughter do I have to be to feel justified in visiting her grave? In asking for a more solid headstone? In asking to be remembered within this family, this tribe? What right of claim do I have to anything? I can't blame others for asking these same questions, when they rotate within me. This place of between is still so barren, and this barrenness is where I exist each and every time I return to this land. I look at Vern and force a small smile. "Have any of my questions ever made you feel uncomfortable?" I ask suddenly and return my gaze to the road.

Vern's reply is simple, and I can see him shaking his head in my peripheral vision. "No. No, I've never felt uncomfortable with any of your questions." I once more turn toward him and study his face. The half smile he gives in return indicates he already knows the answer to his next question. "Are *my* questions making you uncomfortable?" He laughs.

"Yeah." I can't help but chuckle at his laughter, but at the same time I continue the compulsive massage. I release a heavy sigh. "Yeah, they are." The sigh has released a tension within me. I can finally say, "I guess I don't want to answer because I don't think any of my answers will make sense to you. I don't know that they make sense to me. But I don't know what else to say." I shrug apologetically and turn away. And we drive and look at the deer, at the stream, at the antelope, at the various ambers and russets that cloak the ripples of ancient Lake Missoula, over which we drive.

We agree to go halves on a headstone.

We agree it will happen next summer.

But within my head the arguments and counterarguments still continue. Vic is part of me. With all her foibles, with all her mistakes, her harsh nature, her forgetfulness of her children, she is still part of me. She is who I wanted to know since I was sixteen; she is who I feared when I eventually met her. She holds my memories, of who I wanted her to be, of who I thought she was, maybe even who I think she wanted me to be. I feared being forgotten but then constantly prepared for that outcome.

"Did I ever tell you about the last time I visited Vic? The fourth time I went to see her?"

When I look at him, Vern stares straight ahead, but his face is taut. He shakes his head. "No. I didn't realize there was a fourth time."

"I'm not proud of it. I certainly didn't show myself well. But it's something that has bothered me for a long, long time." I pause. This seems to be the trip of confession.

"What happened?"

That's what I like about Vern—there's no tone of judgment in his voice. But I don't ever kid myself in thinking that it's not there, somewhere.

I saw Vic five months before she died. I'd dropped by, and the teen-something girl who answered the door acted as if she knew me. "She's asleep, but she'll probably be awake in a little while. Come on in."

Whenever I come back to the reservation, I find myself in a difficult position: I never fully know what my relationship is to other people I come into contact with. Are we blood-related? Related by marriage? Related at all? And like most American Indian families, it's pretty convoluted. Brittany, the girl who answered the door, is Robin's daughter. Robin is my half sister, Vern's full sister, who died in a car accident three years before I met the family, the one whose son is now buried at her feet. Therefore, Brittany is my niece.

Brittany and I talked for perhaps an hour, where she spoke about her life, her ideas, the friends she's lost through the various ways people die on the reservation: car accidents, drug overdoses, binge drinking, suicide. Within a period of five minutes she'd ticked off twenty people, touching the tips of her fingers as she recounted their brief stories. And I couldn't help but think, *This is just one kid on the reservation. Every kid has this story.*

Afterward Brittany got up from the lounge chair, walked the hallway to the back of the house and disappeared into a side room. She spoke in quiet tones and then beckoned me back, saying, "She's awake." She turned her attention back to the person in the room. "Grandma, it's Vicki Charmain."

I stepped through the doorway and stopped.

I was so unprepared for the sight of the small, emaciated woman who sat on the edge of the bed, her hair dyed dark, her eyes blurred with medication. She looked at me and blinked but didn't say anything. I was unprepared for the image of her skeletal legs and arms that extended out of her cotton pajamas, the bony structure of her face. Her face, its features, stark and angled, belonged to a woman I didn't know, had not really ever known. She was dying, and I was unprepared to say good-bye. We hadn't even been able to say much of a hello.

Tears. Fear. Shock. Guilt. All these ran together in a blur of emotions, like angry chalk colors left out in the rain. So I left. I made a lame, hasty excuse and disappeared down the hallway, where I used the wall as a touchstone in my escape from the tragedy defined by the woman in that room. When I finally reached the car, I turned the ignition and drove away, as tears coursed down my cheeks so fast my lap was soaked within moments. I didn't tell anyone about that experience. I, the daughter and not daughter, never returned until the day before she was buried.

"Did you talk with her at the grave?" Vern asks at the edge of McDonald Lake.

"Yeah." I am embarrassed.

"What'd you say?"

"I don't know." I'm tired. There's been too much prodding around in such private corners, places I've protected for so long. Now with these past few days of conversation, presentation, emotional bartering, I feel like an emotion-hoarder who has been assaulted by the "clean police."

"Dad used to talk to people in the cemetery all the time," Vern added, his voice quiet as he slipped into memory. "I used to sit on his shoulders and listen to him."

I let that hang in the air. When I look at him, I see the strong man who holds his own cards so close to his chest. In the times we've spent together, I'd seen two emotions: calm and restrained joviality. "Did you cry when Vic died?"

Vern shakes his head. No, he'd been prepared for that for a long time. He looks out across the lake. "I cried once when my dad was dying, and we were at the hospital. But I didn't cry when I buried him." Silence. "I cried when I had to pull the plug on Nathan, Robin's son, though. That one was hard."

The water of the lake is dark green and calm, its depth unfathomable, while its edges are fringed in the fiery passions of autumn.

I don't know if I told Vern or not, but what I'd said to Vic at the grave was "I am so sorry. For all of it."

19

Losing the Master Key

Flathead Indian Reservation, Polson, Montana, June 2013.

I am here, at the condo on Flathead Lake, to write what will be my memoir. It is quiet and away from the day-to-day events that would typically pull me away: housework, gardening, lunch with friends. But it is also away from the people who could provide the most support, as I examine my life and the events that framed it.

On the first day of my arrival, I question my decision to do this alone, but it is too late. I am here. I soon realize I need no alarm clock. I wake consistently at five each morning, when the darkness becomes confused as to whether it is coming or going. Each morning I pad into the living room and draw the white accordion shade, revealing the Mission Mountains, large black mounds silhouetted against a dark-lavender sky. Within a half hour the sun will come out of hiding, giving me time to boil water for tea, pull on a pair of shorts and a sweater, slip on sandals, and brush my teeth.

Then I start my day.

As the sky turns a light violet I head to the dock. Along the way I see minnows darting in the protective water as well as the beginnings of plant life establishing itself on the sandy bottom. Few boats are moored in the spaces along the wooden arms that are shaped like an E. I settle myself at a picnic table on the farthest edge. I've brought my mug of steaming Earl Grey, my iPhone, a pen, and my green leather writing journal that I'd purchased specifically for this trip. The cover is embossed with Celtic crosses and braided designs, and just holding it provides a sense of calm. I wrap my hands around the hot mug of tea and watch the steam swirl in the cool morning air. Then I close my eyes, and I can hear the world awaken: the quiet hum of cars on the nearby highway, the wings of birds whispering in the disappearing darkness, the gentle talk of ducks from an unknown distance. I pull the morning air deep into my lungs and whisper a prayer of thanks to the Creator. The mountains wear a halo of gold as the sun inches upward. I put down my tea and take up my pen and my journal and begin to write, looking up every so often to see the world change as the sun rises over the Missions.

A colony of insects spins itself into a dust devil, hovering above the water, which froths, as a school of fish spies the column of insects. Nearby small dark birds dip and sway in pairs, gliding above the pane of liquid glass, while overhead an osprey beats its wings, heading quickly for better hunting grounds. All the while tiny minnows migrate along the edge of the jetty near my feet.

When the sun is well up, three families of geese, goslings in the center, swim in front of the condo. The babies are small downy things, their feet paddling easily to keep up with the adults. In contrast, a female merganser's thirteen ducklings swim frantically around her, wearing themselves down until, one by one, they are allowed to climb on her back, seeking respite.

During my month-long stay, every day, except the stormy ones, start like this.

Who else had been privy to our removal? I've turned this question over in my mind long before my arrival; however, now that I'm here, it appears ceaselessly in my thoughts. The first person to ask is Gloria, my sister ten years my senior. She will most likely have remembered something.

Gloria lives in the same tribal housing neighborhood that Vic had lived in. Inside, her house is familiar in that it has the exact same layout. When I knock (*such a white thing to do*, the white voice reminds me), I am greeted by two kids, a little girl who is perhaps five or six and a boy, about age seven. The boy stares at me, sullen and annoyed.

"Is Gloria here?" I ask.

While neither of them moves, the boy yells, "Grandma! Someone's here and wants to talk to you." Then they disappear into the house.

"Well, who is it?" I hear Gloria say, her voice gravelly, like Vic's.

"I don't know. Some woman."

Framed by short white hair, Gloria's face peers from behind the hallway wall. "Well, hi there, Charmain! Come on in." She holds the door open as I step inside. In the intervening years Gloria has taken on more and more characteristics of her mom: she looks like her, sounds like her, and moves like her, which is disconcerting. Vic has been dead for five years.

I wrap my arms around Gloria's thin, petite frame, almost frail in its existence. But her voice reminds me she is anything but frail. It is that voice, coarse and gritty, which she uses to address the two kids, who have come into the living room to stare at me.

"This is your great-aunt Vicki Charmain," she says, as she taps a pack of cigarettes into the palm of her hand. She takes one, cups the flame, and pulls a deep breath, smoke pouring from her nostrils as she exhales. "She's my sister." Each gives me a doubtful stare. I feel awkward under their examination.

Gloria lets them stare a bit longer, then tells them to "Go play, or watch TV." The boy throws himself on the nearby couch, grabs the remote, and turns on the living-room set. "Go watch in your room," Gloria growls and stares him down.

"But I want to watch in here," he counters, throwing me a sharp look.

Her look is sharper. "Go watch in your room."

Quiet settles into the living room, and I sit on the couch while she sits on the lounge chair. We chat briefly about my travels. I finally ask Gloria the question that has dogged me over the past several months. "Were you at the house when social services came to take Ronni, James Allen, and me?" She pauses before shaking her head. She puts a bottle of beer to her lips and soon after pulls another cigarette from the pack.

"I wasn't there," she says. "I wasn't even aware you'd been taken. I was living in Washington at the time, with another family."

I hide my disappointment. This is really the only missing piece of the puzzle; I've struck out.

Gloria's attention becomes focused on a photo across the room. She hoists herself out of the easy chair, complaining of arthritis in her back. She tells me she's on painkillers to deal with that pain. Bent and stiff, she crosses the room and pulls a glossy photo from the corner of the frame, which holds her tenth-grade high school picture, in which she is young and beautiful and without arthritis.

"Have you seen this picture?" she asks, showing me the photo she'd removed. I stand up and reach for it. "I had a larger one, but I loaned it to Vern. He never gave it back!" She sounds astonished at Vern's gall and looks at me, her brown eyes wide in disbelief. I can't tell if her annoyance is real or feigned.

I return my gaze to the photo and furrow my brow. I don't have any memory of this picture being taken, yet there we are, Gloria, Rosa, Ronni, me, James Allen, Roberta, and Vern. "When was the picture taken?"

"Ma's funeral, in 2008," she answers. "The only one missing is Vern's older brother."

And Robin, but she'd died.

All of us are smiling against a background that looks like winter, except it was in mid-March when snow blew harsh against my skin. I am not really surprised I don't remember this photo. It turns out I hadn't remembered much of anything that happened for the three months following Vic's funeral.

Vic's funeral was in March. In June my father-in-law celebrated his seventy-fifth birthday in Colorado Springs, along with his wife, one of his brothers and his brother's family, Rick's siblings and their families, and Rick and me and our sons. I remember standing in the foyer of the upscale restaurant, holding a glass of wine while talking with Rick's sister, Laura, and her youngest daughter, Kendra.

"It is so good to see you!" I exclaimed. "It's been a long time."

"No, it hasn't." Kendra said, giggling. "We just saw you."

"No, you didn't," I said, smiling. "It's been, what? A year?"

They exchanged a look of concern before looking back at me. "We were at your house two months ago," Laura added, as if prodding my memory. She chuckled, thinking I was teasing.

"No, you weren't." My smile faltered, as I grasped around for a memory that would match up with what they were telling me. But none existed. Laura looked from my face to the wine glass and back again, worry etching her features.

She spoke to me, carefully, as one might a child. "No, we were there. Remember? Kendra and I came to visit . . ."

Nothing.

How could I lose two months of time?

The following October I called Laura. "I think I know why I don't remember you visiting last spring. Vic, my birth mom, had died just two weeks before you came up. And from that point on, I really don't remember much of anything, until Bill's birthday celebration. It's as if two months totally disappeared off the radar."

The photo revealed our family in so many ways. Sisters leaned in toward one another; Vern, the protector, was in the back. James Allen wore a broad smile. But my unease was visible, with my stilted body language, arms close to my body, hands folded over my abdomen.

As always, I skim these faces for family similarities. Gloria looks the most like Vic. Vern and his sister, Roberta, are clearly related, with Ronni looking more like them than anyone else. Rosa is a mixture: her eyes are like Gloria's but the same dimples that crease Ronni's and Roberta's face crease hers. Only James Allen and I don't fit quite as easily into this reunion, neither to each other, nor to our siblings. James Allen's face is sharply angular with a strong chin and high cheekbones, his eyes dark and intense. Me? I'm not sure. I'm slightly darker. I have the same nose as several of my siblings. Our eyes are similar, kind of. Then I wonder if I'm just searching, just trying to find something that is the same. I want to see us as related, but it's difficult being outside of this circle. They've known one another, grown up around one another, been used to seeing one another. All that has been overlaid with the concept of sibling, and whether they are full or half siblings, they don't care. They accept the complicated relationships without question. I'm the only one who cares about such labels.

I returned. They never really left.

Ronni and I sit in the early morning on the deck chairs off the condo's patio. The air is still and the water calm, and I watch as a group of Canada geese swim by. There are three adult pairs that surround seventeen goslings. Although I assume these are three separate family units, they are so tightly knit it is difficult to ascertain really which goslings are with which sets of parents. "Don't you think that's unusual? That three families of geese would be swimming together like that?"

Ronni looks at me, a sparkle in her dark-brown eyes. "Oh," she says gesturing toward the group, "those are rez geese."

We laugh.

I spend the first two weeks of June trying to work up the emotional strength to reconnect with other family members. I tell myself that learning more about them allows me to learn more about me. But within the first couple of weeks the goal sounds hollow, forced. I catch up on their lives through other family members, hearing about their ongoing problems with alcohol or drugs. Some are in domestic-violence situations with no intention of leaving; some have lost their own kids to the social-work system, and consequently their grandkids are at risk as well. Some try to be good parents, or grandparents, to fill in the gaps but end up falling back into their old ways of coping under pressure, their own substance use taking a central role in their lives. Some have attempted suicide. Some sell their medications to make ends meet.

I want to scream: You are repeating the patterns that got Ronni, James Allen, and me removed from this family, and you are doing it willingly, with full realization! You are destroying yourselves and destroying your children, your future. Our future, as Indian people! Don't you realize another generation is in danger of being removed? Of leaving? Are you prepared that when they come home they'll come home filled with confusion, hurt, and anger? Like me? Or worse, what if they don't feel anything at all?

With each story I am overwhelmed by such sadness, such hopelessness. And the dysfunctional strings are so intertwined, they look like macramé gone wrong, with no way to resort them and fix the problem. At times like this I feel a twinge of survivor's guilt.

One day, halfway through June, Ronni and I drive the gravel back roads of the reservation, dust boiling behind us, rising on the breezeless air, obliterating everything from the perspective of my rearview mirrors. This road is unfamiliar, as it snakes through the southwest corner of the reservation, where there are no markings to indicate whether I am on tribal land, private ranch land, or government land. Sagebrush carpets the rolling arroyos, while bluebirds and trilling meadowlarks sit on fence posts surveying the land, their voices carrying easily through my open window.

I slow down as I come to a bridge tagged with paint, whose reds, blacks, and blues argue with one another, asserting the importance of their messages, loud and harsh, against the mundane background of concrete. Ronni tells me this is Sloan's Bridge, a concrete kaleidoscope of names, notes, and initials that memorialize the men, women, and children who died in the various ways people die here. No surface is unmarked, a testament to the reservation's high mortality.

A souped-up Ford F-150 is parked midway on the bridge, and I pass it slowly, looking at the two young men who stare, unsmiling, as I drive past. Old habits die hard, as I become acutely aware of the eagle feather, a gift from Ronni, that hangs from the rearview mirror. The movie *Deliverance* comes to mind as we watch one another, the green water below swirling in dangerous eddies. I've been conditioned to fear being marked as Indian in an unfriendly white world.

Over the ensuing days depression settles around me like a wet wool cape, as I think about the way old patterns rework themselves into new generations. In this state I don't visit family; I can't witness the destruction. My heart, already so bruised, shatters as I watch the blind acceptance of living a seemingly predetermined life.

In addition, the condo feels small, and my words, my pages, stack up and cramp my movements, my thoughts. All this simmers into anger, anger at myself for wearing such rose-colored glasses and moving here with no forethought of what was really going on and anger at the family I was born into because, over the years, I had convinced myself we were made of stronger stuff. But now I feel the oppressive nature of the reservation, and more than anything I want to pack my car and drive away from this place, with its wounds and spilled blood, the social body reeking like a gangrene infection.

But I don't.

Deep into depression, I phone Gyda, a psychologist and fellow tribal member. I figure she'll understand where I am and give me direction— because the direction I'm going has bled me out.

Gyda and I agree to meet two days later at the little Victorian restaurant in downtown Missoula. It's clearly the type of place where university professors and urban professionals gather to talk about projects, in progress or upcoming. I listen to their conversations as I wait for Gyda.

She arrives, wearing that familiar beautiful smile that makes the clouds lift. "How are you?" she asks with a flourish, as she slides into the booth, ordering coffee from the server who hovers nearby.

"Fine." I smile, but my smile is forced. I don't want to say anything more because my voice will crack. And there is this facade I have to maintain. *We're fine. Everybody's fine here. We're all fine.* We order breakfast and chat about inconsequential things, my family, her family, our vacations. But once the plates are cleared away and we sit with our respective cups cradled in our hands, Gyda asks how things *really* are. I wince. She's able to read me with an uncomfortable accuracy. And like the deluge of the rains I've watched over the lake in the past several days, I tell her. I tell her of my quest to find witnesses to our removal; my need to connect with, while at the same time distancing myself from, family; and the painful psychic lacerations that happen in the aftermath. Tears form and I look out the window at the cars going by, concentrating so hard on anything else but the heavy heart that keeps me in this booth.

"I wanted to be strong," I say, the tears flowing despite my best efforts. "I'd wanted to prove I was strong, that I was doing the right thing in being here. But the devastation is heartbreaking, and I can't watch the self-destruction because it is heartbreaking. More than anything I wanted to be in this space to prove I belong here, but I don't. There is such pain. I can't witness the pain."

I stop because I can't continue. I breathe deep, take a sip from the cup shaking in my hands, and get myself under control so I can meet her gaze. I feel like such a failure, with my naïveté and Pollyanna ideas of how things should be. When I finally look at her, she gives me a gentle smile, wistful, and her black eyes are liquid. She lifts the cup of coffee to her lips and sips before she answers.

"Oh, I know," Gyda says. "I know exactly what you're describing. Being in love with the reservation is like being in love with a drunk. You can't help but like the place and the people; they're loveable characters, kind and well-meaning, but it's all so damned dysfunctional." She glances out the window and returns her gaze to me, her smile tender. "But you can't spend your life here, or you'll just become part of that pattern. You'll drown."

My heart fractures at the truth of her words. I now understand there is no place for me here. It will destroy me. It has already begun to do so.

Gyda suggests I meet Victor Charlo, a Salish poet. The universe worked its magic, and the following weekend Ronni and I happened to run into him at a local diner, where we'd gone to have breakfast. We invited him to join us, and he did so, happily. He has published a book of poetry, *Put Sey (Good Enough)*, about his life, his family, and his people's experiences as Native people. Born in 1938, Victor lived through many of the policies that ripped us asunder: child placement, boarding school, relocation, and termination—the proposal by Congress to end all relationships between the United States and American Indian tribes. In his poem "Bad Wine" he describes our history, our pain:

> You can love a dying Indian,
> But when he drinks bad wine
> And breaks your best glass
> You give him to the wind.

Before Ronni and I leave, he tells me, "When I wrote this book of poetry, it was to tell myself that I was good enough. *We* are good enough."

Despite these introductions my depression finds a home, digging in as I write page after page, day after day, night after night. Even my trips with Ronni along the back roads of the reservation, or my lunches with Vern, or my visits with friends never hold it at bay for long. It always comes crawling back when I sit in the condo and throw my experiences on the virtual page for sometimes eight, ten, twelve hours at a time. At the end of those days, I flop on the leather couch and turn on reruns of *Law and Order: SVU*, watching episode after episode after episode, downing a beer, eating a sandwich and chips, and remembering nothing about the storyline, not really even caring about the storyline.

"Why do you watch that?" Evelyn asks one evening, laughing, when I tell her how my days are going. "That's filled with awful stuff."

"So I can watch someone else's life go to hell for a change."

Ronni provides a foundation for me as we spend days driving the dirt roads of the reservation. We visit the tribally owned Kerr Dam and marvel at the Flathead River's steep, rugged channel cutting through the wide, flat landscape on either side. We tour the reservation's southwest corner, which lies seemingly forgotten among the sagebrush-covered hills, where the road zigzags and twists in the ripples of ancient Lake Missoula.

On several occasions Ronni and I drive along the western edges of the Mission Valley. Here the land is sectioned like patchwork, agriculture at the center, where mansions, trailers, and log cabins that cave in on themselves exist. Colors, like a blurred Monet, come into focus as short grass, sagebrush, wildflowers, and Victorian gardens follow the land's undulations. My thoughts continually drift back to Vic, her need to escape using whatever method best served her interests: automobiles, men, alcohol, drugs. I think about violence with her as the victim, the ways she placed herself in dangerous situations: new boyfriends, another marriage, another child, another stab at "normal" when normal didn't feel comfortable.

We, her children, have paid a high price for her choices. We are still paying the price with our own addictions, our dysfunctions, our need to be a part of something larger than ourselves: the family, the tribe. And the bruising grows deeper and more pronounced. As a result of my musings, I become more and more of a hermit, living in the condo, too exhausted to cook myself a small meal or write or read. Instead, I watch TV, or, on days where my thoughts are too jumbled, I just sit and watch the light move from day to evening over the lake.

One afternoon, on a whim, Ronni and I decide to drive the Jocko Canyon Road. I had checked the road on Google Earth and witnessed its twists and turns as it climbs over a pass through tribal and Forest Service land, eventually intersecting with the Seeley-Swan Highway forty miles later. We stop in St. Ignatius to fill up the car and shop for groceries—sandwich fixings, soda, and chips—and begin our drive along the narrow, paved road, where intersections of culture are the most visible. We pass Mennonites on bikes, the women wearing colorful dresses, their hair drawn neatly into a bun, the strands barely visible under the white eyelet lace caps. We pass American Indian kids walking by the side of the road, laughing. One swings a stick through the tall grass that threatens to grow into pavement. We even pass an Amish buggy, whose occupants are shaded from our eyes beneath the broad, black enclosure.

As we pass a meadow of tall green grass, Ronni points out the window and says, quietly, "This is where they found the body of that woman who'd been missing for several days."

"I read about the incident on Facebook, but I never heard what happened."

"No sign of foul play," Ronni assures me. "But it's like she wandered off and half fell into an irrigation ditch and died of hypothermia." She pauses. "That just happened a few days ago."

The living and the dying exist in the same space.

We drive through dark forests, then stop and cool our feet in the frigid waters of the Jocko River, moving carefully on top of the colorful stones, whose edges had been smoothed by aeons of grating along the stream's rocky bottom. Driving again, we gain elevation and go through acres of timber, both cut and charred, the latter from fires that had ravaged the high mountain plain many years before. I spot clumps of bear grass, with their ecru cones of densely packed flowers, my favorites, second only to the bitterroot. At this point peace begins to sift into my soul. I breathe easier, my shoulders relax, and a smile, unbidden, unfolds as we move silently through a landscape of mountain flowers, explosions of red, purple, white, and blue. On the fine sand, my tires are silent, and the backside of the Mission Mountains drifts by as if on its own accord.

This is the Montana I love. The people I am learning to dislike and lose respect for don't exist here: people who hurt one another, who forget about one another, who fail to cherish the existence of one another, who destroy one another. They exist in the mileage behind us, and they'll exist in the mileage coming up, but right here, on top of the pass, among the bear grass and the lupine, there is no pain.

Before I leave Montana I want to obtain my adoption files, all of my files, from the tribes, the Bureau of Indian Affairs, and the Montana Department of Public Health and Human Services. I'll start with the DPHHS, asking for the files that a tribal judge certified I had a right to access. But I am hesitant, afraid that court order won't be as strong as I initially believed it would. Currently, all I have is a myriad of documents carefully filed in labeled manila folders that I've collected or been given, over the years; these are all the things that tell me about me: copies of my legal adoption records, my enrollment information, ancient per capita correspondence, Vic's obituary, copies of the letters to the editor that had powered the reunion, and a family pedigree, as well as copies of newspaper articles and transcripts of interviews and podcasts. Some are legal documents; most are interpretations of my life. Although the files are thick, the information is insubstantial. I know nothing about social-worker visits, about decisions, about whether or not Vic had fought, even a little bit, to keep us. These files indicate the end results; I want the introduction.

I extract the court order to open my record, beginning to truly appreciate the fact that right now, there are a lot of people who have far more information about me than I have, including the organization that handled my adoption in 1961—Child and Family Services within the Department of Public Health and Human Services. I find their number online, scribbling it on the pad next to me. But instead of dialing, I stare at the number for a long time, gathering my courage to call. What if they say they can't give me that information? I think of all the ways "no" has been said: no, you shouldn't be in anthropology; no, you shouldn't be in college; no, you don't have any family; no, I can't give you that information. But this particular "no" matters more than the previous ones.

I dial and take a deep breath. It rings twice, and a female voice answers. I state my name and my request. "Please hold," she says and transfers me. I am transferred two more times, until I talk with Heidi, the woman who assures me she is in charge of the files I seek.

After listening to my request, she asks, perplexed, "But why do you want them?"

"Because I want to know what's in those files," I respond. I had planned on this being a yes-or-no answer, not a question with which I have to defend my need for information.

"But why do you want to know? What exactly are you looking for?"

"I'm looking for information about my adoption." My face reddens, and I wonder why I am embarrassed for pushing this issue when no one can see me. But I am begging. For my baby information. Who else does this?

"But what are you looking for exactly?" she prods. "Perhaps I can pull the information most pertinent for you."

"I want the entire file that concerns me and my adoption." My voice shakes.

"Well, that's not something we do," she explains carefully. "I can give you some information, but not an entire file."

"I have a judge-signed court order that says you can." I play my ace.

"Which judge?"

"Judge Winona Tanner."

"I don't know her."

"She's a tribal judge here on the Flathead Reservation."

"Oh, I don't know that we consider that kind of court order official. I would have to look at it."

"Look, this is what the court order says," I answer and proceed to read the document aloud over the phone: "Having read the Petition with attachments filed by Susan J. Harness and having heard her statements, the Court finds good cause to authorize the release of any and all records pertaining to the circumstances surrounding her adoption as a child."

This sounds like a court document the state should honor.

"This is what you need to do," she advises, when I'm finished reading. "Tell me which documents you want, and I'll make copies and mail them to you. You'll need to email me your request and what you would like from the file and send it to me as PDF. I will also need a copy of your photo ID and your current mailing address."

"Look," I bargain, "I'm only two and a half hours from Helena. I can be there any day this week, and I can get the information from you then, in person."

"That's not how we do it," she clarifies. "You need to make the request in writing, and I need to mail you the contents. We just don't hand out those files to just anyone."

"I'm not just anyone," I say, my voice rising in frustration. "I'm the person those files are about. And it's not as if I'm asking for something I don't have a right to. I received that court order because both my birth mother and adoptive mother signed affidavits that they agreed those files should be open. I've met my birth mother. I've spoken with her. My adoptive mother agrees that information is mine; it is a significant part of who I am. It's not as if there are any more family secrets."

"I'm sorry, just email me the information, and I'll see what I can do."

I know I won't write the email. Not now. I feel defeated. I decide to try to obtain the information through the tribes. I call Evelyn and ask who I should talk with to obtain my files. She gives me a couple of names and the departments to start with—Enrollment and then the Bureau of Indian Affairs. "Call them ahead of time so they can have the files ready when you arrive," she advises. Before returning the signed court order to its manila folder, I once more run my fingers along the raised-letter ridges. Its strength seemed so official, so filled with power. But unless I have an explanation deemed worthy, I am losing hope that it is worth anything.

It is ten miles between my house and the Tribal Complex. In route I contact Enrollment to give them a heads-up. A man answers, whose voice is kind and gentle. I briefly introduce myself and my reason for calling, but then I wince at the dead space of his pause. "I have a judge's court order, signed by Judge Tanner," I add.

"Well, I do have a file," the man at Enrollment explains, not unkindly. "But I can't give it to you. If you need something specific, perhaps I can find that and have it ready when you get here."

"No, I'm not looking for anything specific. I just want to see my file."

"But why? I mean, if there was something you were looking for I could get you a copy."

The fatigue, I was fighting the mental fatigue of begging. And I hadn't expected to do that here. "I just want to see my file. I have a judge's court order that says I can do that." I can feel my throat tighten up.

"We don't typically allow people into the files. Again, if there is a document that would help you find something specific that you're looking for, I can make copies of that and give it to you."

My throat hardens to glass. "I just want to see my file." The line between being difficult and being frantic is thin.

"Look," he said, as if explaining it yet another way, his voice still gentle, "if there's something you were looking for, I can certainly pull the information and have a copy ready for you when you arrive."

"Why can't I see my file when I have a judge's order?" My throat shatters, and I wonder why my reasons are not acceptable.

"Do you have the order with you?"

"Yes, I'll be there in about ten minutes."

"Well, I'll see what I can find, but to be honest," he said, almost apologetically, "I don't understand why, exactly, you want to see your file."

Tears gather and my throat breaks. "Because it's my file," I choke. "It's about my life."

He pauses, and his voice becomes quiet. "Okay. Well, I'll be here, waiting for you."

And he is. The front-desk receptionist points me back to his office, and this tall, slender man, with a neat braid down his back, stands and shakes my hand. His face is brown, kind, and I am silently grateful he agreed. He returns to his Office Depot executive chair, adjusts his glasses, and examines the court order before placing it in the manila file folder labeled with my legal name. He types in the password on his keyboard, and his virtual files pop up, including my official pedigree. I'd always been told I was half Indian; no one knew, or cared, what the other half was. Actually, the pedigree states, I'm five-sixteenths. "Why is there a difference between what I'd been told by my birth mom and what you have?"

"See," he said, pointing to the genealogy chart on his computer, "this is where you lost it." He scrolls over and plants his finger over one of the names. "This is where your family began losing that blood, back here in this generation." I'm not even sure how long ago that was. I don't ask. But in our family the quantum has steadily decreased over generations. My children cannot be enrolled; their quantum is too low. I sigh and remind myself the official purpose of blood quantum was to ensure we, as Native people, obtain what was rightfully ours. Unofficially, it ensured we would eventually breed ourselves out of existence.

I stare at the computer screen and process the information that glows before me, my birth family's records, which stretch back to 1748 and contain ancestors who are Iroquois, Chippewa, Assiniboine, Kootenai, Cree, and French, the latter provided by a Frenchman named Baptiste

Losing the Master Key

La Jieux. And here I am, scrabbling to hold onto a fragmented identity someone allows me to have, because those files can't be given "to just anyone."

By the time we're finished, I believe the gentle man in Enrollment understands the importance I have placed on these papers. He offers me a copy of everything he has, which I will add to my files. Before saying good-bye with a formal handshake, he points me in the direction of my next appointment: the Bureau of Indian Affairs Tribal Lands office. It is in the building across the parking lot.

He gives me the name of the person to ask for, and I find her sitting behind the desk in a small, overcrowded office. She is serious; she offers no smile. My gaze wanders over the office, across some small memento that indicates she is a Flathead Reservation tribal member, a photo, and large bound files, until it finds the wall-mounted, framed Certificate of Appreciation for her efforts in successfully moving unending files through probate effectively and efficiently. She takes my court order, glances at it, and puts it aside on her desk. I watch this action with a certain amount of frustration. I'd purchased three copies of this order for ten dollars each, and so far only one person has granted my request.

"So what are you looking for, exactly?" she asks after I explain my mission.

"I'm looking for my file."

Uninterested, she rephrases her question. "Are you looking for a specific document?"

And the tape hits rewind.

People don't seem to understand why this piece of paper is so important, that it has the power to unlock a life, an identity, that until now has been inaccessible because of sealed records. They, with their full lives, genealogies, and unquestioned documentation, don't understand that my life book begins on chapter 3. Chapters 1 and 2 are located in various bureau drawers and file cabinets, three-ring binders, and other people's memories. The people who are the gatekeepers for my information have all grown up with parents and siblings, aunts and uncles, cousins and assorted relatives, who all have snippets of recollections tucked behind their ears like accountants' pencils. I imagine they heard the sordid family details of breakups, of babies, of boredom, of booze or worse, from family members themselves or from someone who knew the family, who cared about the family. They've heard the stories of themselves as infants, probably their first steps; they've been compared to parents and siblings, aunts and uncles, or grandparents for their looks, their idiosyncrasies, their characteristics.

When considered from this perspective, their questioning seems innocent. What could these files possibly contain that was so important? Yes, they might think only portions of that file are pertinent proof of a lived experience, but whatever reason I provide is not deemed good enough.

"The file is still in probate," the woman continues.

"I thought probate was for when you had an estate. Vic didn't have anything."

"Perhaps she had an allotment. I don't know. But after it goes through probate it will go to the Clerk of Courts Office. Just make sure they have a current address, and they can mail it to you."

"How long will that take?"

"I have no idea. Just make sure you have an updated mailing address and leave it with the Clerk of Courts Office."

And just like that, I am dismissed. As I leave, I glance at the court order that sits forgotten on her desk, and I wonder where it will end up.

I once more make my way through the maze that is tribal headquarters to the Clerk of Courts Office. I stand at the window and am glanced at briefly by a young Native woman behind the desk. The Native woman who eventually addresses me, not the woman behind the desk, is brisk, and I feel as if I am taking up her time with such a frivolous request. She leaves in an officious manner and disappears behind a row of files; the woman who now faces the window actively avoids my gaze. There are no smiles, at least toward me. But these women smile at each new person that comes to the window, and there is an exchange with marked differences: there is recognition, interest.

"Hey, Doris," the gaze-avoider greets a newcomer to the small room. "No, Charlie just left. Yeah, I heard he won two hundred bucks at the casino! What are you looking for?"

I had been helped with a short, concise "What do you need?" My reply had required no further interaction. My blood pressure rises, and I feel a familiar headache begin at my temples. The longer I remain in this building, walk these halls, knock on doors, talk to strangers about why they have the information I need with no success of actually obtaining anything useful, the more frayed my nerves become. And as I stand here watching people ignore me, step around me, avoid me, I realize something disconcertingly important.

I don't want to be here. I want to get in my car and drive to Polson, where I can enter the white-owned business near the condo where I live and talk to the owner about trivial things, and I know what the rules of those discussions will be. When I walk in, I will be greeted; I will extend greetings in return. I know when I see him slip his hands easily into his khaki pockets, he is relaxed, and we'd talk about the weather, about the summer traffic, about the noise of the boats on the lake in the morning. I know when he frowns he's considering my request for information and how he can fulfill it; it will not be because he is annoyed I'm in his store. And once these niceties are completed, we'll get down to the business of sending a package or pricing shipping options or whatever it is I'm there for.

I know this because this interaction is culturally defined. I've spent my life learning it, using it, perfecting it. I can translate people's facial expressions, body language, subject matter, with amazing clarity. I've spent a lifetime doing it. In the white world. But here on the rez, I know nothing. I can't read these faces; I can't read their body language. I can't interpret their responses or lack of responses. I can't read between the lines of what is being said because I've never been taught how to. Those within this culture don't see these ways of communicating as unique; they just *are*. I imagine the people I find myself surrounded by at this moment may feel as uncomfortable in my world as I do in theirs—we are outsiders together but for different reasons. I am not only an outsider within this group; I am located so far at the edges of the margins that I will never be fully accepted by the core. I don't have the master key.

During the 1960s and 1970s the whole purpose of placing Indian children with only white families was to force us to become assimilated, to become white. If this social program was proven successful, we, as children, couldn't afford to be around the people most influential in "holding us back," that is, family members or tribal members. Therefore, we were not encouraged to play with American Indian children or otherwise engage with American Indians in general. We were not introduced to Native people. If we traveled to the reservation, it was clear we were on "their" land, not ours. Yes, we were outsiders within.

Thinking back to the three families of geese that swam each morning in front of the condo, I am stunned with the care that existed within this small flock: the group was always together, the goslings swam within the pairs of adults, and the goslings were never out of the parents' sight. Any sojourns goslings took onto shore to graze the healthy green grass were heavily monitored by the adults. It was amazing that in the three and a half weeks I'd been there, the parents hadn't lost a single gosling.

These were definitely not rez geese.

Epilogue

Bitterroot Valley, Montana, June 29, 2013.

Two days ago, over breakfast, I'd asked Uncle Albert for another favor: could he please take me to a place he felt it was important for me to see, to know. He was my guide, talking about my birth father, sitting with me at Vic's funeral, walking with me as we visited the homestead. I felt there was at least one more place, but I didn't know what it was.

"Well," he chuckled, his eyes bright. "What do you want to see?"

"I don't know anymore. You pick." My smile was slight and my words limited because I was tired. This place has worn me down. I need him and his wisdom to help me rebuild the person I thought I was.

As if reading my mind, he said, gently, "Well, let me think about it."

He'd telephoned last night and, without preamble, asked me to pick him up at seven thirty the following morning. My mind flew with the possibilities.

"Are we going a long ways away?" I asked, trying to figure out why we were leaving so early. Maybe to visit the sacred pine tree? A place on the Jocko? Somewhere in the Missions?

"I'll tell you tomorrow," he said, laughing. "It's a surprise. It took me a while, but I've finally thought about what I think is important for you to know about yourself."

At seven in the morning the highway is quiet; I meet only a few cars on their way to work. With my eyes acting as a camera, I snap memory images as I drive through the Mission Valley, noting its fields, its houses, its graveled roads that intersect every mile or so with the highway. I want to capture this landscape, take it home with me to review on a cold winter night.

The Missions have not yet released the sun, so it is with a quiet beauty that the kettle ponds of Ninepipes National Wildlife Refuge reflect the peach sky in their still waters. By the time I am near the Bison Range, the sun is awake, but it disappears again as I drive the deceptively sharp curves of the canyon that follow the Jocko River.

I pull into Albert's drive just a bit past seven thirty and watch as he, deliberate in his movements, checks the spaces around his house, opening and closing car doors, locking storage doors, checking the house door. When he climbs into the passenger seat of my car, he looks at me, smiles, and says one word. "Ready?"

It turns out we are on our way to Hamilton. In the last five years I've driven this corridor several times, either by myself or with a member of my family, blood and legal. As we head south, time collapses until I am young, driving with Mom and Dad by the towns of Florence, Victor, and Stevensville, watching the cottonwood trees along the Bitterroot River blur as they fly past my window. But I am not young. I am fifty-four. I notice that many of the farmhouses that occupy sizable acreages haven't changed in the past fifty years, except for a new coat of paint or maybe some repairs. They still stand stalwartly on the land. I recognize the bars that Vern pointed out five years ago and the campground whose dirt road snaked down toward the river, the one they'd stayed at. The one of many.

Roads take off from the highway like irrigation tubes, twisting and turning their way toward the Bitterroots. We turn off on one of these roads, a one-lane paved asphalt ribbon, and follow its convoluted path. Overgrown shrubs and brambles blind the corners, so it's kind of an exciting drive. As we near the base of the mountains, the road undulates, and we drive by the remains of almost-forgotten orchards that stand bent and gnarled on the brilliant green landscape of late June. Dark, plowed earth releases bursts of color, as vegetable and flower gardens vie for attention, the cottage-like homes nearly lost in the visual cacophony.

"Okay," Albert says, his voice tinged with excitement. "We're almost there." He scans the landscape. After a few moments he raises his index finger near the glass and says, "Slow down. I think it's near here." I allow my car to creep up the steep incline until the fork on the road, then I pause. Albert hesitates only for a moment. "Yes, here. To the right. Slow down because it's coming up." We catch a rise and follow a gentle L, and as we round the corner, Albert says, "Okay, stop here."

Even though I pull over as far as I can, my car still occupies a good part of the lane. I lower the power window and cut the engine, and silence descends. After a moment I make out the buzz of insects that dive-bomb our car and, a little farther away, the hum of bees as they dip and sway over the nearby garden. Beyond the garden sits three small, white, dilapidated buildings, each perhaps fifteen by twenty feet. Each has a door flanked by a couple of windows. Albert is silent as he studies this space. A few moments later, when he speaks, it is with deliberation.

"See those sheds there?" he asks, pointing at the buildings. "That's where we used to live in the summer. Your folks and you kids would stay in the middle shed; my mom and dad would stay in the front one; and I'd stay with some of my older brothers or sisters in the one in the back." He turns and looks at me. "We'd come here every summer to pick strawberries, and this whole hillside was filled with strawberries. Those were long, hot days." He pauses, then gestures to the adjacent white house. "The guy who owned this field lived right up there."

"How old were you?" I ask.

"Fourteen, fifteen, sixteen, somewhere around there."

I do the math with what I know. He is fourteen years older than I am. If I was here, he was probably fifteen. "Were you here all summer?"

"As long as the berries produced. But once they stopped, we worked fields all over this valley. We picked berries, apples; we worked the potato fields. And sometimes my brothers and sisters and I would walk into town, maybe three or four miles, and go to the movies or to the skating rink, when it cost a quarter. But that money was hard-earned." He looks back to the field, and his voice becomes strained. "We were so poor then." When he turns toward me I see sadness in his eyes, on his face, and I hear almost an apology in his words.

"I used to be embarrassed of the life we lived," he continues. "Of the places we lived, this being one of them. I was embarrassed at how poor we were. I was embarrassed for a long time. I had no reason to be ashamed of who I was or the work I'd done; it was honest work. But I was ashamed for a long time. But at some point I stopped being embarrassed and accepted that this was the life I was given."

He grows silent again. His gaze blankets the scene once more before it returns to me. His voice is strong, sure, and the smile is filled with compassion; I think for both of us. "This is what I wanted you to see because I thought it was important for you to know that you lived here, with your folks. With us. Even if it was just a little while."

The tribal council never did anything about the resolution for the home-coming for adoptees or fostered people separated from the tribe. I was also never able to obtain my full adoption records, but I doubt I'm done fighting for them. They are my Rosetta stone, allowing me to interpret my whole life, not just the life that started on chapter 3 but is now, somewhere, on chapter 2. But really, I want to read the prologue, the writing of how everything came to be.

The morning before Rick is to arrive at the condo, I see several gray shapes through a gap in the blinds. It is the three pairs of Canada geese with their seventeen goslings, spread out on the lawn, pulling at the new grass. They panic when I pull open the shades, the adults pushing the adolescent goslings ahead of them, into the water. They wag their tails in agitation and their voices in protest at my presence. Only when all the goslings are safely in the water do the adults follow them.

How I wish my reservation family had watched us children as carefully as this group of geese. But they didn't, for whatever reason. But other adults attempted, with varying degrees of success, to fill that role. Although Dad started out trying to do the right thing, he was haunted by his own demons, who chased him relentlessly down his alcohol-induced path. After the damage had been done, I wouldn't let him fully return. I don't know how I feel about that now.

Mom's number-one interest was raising me to be confident, successful, generous, and kind; I think for the most part, she was successful. But there was a whole society out there that undermined much of what she tried to do. Children, I realize, are raised in a society, not just a family, and families need to prepare them for that. As I've become older, I've also become more confident, and in looking back I see that I have surrounded myself with warriors fighting for the best interests of children in all kinds of ways.

Vern Fisher, my brother who works for Tribal Law and Order, could have fallen into the patterns so many of our siblings did. Instead, he chose a path that guides and protects the people of our tribe. I asked him once how he wanted to be remembered. "I am sure I will be remembered as a firm, but fair, police officer. . . . I have an impact on a lot of lives. . . .

Most of the impact is viewed as negative at first . . . but I think people will remember that I was trying to help them and their families. And I would like my kids to remember that I love them."

Evelyn Stevenson, a lawyer for the Salish Kootenai tribes, passed away in March 2015. Over our ten-year friendship, she was, in a very real sense, my surrogate tribal mother. One story stands out, over the many we shared around her dining table: "I remember my grandma would how say proud she was that she'd never lost any of her kids to the social worker. And then when I got older and left home, I thought, people don't normally say that. People don't even think about losing their kids to the social worker. But every Indian family in the history of time has worried about losing their kids to the social worker." This insight led her to not only become a lawyer but, after listening to testimony in Washington DC from tribal people whose families had been shattered, begin crafting what would become the Indian Child Welfare Act of 1978.

Judge William Thorne has presented with me on a few occasions at conferences hosted by the Casey Family Foundation's Indian Child Welfare Division. I met him for the first time at the conference held in Great Falls, Montana, in 2013, recognizing him from a video created by the National Council of Juvenile and Family Court Judges used to educate judges, lawyers, and social workers about the Indian Child Welfare Act of 1978. His interest is in promoting "customary adoption": "If a child needs new parents, we can replace their parents, but that doesn't mean we have to replace aunts and uncles, cousins, or their siblings." As soon as I heard his argument, I knew this was the kind of adoption I wanted to advocate for. At the end of the conference, I approached him and shook his hand, telling him, "You are my hero." I wasn't able to stop the tears. He hugged me and thanked me for telling my story; it gave context for his argument for policy change.

Uncle Albert's strength and his careful and thoughtful way of speaking, as well as his concern for the welfare of the people, captured my attention immediately. Heavily grounded in his traditions and spirituality, he is a man with a strong sense of self and purpose. As a result, I turn to him for advice, solace, and answers. I think if my parents had met him in an age where that was not just acceptable but encouraged, they would have, like me, been drawn to his quiet ways and strong values, his gentle sense of humor, and his compassion. Like Albert, I felt different, inferior, not good enough to walk upright in the world. Except I had the additional complication of feeling like I couldn't walk upright in the Native world either. In both realms I was expected to be invisible.

Yes, parents lost us as adoptees, but we have lost our entire family, entire tribes, who could have helped us navigate the dangerous waters we crossed, in ways our adoptive families could not. We needed them in our lives.

But even members of my family don't fully understand the complicated betweenness of being. In one of our early conversations about this topic, Vern told me, "You think too much about being Indian." That was easy for him to say, with his unquestioned and unchallenged tribal and family membership. Plus, he had an identity of which he was proud, but it didn't define him; it was taken for granted. But me? I was made to think all the time of what I was allowed and not allowed to be by entire groups of people. Their applied pressure didn't stop the bleeding but instead became a tourniquet, where I almost lost a piece of myself in the process. In this pressurized system bounded by race and ethnicity, I allowed other people's problems to become mine.

But somewhere along the line I changed. I no longer accepted responsibility for how other people thought or behaved. I no longer feared the spaces around me. I no longer accepted my placement in the societal space to be determined by others. I like to tell people that my master's research in cultural anthropology was the most successful, and expensive, counseling session I'd ever attended. Through this I understood the social hierarchy, the ways we, as adoptees, acquire and exchange material goods, cultural characteristics, and social networks that increase, or decrease, our perceived human value. I also understood the role social memory plays, by determining what is remembered but, more important, also what is forgotten. Social memory is what ties all these perceptions together, allowing them to be regifted from one generation to the next.

I was not responsible for not fitting in. Society holds that responsibility.

I am able to breathe a sigh of relief to put down that burden.

I have been invited to be the keynote speaker at a conference sponsored by the American Indian Council in Kansas City, Missouri. Before the program starts I stand and watch the color guard, a group of American Indian veterans, enter the hall, their feet moving to the rhythm of the traditional drummers and singers that occupy one of the corners. One of the veterans in particular captures my attention; he looks the most "Indian" of the group. His skin is dark, and his black hair is pulled back into a ponytail that falls halfway down his back, revealing a sharp, angular face. He moves with such pride, as if he knows exactly who he is and where he's come from. And to be honest, I feel a sense of envy at his unquestioned confidence.

It is time for my presentation, and I climb the steps, walk behind the podium, and draw a calming breath. Then I begin to talk about my adoption experience, with all its beauty and all its ugliness. I tell the audience about how I grew up, of finding my family, and of still feeling ungrounded. And I tell them why: I carry the burden of colonization. I don't belong; I find myself on the outside looking in, no matter where I am. Tears drift down my face, uninvited. I tell them that transracial adoptees carry a lot of baggage, and I want people to understand how much that burden weighs. I want people to understand how their words, their actions, have far-reaching consequences.

Their applause tells me they heard my message.

After my talk the man in the color guard, the one I noticed, approaches me. Up close I can see he is about my age. He leans toward me and shakes my hand, talking quietly in a conversation for my ears only. "I am

12. Susan, Ronni Marie, and Vern. Photo by Rick Harness. Courtesy of the author.

giving you this gift in a traditional way, so you understand how much I appreciated that you told my story. That was my story you told up there. All those things happened to me. And people need to know that. But I wasn't able to tell them. So thank you for telling them."

He presses something into my palm.

I wait until he disappears into the crowd, then open my hand to see what had been exchanged: a carefully folded bill.

The amount is not important.

The message is.

Telling a Good One: The Process of a
Native American Collaborative Biography
By Theodore Rios and
Kathleen Mullen Sands

Muscogee Daughter: My Sojourn
to the Miss America Pageant
By Susan Supernaw
Foreword by Geary Hobson

William W. Warren: The Life, Letters,
and Times of an Ojibwe Leader
By Theresa M. Schenck

I Tell You Now: Autobiographical
Essays by Native American Writers
Edited by Brian Swann
and Arnold Krupat

Sacred Feathers: The Reverend
Peter Jones (Kahkewaquonaby)
and the Mississauga Indians
By Donald B. Smith

Postindian Conversations
By Gerald Vizenor and A. Robert Lee

Chainbreaker: The Revolutionary War
Memoirs of Governor Blacksnake

Grandmother's Grandchild:
My Crow Indian Life
By Alma Hogan Snell
Edited by Becky Matthews
Foreword by Peter Nabokov

As told to Benjamin Williams
Edited by Thomas S. Abler

Standing in the Light:
A Lakota Way of Seeing
By Severt Young Bear
and R. D. Theisz

No One Ever Asked Me: The World War
II Memoirs of an Omaha Indian Soldier
By Hollis D. Stabler
Edited by Victoria Smith

Sarah Winnemucca
By Sally Zanjani

Blue Jacket: Warrior of the Shawnees
By John Sugden

To order or obtain more information on these or other University
of Nebraska Press titles, visit nebraskapress.unl.edu.